IMAGES
of America

ROCKLAND AREA LIME INDUSTRIES

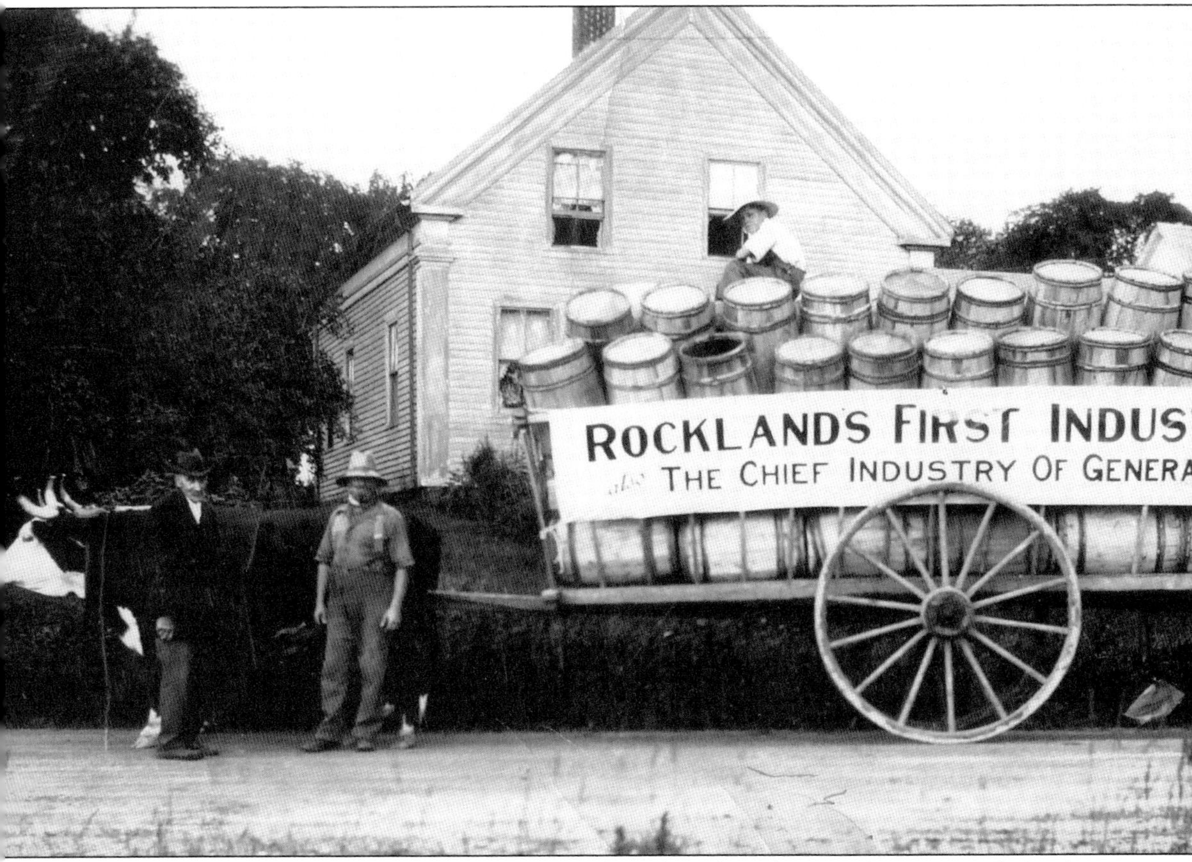

Hayracks made perfect conveyances for hauling lime barrels. Barrels were made by farmers who operated small cooperages as a second source of income. This wagon was in a parade in Thomaston at the dedication of the Thomaston Mall. A note on the back of the picture says, "Father beside the oxen." (Thomaston Historical Society.)

On the cover: A crew is replacing the rivets in the kiln stack. Constant attention was needed for upkeep on kilns, which sustained rough treatment from the heavy rock and high temperatures. (David Hoch Collection.)

IMAGES
of America

ROCKLAND AREA LIME INDUSTRIES

Courtney C. MacLachlan, David R. Hoch,
and Paul G. Merriam

ARCADIA
PUBLISHING

ISBN 978-0-7385-4485-4

Published by Arcadia Publishing
Charleston, South Carolina

Printed in the United States of America

Library of Congress Catalog Card Number: 2006924627

For all general information contact Arcadia Publishing at:
Telephone 843-853-2070
Fax 843-853-0044
E-mail sales@arcadiapublishing.com
For customer service and orders:
Toll-Free 1-888-313-2665

Visit us on the Internet at www.arcadiapublishing.com

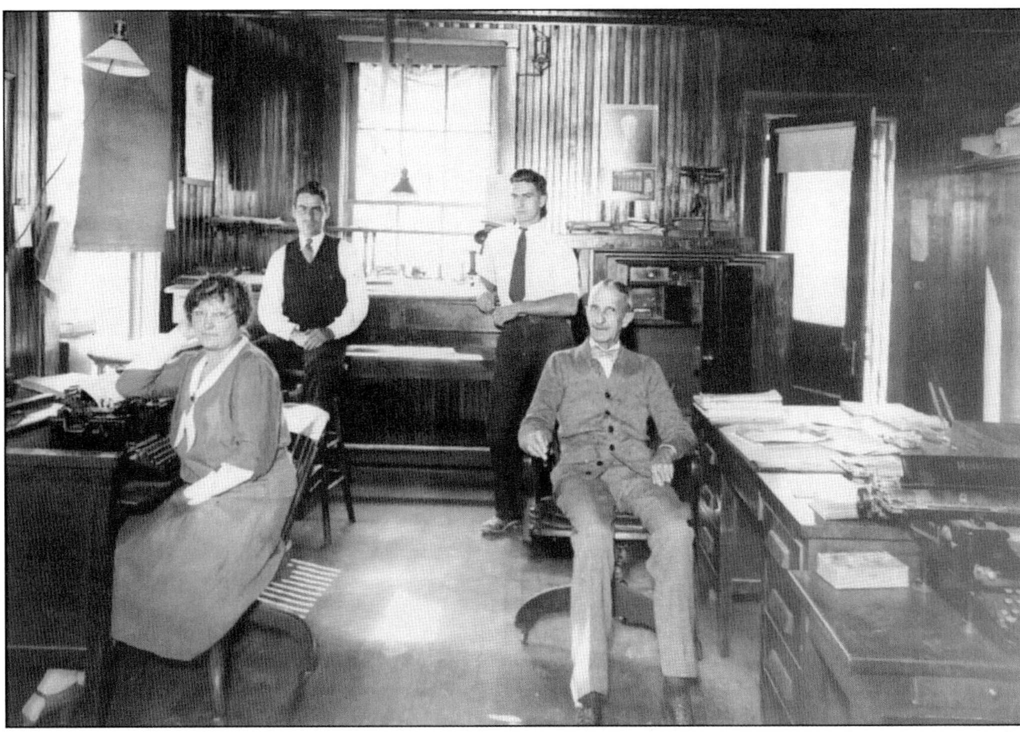

Employees at the main office of the Rockland-Rockport Lime Company pose for a picture. The seated man on the right is H. W. Huke, president of the company from 1911 to 1917. Rockland-area lime manufacturers had developed a reputation for having a specialized body of knowledge on the properties of lime, and their knowledge was in demand. They traveled to other lime-producing facilities in Virginia, Missouri, and to California to share their expertise. In California, they helped develop lime quarries on the Big Sur coast, and the area is known today as Lime Kiln State Park. (DH.)

Contents

ACKNOWLEDGMENTS

Special thanks are extended to the following individuals for their many and varied contributions to this book: Margaret Gagnon of Friendship; Brian Harden, mayor of the city of Rockland; Wayne C. Gray of Rockland; Margaret S. McCrea of the Thomaston Historical Society; Ron Raiselis, cooper at Strawbery Banke Museum in Portsmouth, New Hampshire; Ted Skowronski of Chelted Gallery in Rockland; Bethany Engstrom of the Farnsworth Museum in Rockland; Capt. Douglas K. Lee and Capt. Linda J. Lee; Barbara Perkins and Bertram Snow of the Rockland Historical Society; Paulette Stewart of Rockland; Constance Parker of the Lincolnville Historical Society; Richard Ferren of the Warren Historical Society; and Gail Frye of the Camden-Rockport Historical Society. Their willingness to share time, knowledge, and support throughout the project is deeply appreciated.

Photographs are keyed to the source by the following notations: Camden-Rockport Historical Society (CRHS); Edward Coffin Collection (EC); Farnsworth Museum (FM); Mervin Harriman Collection (MH); David R. Hoch Collection (DH); Douglas and Linda Lee Collection (DLL); Lincolnville Historical Society (LHS); Courtney C. MacLachlan Collection (CM); W. J. Lewis Parker Collection (LP); Penobscot Marine Museum (PMM); Rockland Historical Society (RHS); Thomaston Historical Society (THS); Waldo Tyler Collection at the Rockland Historical Society (WT); and the Warren Historical Society (WHS).

INTRODUCTION

Today Rockland is known as the lobster capital of the world, but this was not always the case. Until recently, Rockland was the "Lime City," the center of lime manufacturing on the East Coast. Limestone is an essential ingredient of modern life. It is used in agriculture, papermaking, steel refining, soil stabilization for large construction projects, and in environmental cleanup. For years, it has also been basic to the building trades as an ingredient in cement, plaster, and mortar. For well over a century, the high-quality lime rock that stretches from Thomaston to Union and up to Lincolnville provided the essential plaster and mortar to the growing towns and cities along the East Coast.

Lime has had some specialized uses, too. One use was as a "magic lantern," a precursor to the spotlight in the theater, in the days before electricity. When heated, the lime gives off an intensely white light, which spotlighted the person on stage. This gave rise to the term "in the limelight," which we still use today.

The 12-mile vein of lime rock in the Rockland area became famous for a number of reasons. First, there were no other known deposits near the ocean along the East Coast of this country. Second, it was a large deposit of excellent quality. Third, it was near the seacoast, which meant that transportation of the heavy limestone to the kilns was economically feasible. And lastly, inexpensive ocean transportation to market was available in vessels built from abundant local timber. This confluence of conveniences made the development of the lime industry almost inevitable. It was the basis of a regional economy that involved a range of secondary support industries.

Henry Knox, secretary of war in George Washington's administration, built a lavish home in Thomaston and had great plans for several enterprises in the area. Foremost in his plans were lime manufacturing and shipping. From his efforts, and the efforts of others who recognized that they had found a gold mine in lime, a major lime manufacturing industry developed in the 19th century. By 1900, numerous jobs involving a wide variety of skills provided employment to more than 1,000 men: laborers, quarrymen, teamsters, kiln tenders, kiln masons, lime trimmers, lime manufacturers and their business staffs, lime burners, coopers, railroad men, longshoremen, stevedores, shipping agents, ship captains and mariners, and shipbuilders, ship joiners, block makers, and sailmakers. All were involved in various aspects of lime production and its transportation.

The product was known originally as Thomaston lime since Thomaston was the name of the land area that now encompasses Thomaston, South Thomaston, and Rockland. Many of the large quarries were located in Shore Village, in an area just inland from tidewater called the

Meadows. As the number and size of these quarries grew, population increased, so that in 1848, the Shore Village separated from Thomaston to create its own community. As an indication of the importance of lime rock, it named itself Rockland in 1850 and was incorporated as a city in 1854. The name was as pervasive as the industry: a main street in Rockland is Limerock Street, its first bank was the Lime Rock Bank, a prominent business was the Lime Rock Fire and Insurance Company, and the local newspaper was the *Lime Rock Gazette*. Other quarries existed in Camden-Rockport, Warren, Union, Lincolnville, and even on Islesboro, but the bulk of the vein of lime rock was centered in Thomaston and Rockland. Rockland was rightly nicknamed "Lime City."

Despite economic fluctuations, the population of the East Coast cities continued to grow throughout the 19th century, and lime had a guaranteed market as long as new buildings were being constructed of brick and mortar. Annual lime production in the area grew steadily until the Civil War. The war and its aftermath created a disruption, but by 1870, business had picked up again. By the late 1880s, the city of Rockland was producing up to 1.4 million barrels annually. By this time, Rockland had cemented a trade relationship with builders in New York City, and a fleet of schooners sailed regularly between the two ports, carrying barreled lime to New York and often returning with a cargo of coal.

By the beginning of the 20th century, major changes were affecting the production of lime in Knox County. The use of steam and electricity in the quarries enabled men to dig to ever-deeper depths in the narrow-pit quarries. A railroad system was built in 1888 to carry rock to the kilns. This displaced many teamsters. Coal became common as fuel for the kilns, displacing wood and the accompanying fleet of wood boats and lumber coasters that supplied the kilns. A fleet of steel barges towed by tugs displaced the schooners, giving Rockland Harbor a radically different look. Most important, most local lime companies were consolidated into the Rockland-Rockport Lime Company in 1900, a conglomerate backed by money from Boston. All of this reflected national changes from wood fuel to fossil fuel and from a regional economy to a national economy.

There were major changes in the building trades, too. Finish plaster was being used less as wallboard and Sheetrock came into common use, so there was less demand for fine lime. This occurred at the same time that, despite efforts to cut production and shipping costs, the depth of the quarries made it harder to retrieve the high-grade lime. In the end, local quarrying for the building trades ended when the high-quality lime was dug out. The last fire from the last harborside kiln in Rockland was extinguished in 1958, after millions of tons of lime rock had been quarried for the building trades.

Today, although the abandoned quarries are in evidence everywhere, there is still active quarrying in the same vein of lime rock. Dragon Cement Company of Thomaston has been in operation since 1928 and is the only cement manufacturing facility in New England. Annually it produces 750,000 tons of cement, the key ingredient in concrete and one of the major engineering materials in the country. The plant and quarry recently received designation as a State Significant Historical Civil Engineering Landmark.

The uses may have changed, but the lime rock itself still provides employment and economic vitality for the Rockland area.

One

Quarrying

The quarrying process itself began when local farmers recognized seams of lime rock protruding into their fields. They dug the surface rock out with pickaxes and burned it in homemade field kilns. As the industry grew, the quarries deepened and broadened. Quarrymen reached the bottom of the quarry in rock wagons, which followed a steep narrow road cut into the side of the quarry. Workers then climbed up to the quarry face where they were working via a system of ladders arranged on the quarry wall. The mechanics of quarrying limestone involved several basic steps. First, quarry workers drilled holes into the rock and forced powder or dynamite charges into the holes. Next, the powder was set off, and the rock blasted loose. Workers then broke up the large pieces with pickaxes and sledgehammers to roughly the size of a man's head. Last, they loaded the limestone by hand into the rock wagons (or later the large steel buckets called drags), which were hoisted out of the quarry. An average workday was nine hours; typical wages in 1900 were $11 per week. In the 1880s, mechanization moved in, but the same basic processes continued.

Work in the quarries was backbreaking and dangerous. Local newspapers described a variety of accidents; premature discharge of powder was a common one. Unintended early explosions could result in loss of limbs, loss of eyesight, or even loss of life. Other accidents abounded involving falling rock from unstable quarry faces, falling equipment like derricks, and falling rock from overloaded drags. The number and seriousness of accidents mounted with the increased use of heavy steam and electrical equipment. For example, after dynamite was introduced, workers fired a row of dynamite charges by battery, which was a safety improvement. But not all charges exploded, leaving an unexploded charge in the rock face for someone else to hit unwittingly. There was no accident insurance or workman's compensation, so disabled workers were cared for by their families. Sometimes an injured quarryman was aided by a one-time "subscription" from other workers. If either of these supports failed, he became a ward of the town.

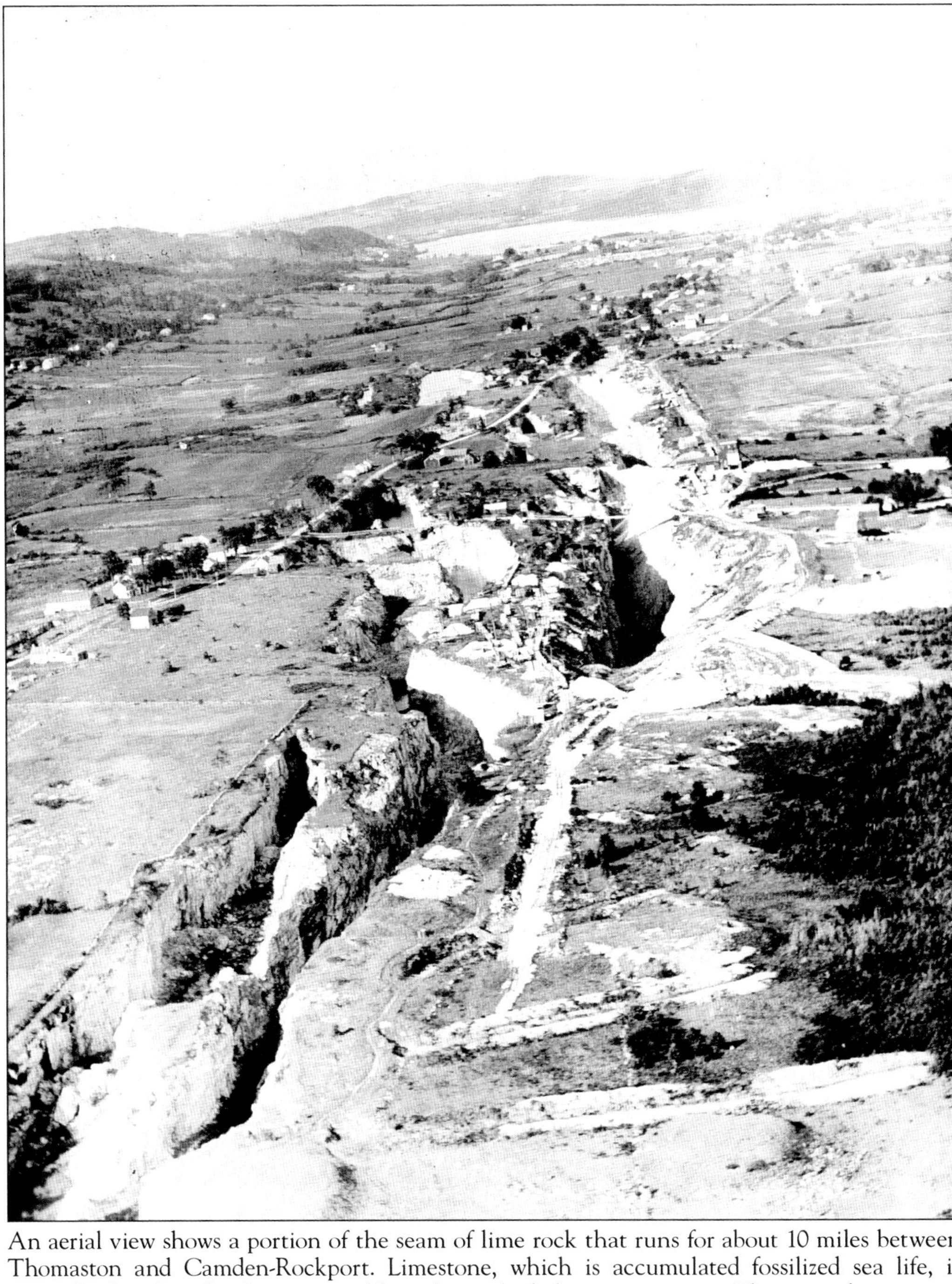

An aerial view shows a portion of the seam of lime rock that runs for about 10 miles between Thomaston and Camden-Rockport. Limestone, which is accumulated fossilized sea life, is normally found in flat layers resembling the seabed that it once was. This vein, however, is unusual because it has been compressed and turned by geological forces into a vertical position, necessitating the deep, narrow quarries for which the Rockland area is famous. (DH.)

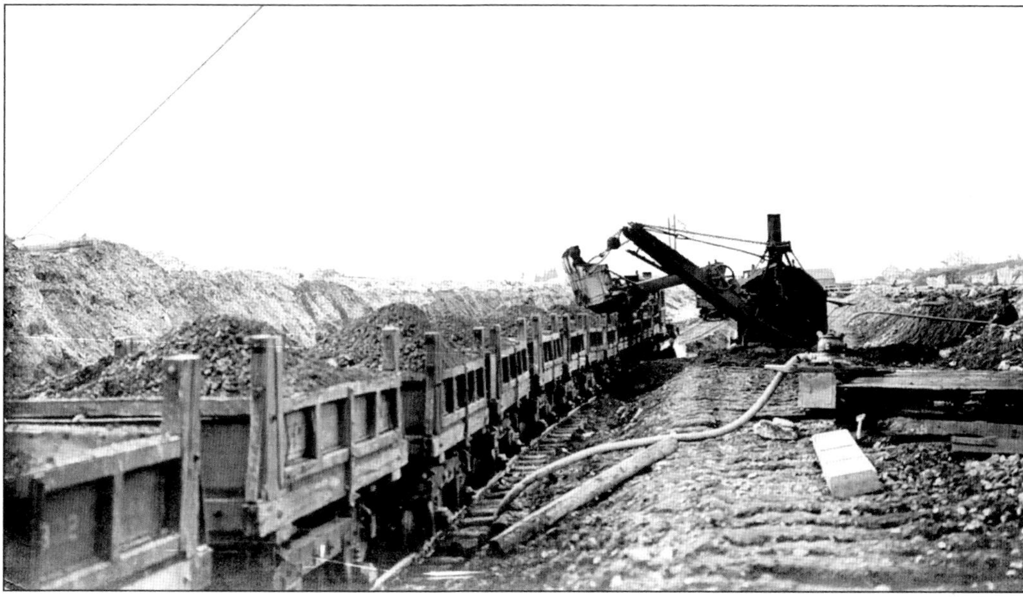

This photograph illustrates the application of steam technology to the opening of a new quarry, a process that came into play in the Rockland quarries in the last quarter of the 19th century. Here a steam shovel is loading rock cars with overburden—the top layer of soil and rock—to uncover the limestone. The train is on a temporary track. After the quarry is defined and quarrying begins, a permanent track will be laid. Before the use of steam, this process was done by hand, horses, and sometimes explosives. This photograph was taken on October 15, 1912. (DH.)

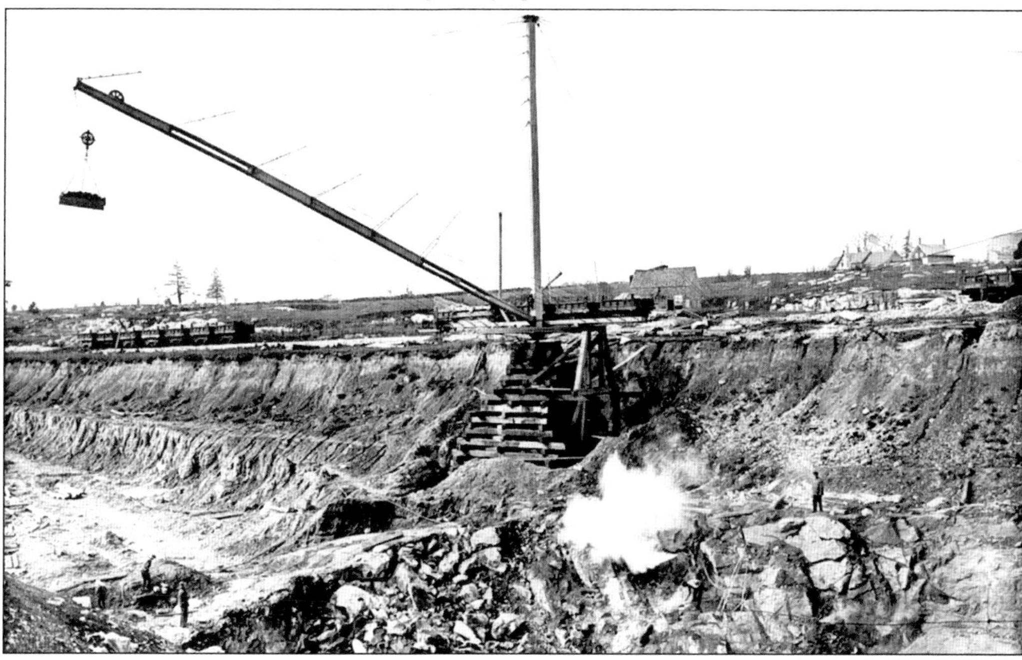

The Blackington Farm quarry in Rockland is shown here in the early stages of quarrying rock after the overburden has been removed. The broken lime rock in the foreground is being hoisted out of the quarry in a drag by a steam-powered derrick. Note the Lime Rock Railroad rock cars at the edge of the quarry. This photograph was taken in October 1912. (DH.)

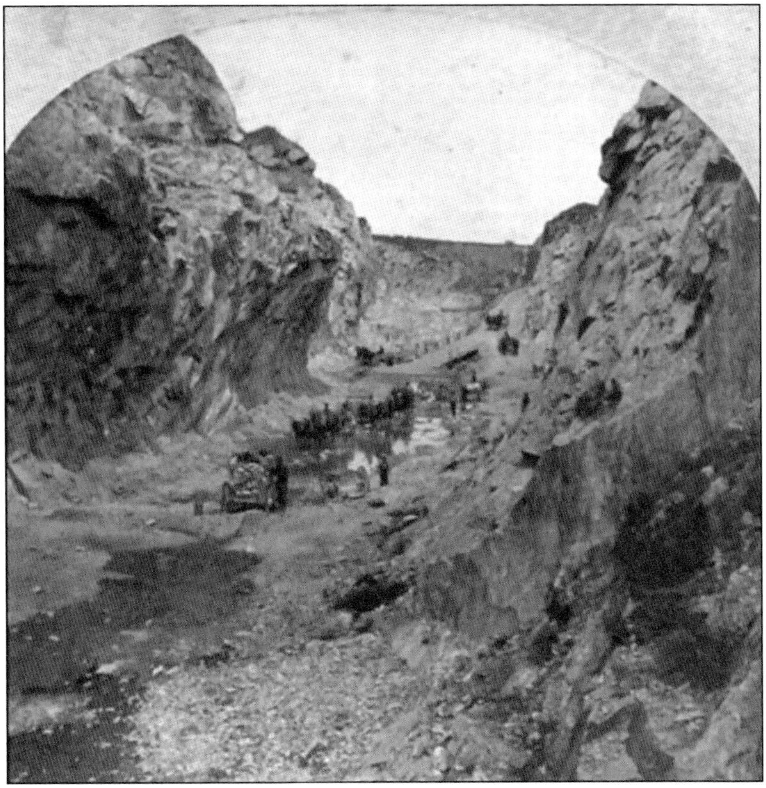

This early picture shows the interior of a quarry before the quarry became deep and the equipment became mechanized. In the 1850s, hand pumps were used to keep quarries dry, "church drills" were used to set the explosives into the rock face, and the lime rock was "doubled out" of the quarries on horse-drawn wagons. By about 1890, steam pumps kept the quarries dry, steam drills were used to set the dynamite, and rock was hoisted out on drags by steam-driven derricks or tramways. (DH.)

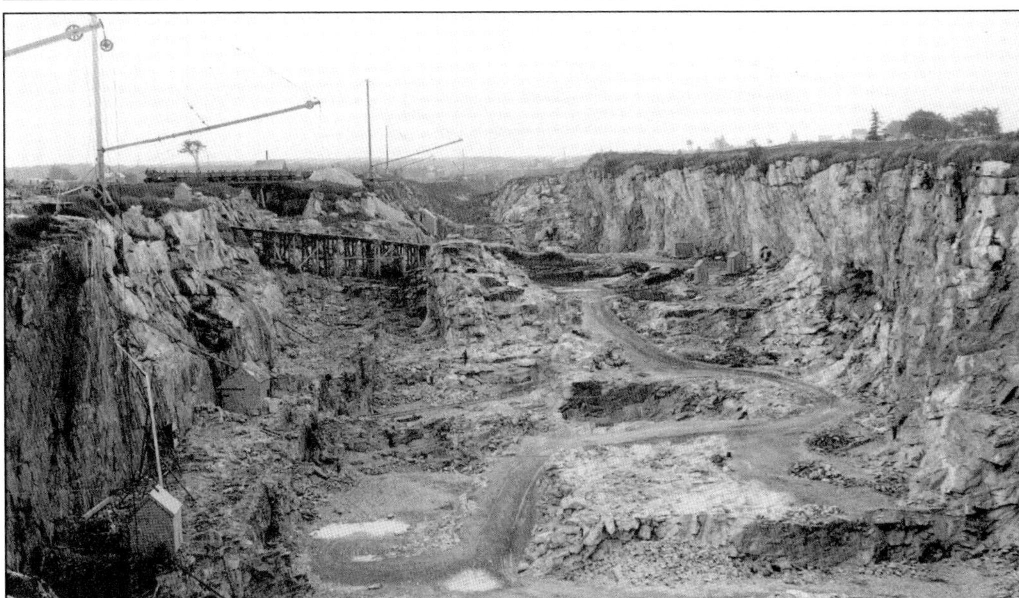

In the left foreground of this quarry, in the West Meadows of Rockland, is the pump house, used continuously to keep water out as the quarries deepened. Note the derricks on the left side of the image and the switchback and trestle, formerly used by horse-drawn carts to take rock out of the quarry before the derricks were installed. In the distance one can see smoke from the engines at the Williams and Doherty quarries. (THS, photograph by Levi Morse.)

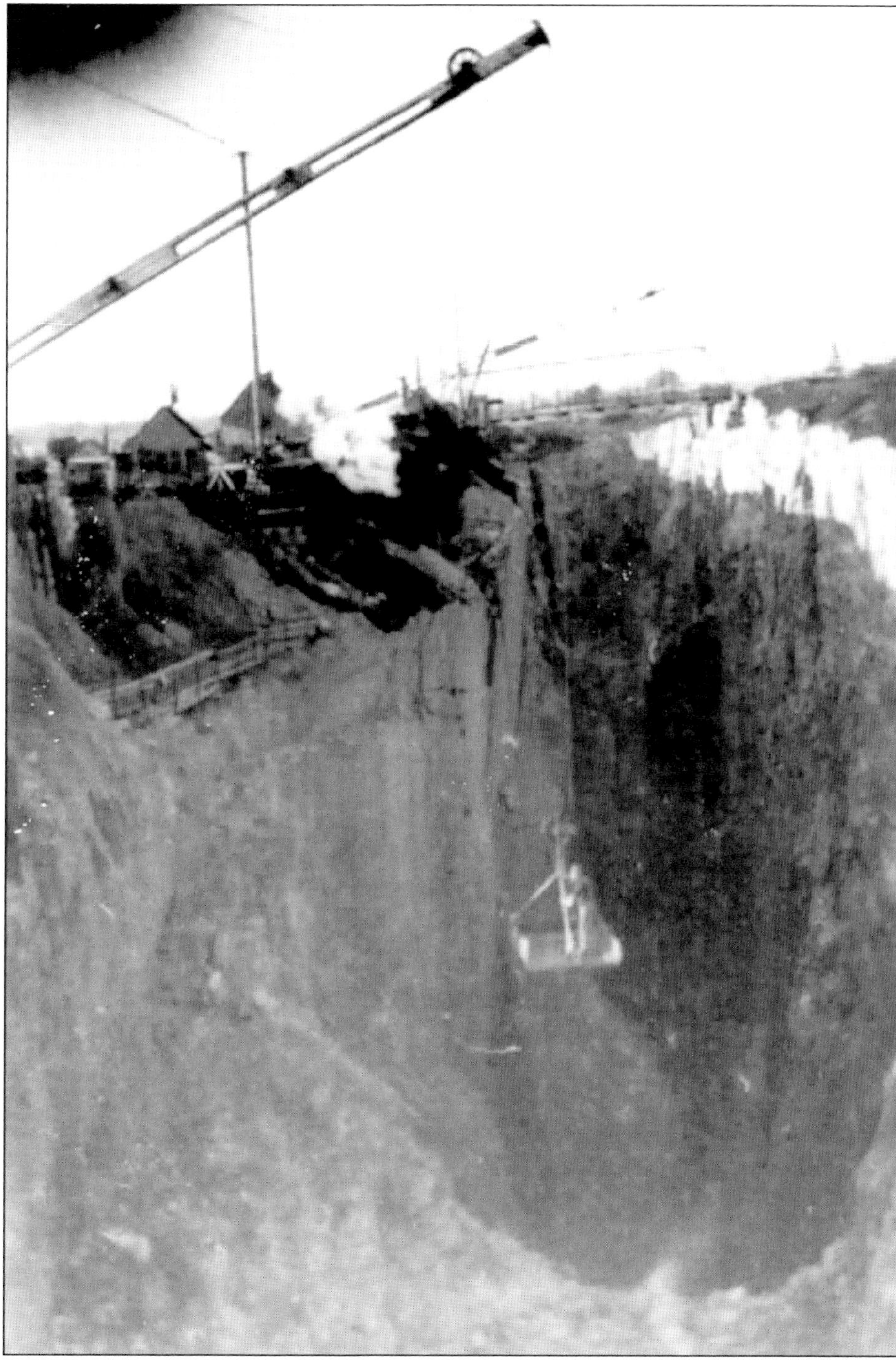

A lone worker is being lowered, or lifted, in the quarry on a drag. Derricks and drags were employed when a quarry became too deep for horses to haul the rock. Workers crowded onto these drags to be lowered into the quarry at the beginning of the day's work and were hoisted out at the end of the workday. The men either had to hold on to each other or the cable since there were virtually no sides to contain them. (DH.)

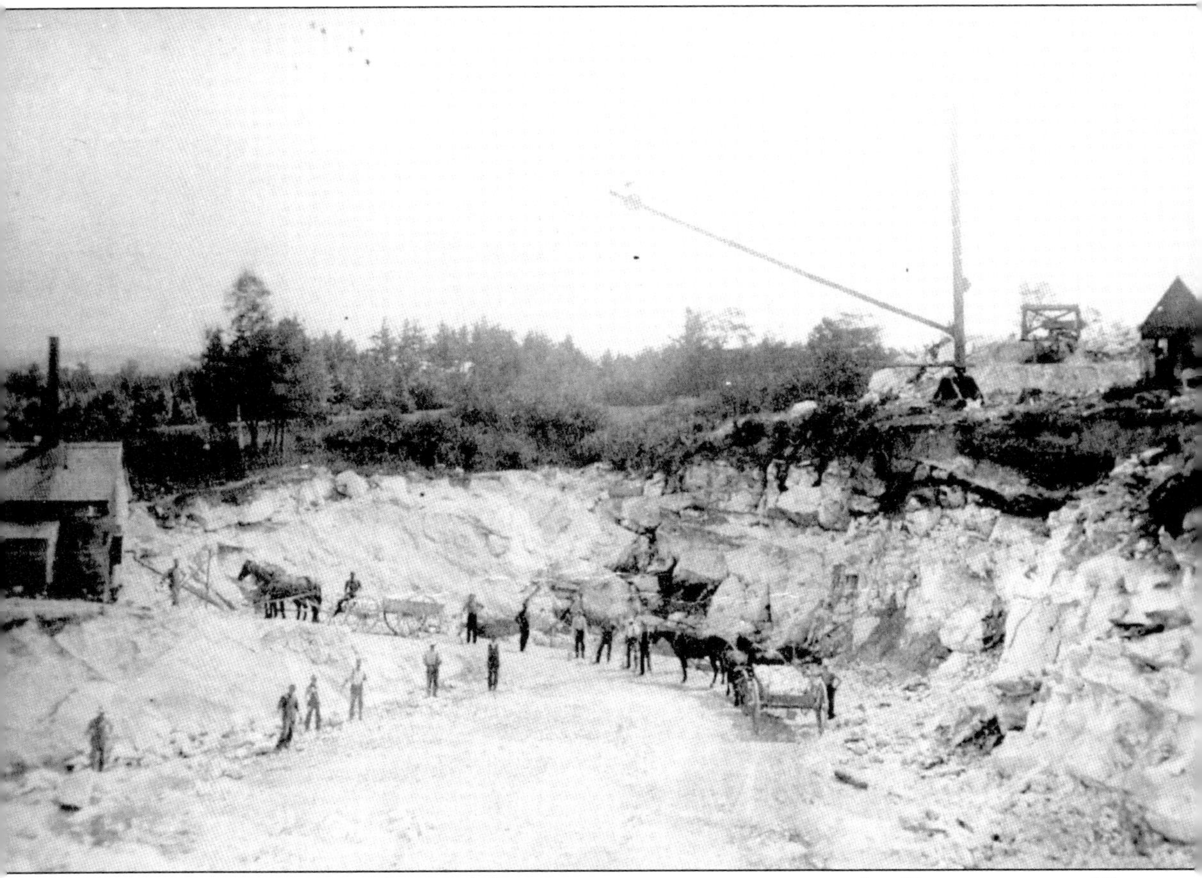

Keeping a quarry pumped out and dry was an expensive requirement for all quarry owners. This unusual quarry in Warren, however, was an exception. Built into a hillside, it was self-draining, which meant no pumping expenses for the owners and, therefore, higher profits. (WHS.)

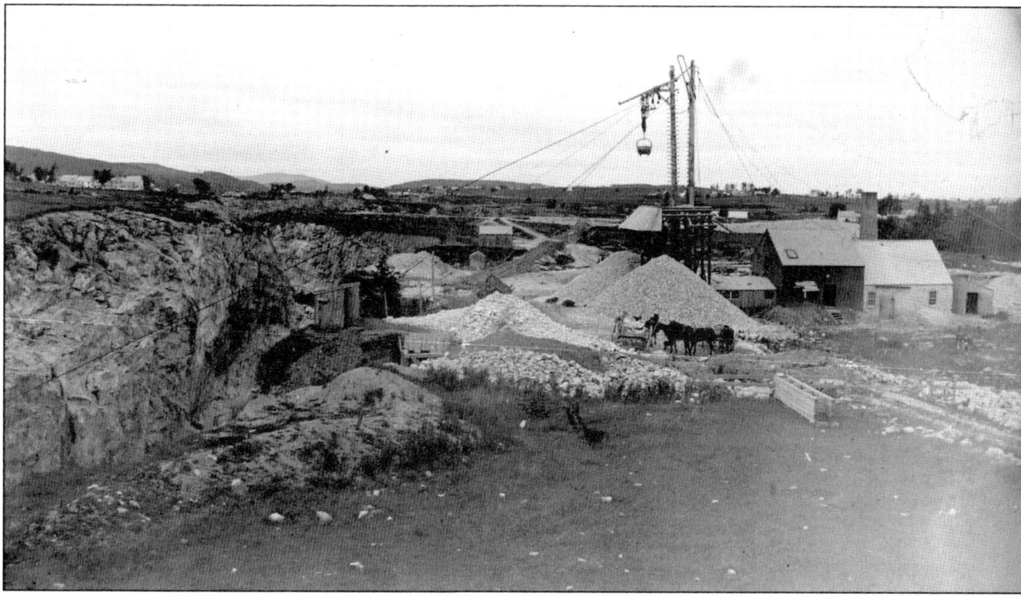

When a quarry became too deep to carry the broken lime rock out by wagon, derricks and tramways were introduced. This 1888 image shows a tramway quarry in Rockland—the Cobb Lime Company Quarry No. 4—just prior to the opening of the Lime Rock Railroad. The large steel bucket travels by pulleys along the cable carrying the chunks of lime rock from the quarry floor to the large rock pile at the rim. (WHS.)

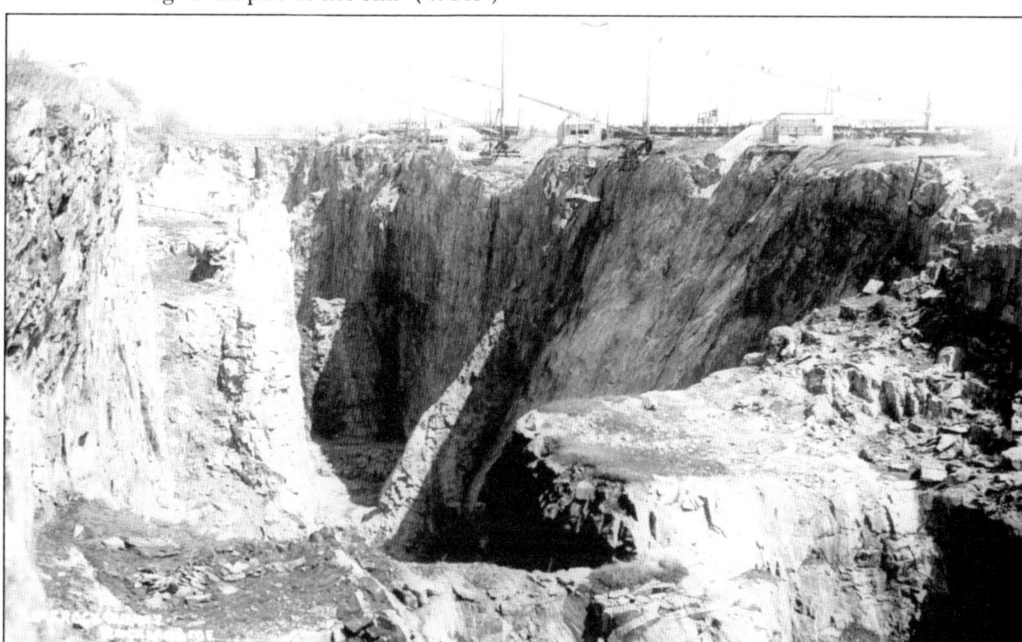

On the far side of this deep derrick quarry, a hoisting derrick and a string of rock cars of the Lime Rock Railroad can be seen. By the 1890s, steam was the prime source of power used for drilling, pumping water, and transporting the rock from the quarry floor to the surface and then on to the kilns. Beginning in that decade, however, electricity was introduced in some quarries for pumping and for creating compressed air for drilling. (DH.)

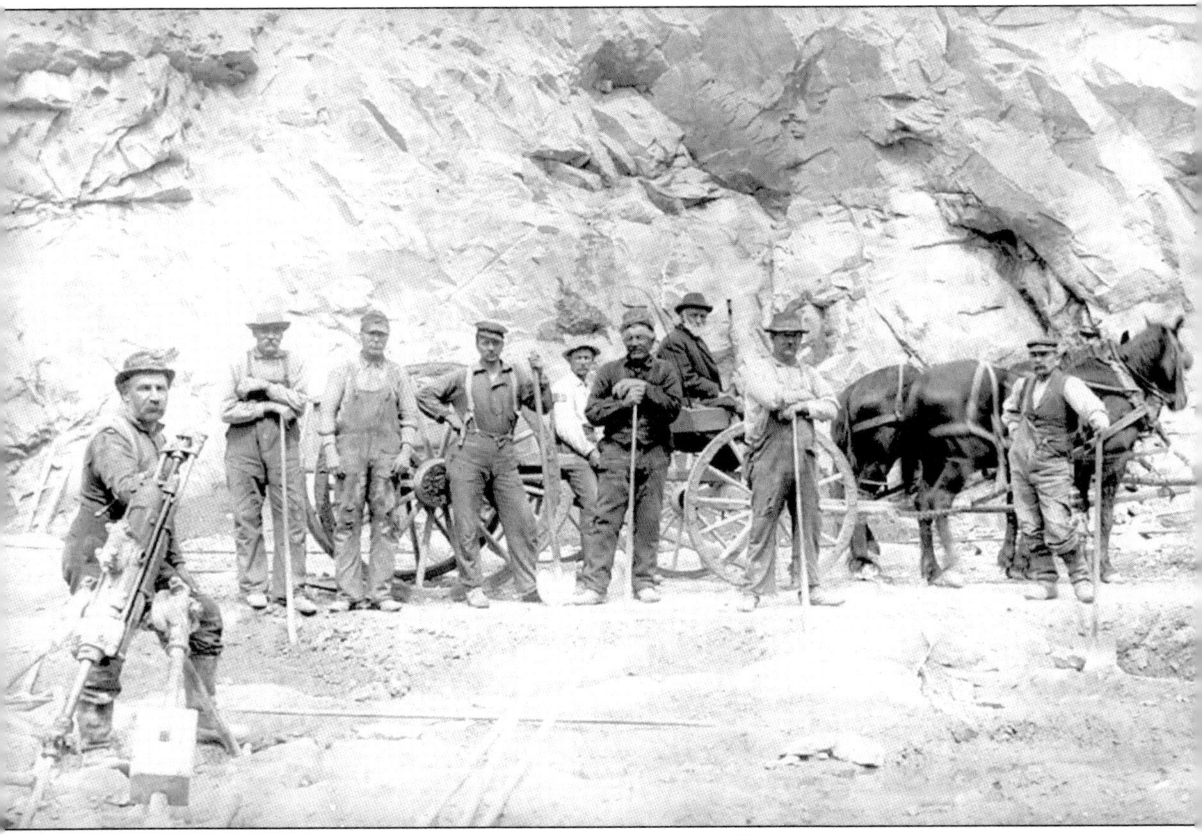

An unidentified quarry crew poses for a picture around 1900. The man on the left has a steam drill for drilling holes in the rock to place the charges of dynamite. Several men lean on poles used to tamp the charges into those holes in preparation for blasting. The bearded man in the wagon may be the owner or an overseer. This photograph is attributed to Ida S. Crie, a well-known amateur photographer from Rockland. (DH.)

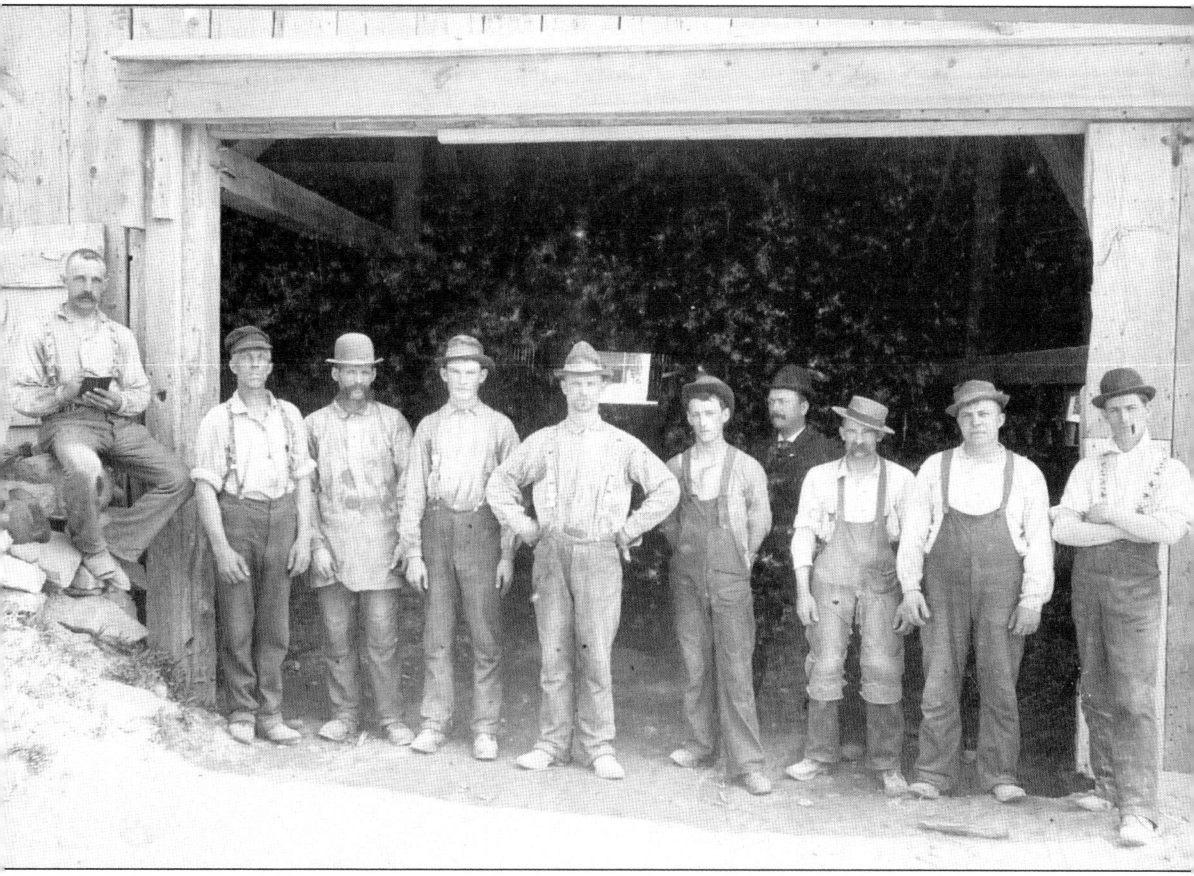

This image of another crew of quarrymen was taken in the early 1900s. Some quarry workers were young single men who came from the surrounding inland towns and lived in boardinghouses in Rockland. (EC.)

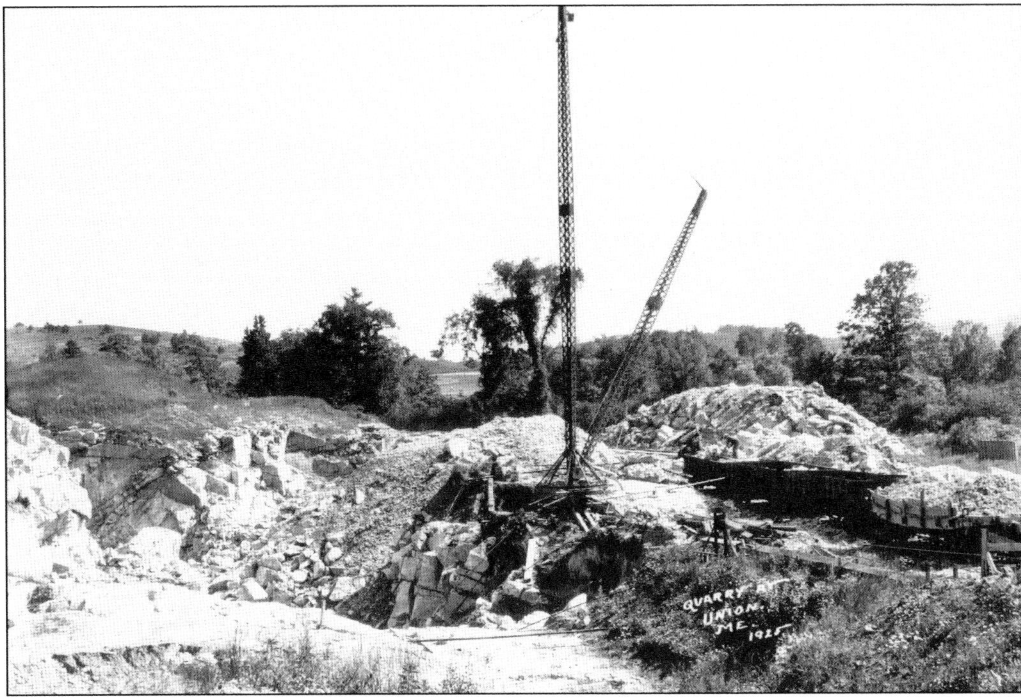

Union, about 12 miles from Rockland, was also involved in the lime industry, both in quarrying and in barrel making. This is an undated view of an operating quarry in Union. (RHS.)

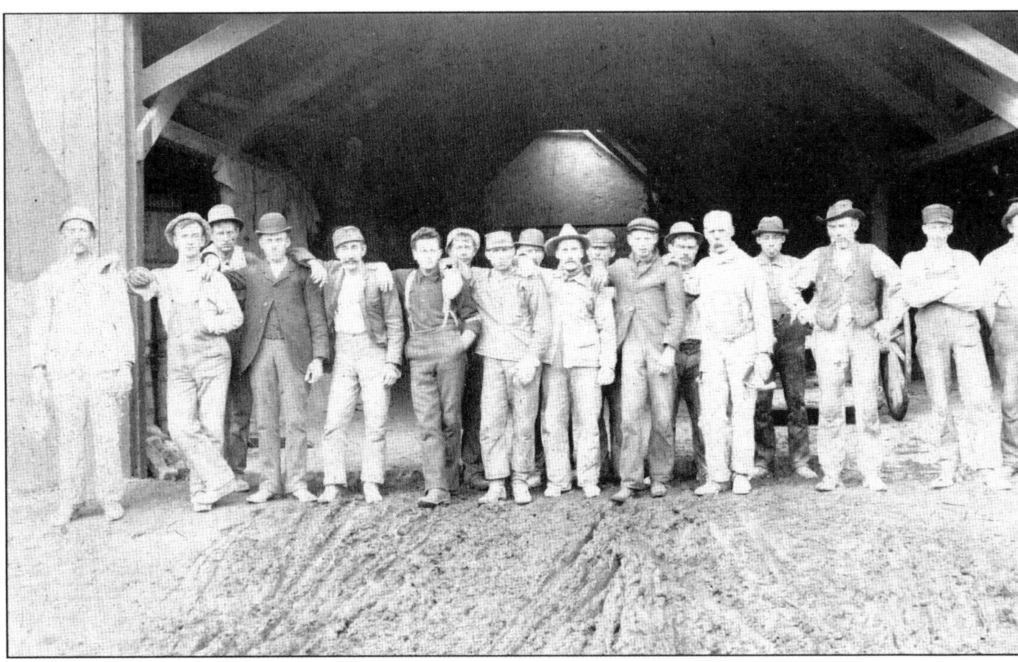

This large crew of a lime kiln poses at the entrance to a kiln shed. Except for one man on the left who is dressed in business clothes, everyone wears work clothes. Kiln tenders often wore bandannas that they pulled over their faces when they shoveled the caustic lime. Men also wore large leather mitts to avoid any lime burning the flesh. (RHS.)

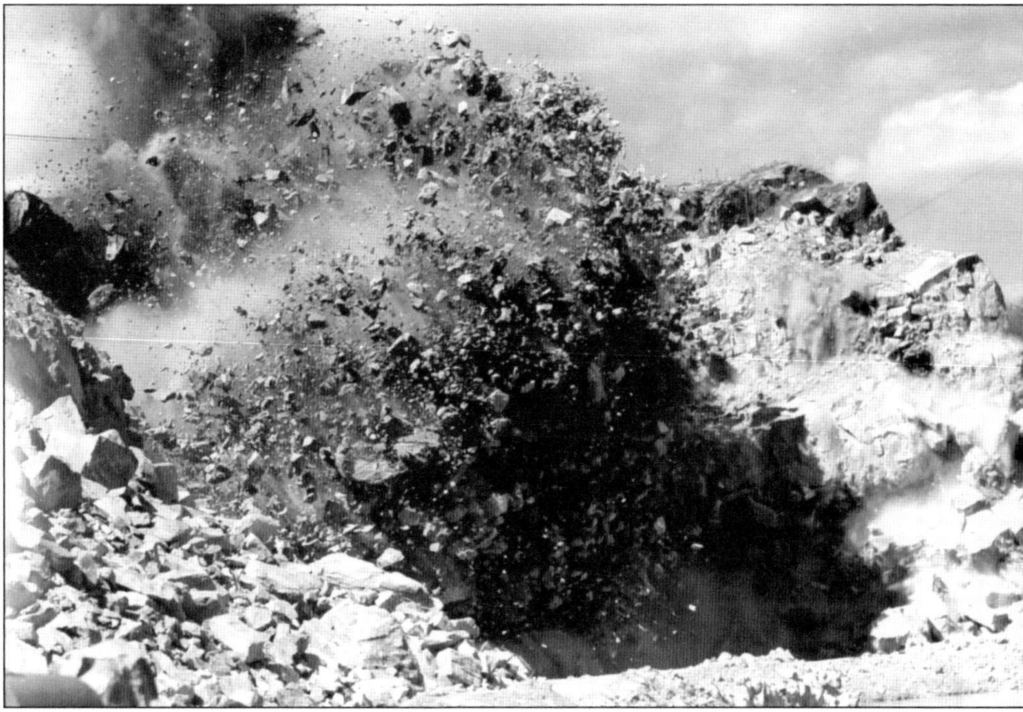

In this blast at the Mag Quarry on May 5, 1959, a total of 7,200 pounds of dynamite were used. One safety feature that was always followed was the 15-minute warning given before a blast. This gave workers time to take cover. (DH.)

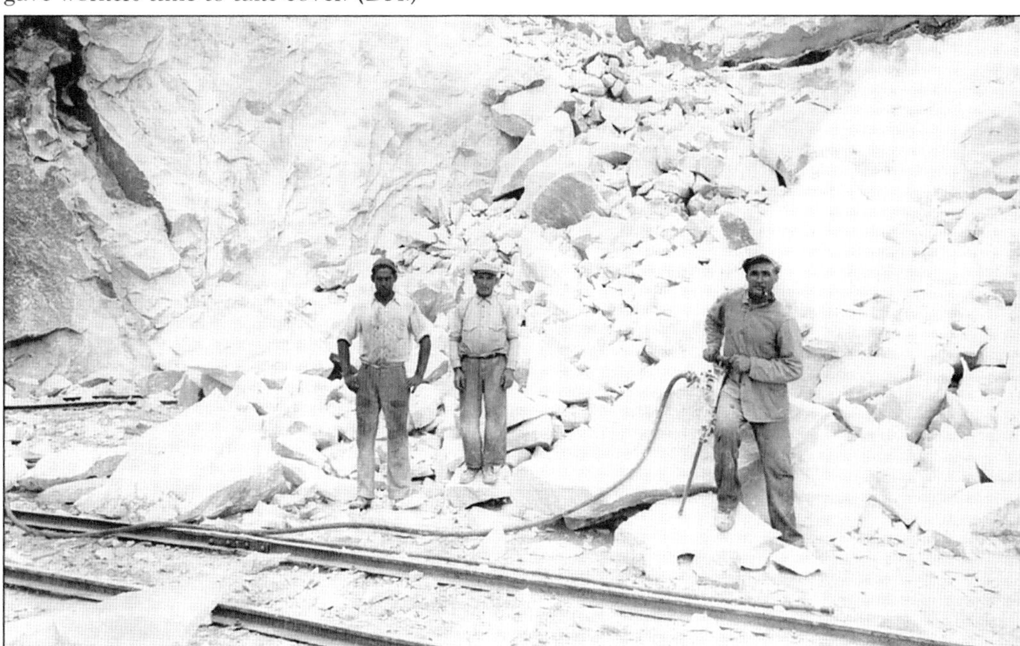

Quarrymen are drilling a blasting hole for a charge of dynamite, to blast the large rocks into smaller pieces. This was called squibbing by quarrymen. The large pieces, or squibs, may have to be broken again with a hammer to achieve the required head size of the rock. (DH.)

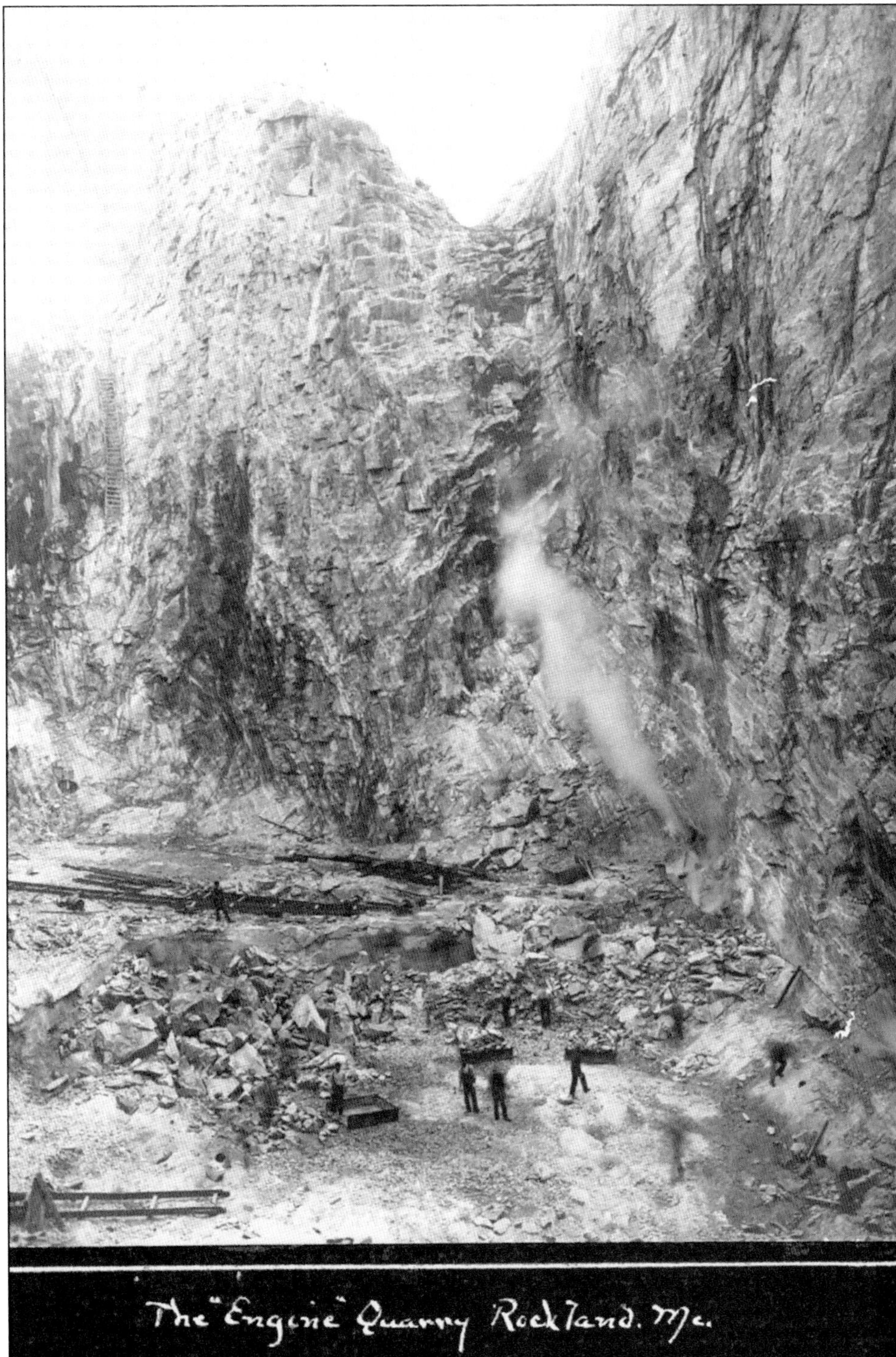

This is the Cobb Lime Company's Engine Quarry (pronounced with a long *i*) at the head of Limerock Street in Rockland. In 1895, it was the first quarry in the United States to change from steam to electricity to hoist the rock drags and pump the quarry. (DH.)

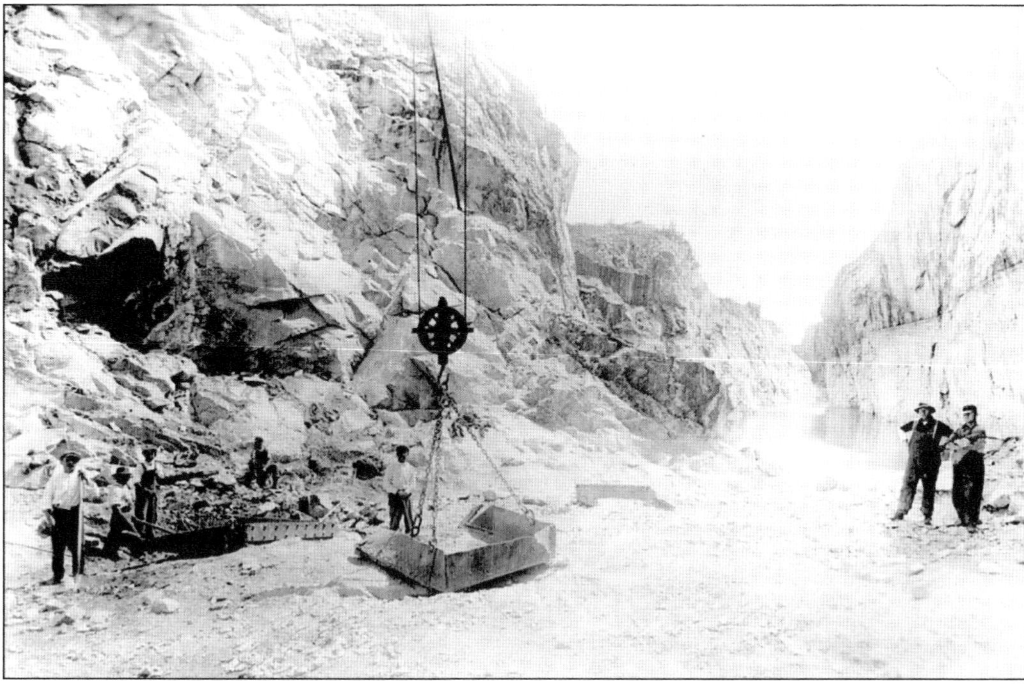

The quarry crew poses by two full drags ready to be hoisted to ground level and an empty drag hooked to the derrick cable that has just been lowered to the quarry floor. (DH.)

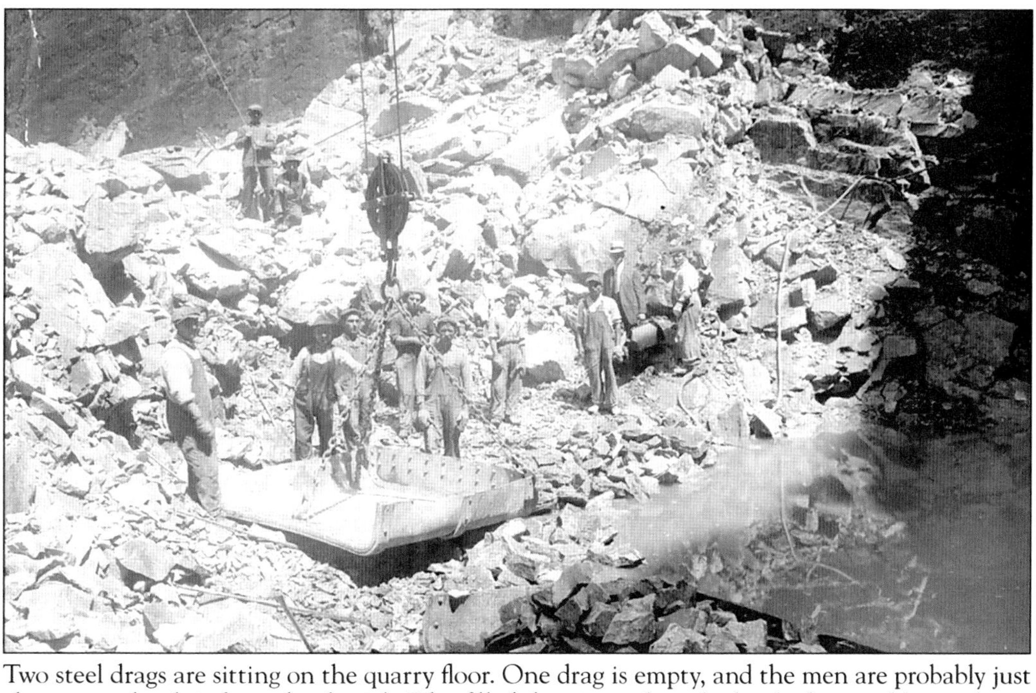

Two steel drags are sitting on the quarry floor. One drag is empty, and the men are probably just about to unhook it from the derrick. The filled drag is ready to be hooked up and hoisted out. Rock crews dug and blasted out rock of all sizes, but each chunk of limestone had to be broken up by hand to about the size of a human head before it could be taken out of the quarry. (DH.)

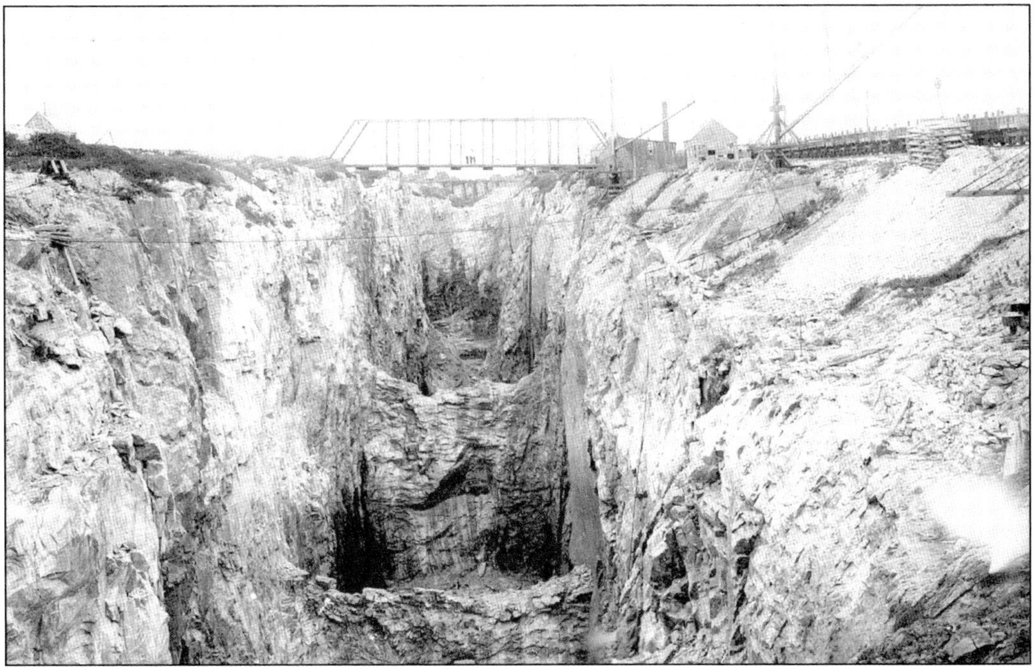

This is a typical quarry scene that shows the growing depth of the quarry using intact sections to support the quarry walls. Note the many derricks and rock cars on the Lime Rock Railroad. (DH.)

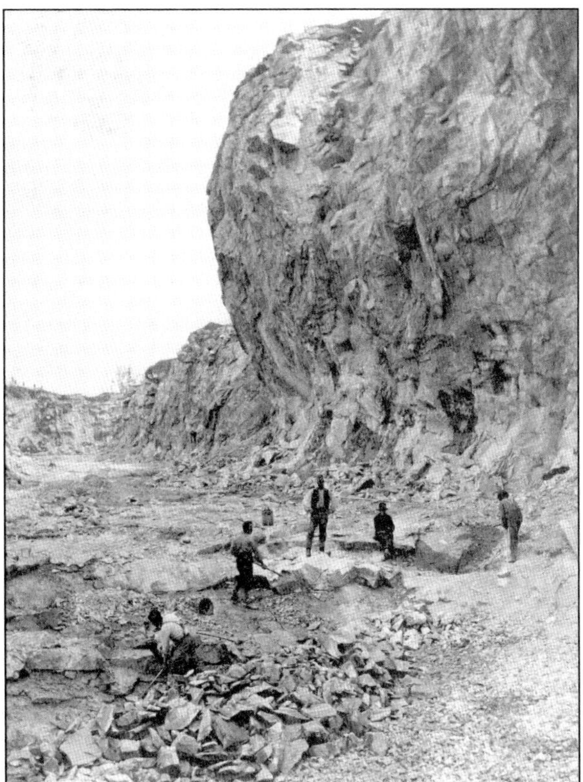

This image shows a quarry crew with a background bulge of low-grade limestone. This illustrates the care taken to quarry only high-grade rock. (DH.)

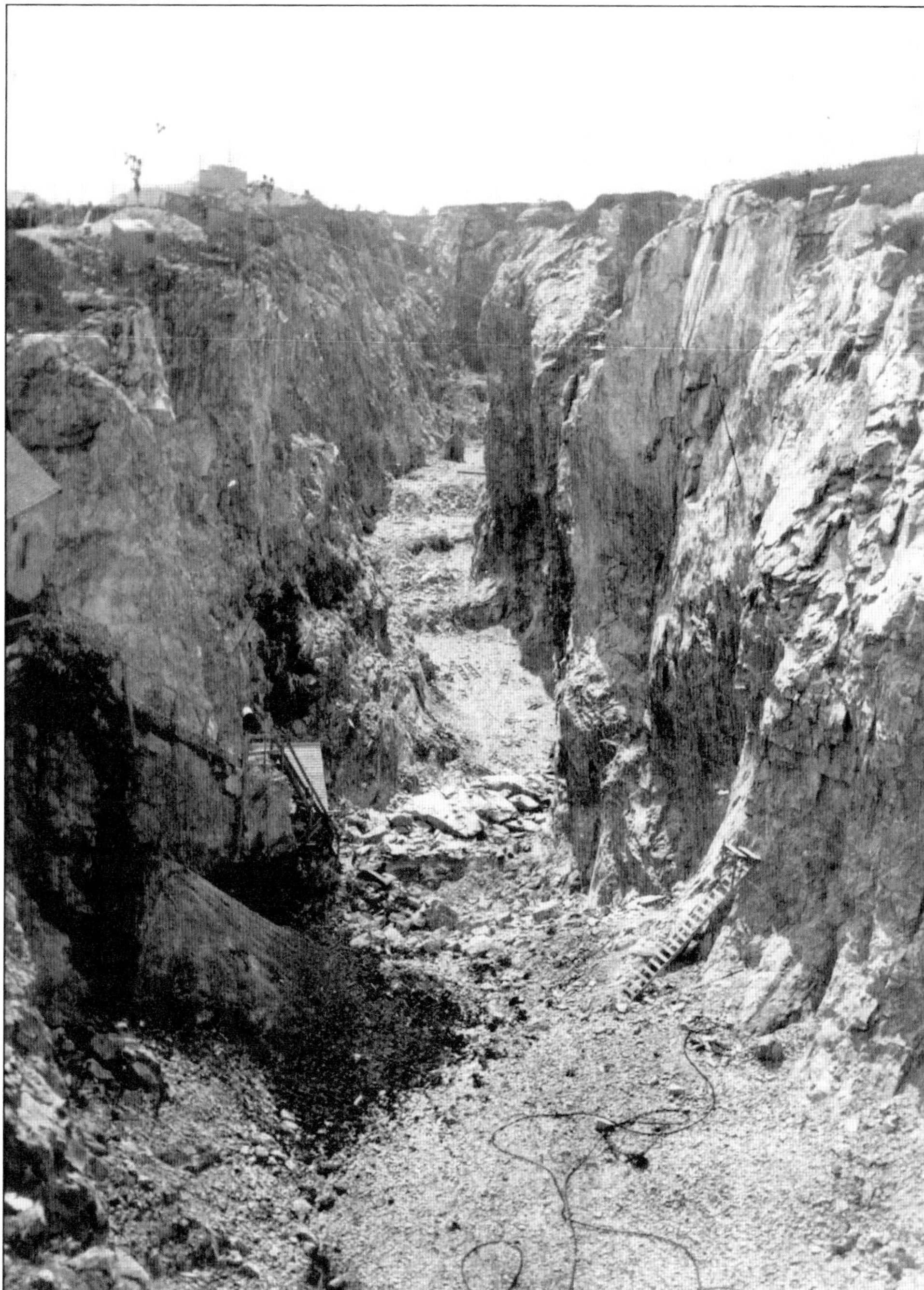

As quarries in the Rockland area deepened, quarry work became more dangerous. Large charges of dynamite called "giants" would occasionally discharge prematurely, or sometimes not at all. Later an unsuspecting quarryman might drill and hit the unfired charge. Some discharges would dislodge rocks in neighboring quarries. When steam drills and donkey engines were installed, both steam and hot water were released, which sometimes resulted in serious scalds and burns for the unwary worker. (RHS.)

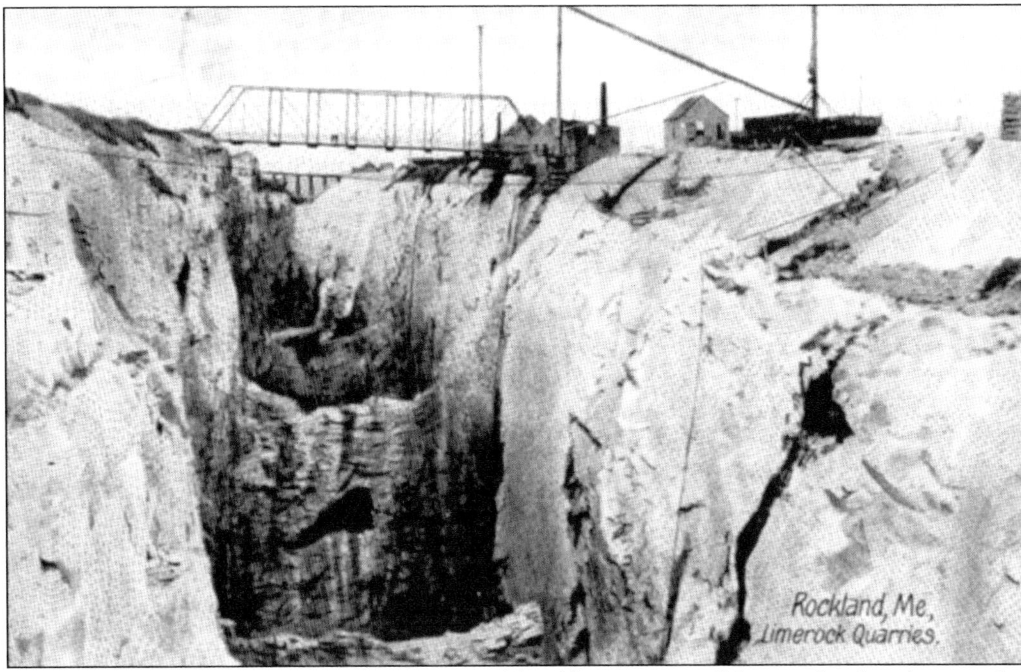

The Park Street bridge at the Thomaston-Rockland line was a well-known landmark in its day. It spanned the Williams Quarry, which became the deepest lime rock quarry in the world. The rock quarried west of the Old County Road was carted to the harborside kilns over this bridge, which connected Old County Road to Rockland's Park and Pleasant Streets. (CM.)

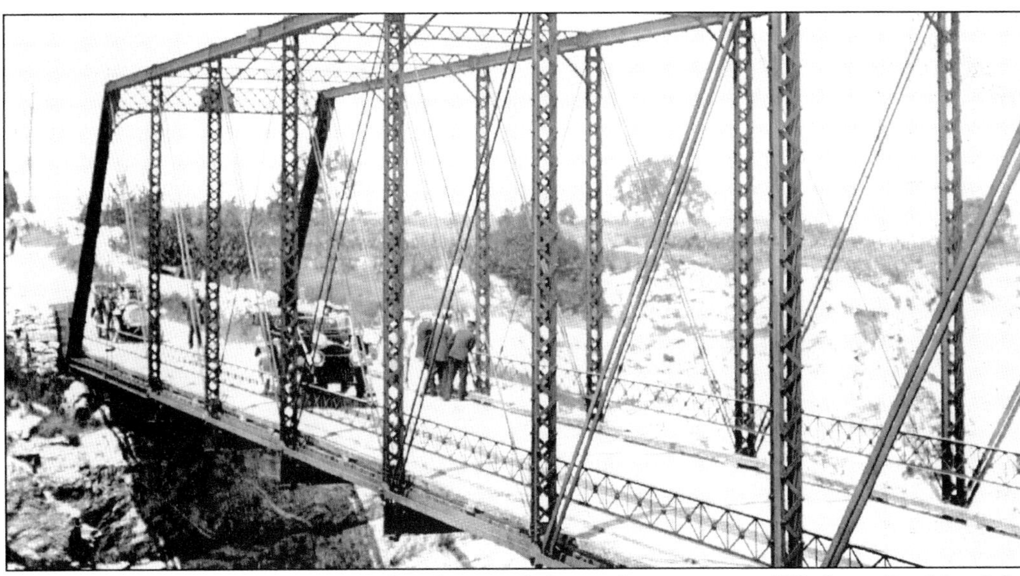

In July 1910, Pres. William Howard Taft visited the midcoast region. While in Rockland, he wanted to see the world's deepest open-pit lime quarry, the Williams Quarry, then about 400 feet deep. This is a picture of the president's party as they pause on the iron bridge, which allowed them a full view of the quarry. (DH.)

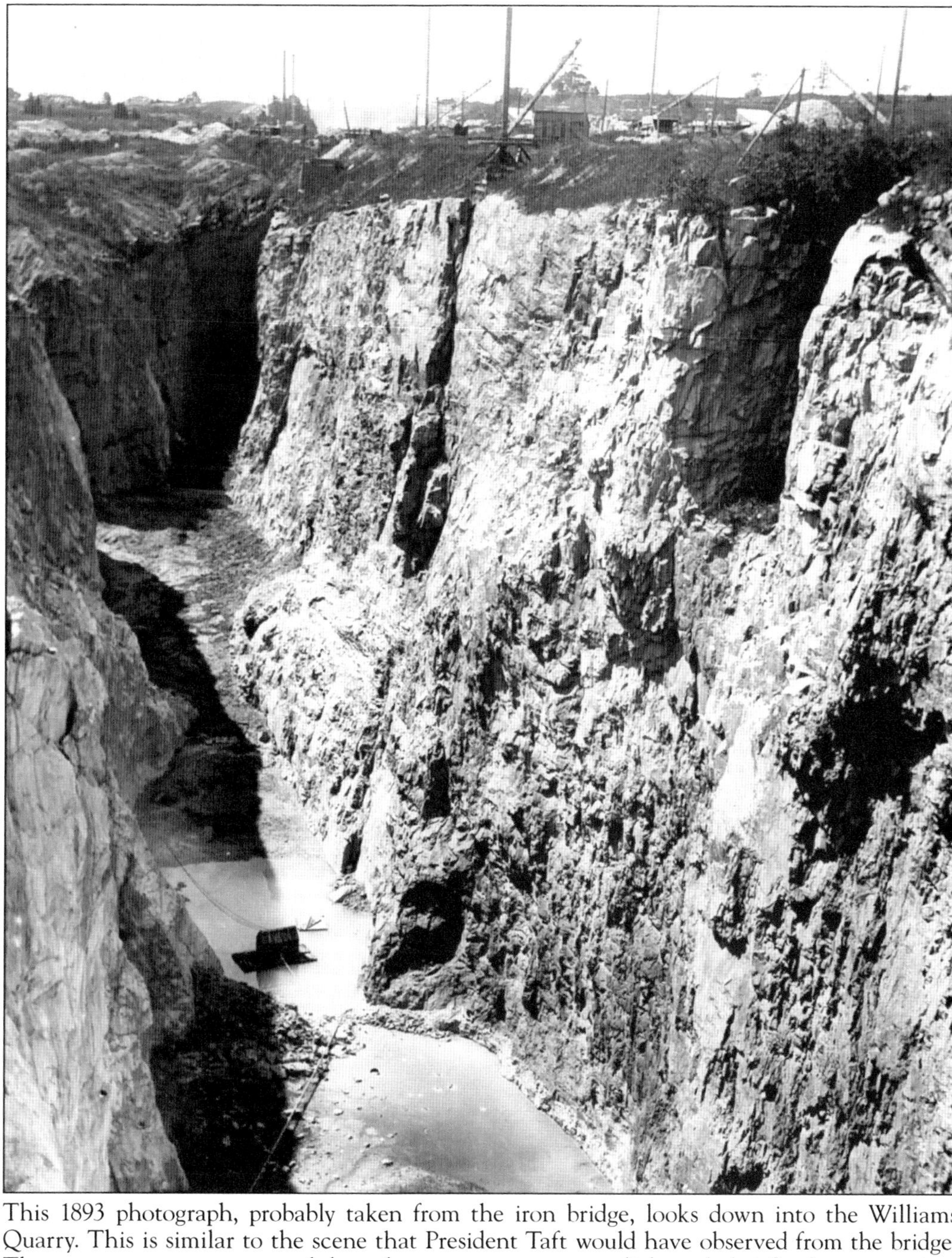

This 1893 photograph, probably taken from the iron bridge, looks down into the Williams Quarry. This is similar to the scene that President Taft would have observed from the bridge. The quarry was so narrow and deep that quarrymen saw sunlight only briefly about noontime when the sun was directly overhead. The rest of the day, they worked in shadow. (DH.)

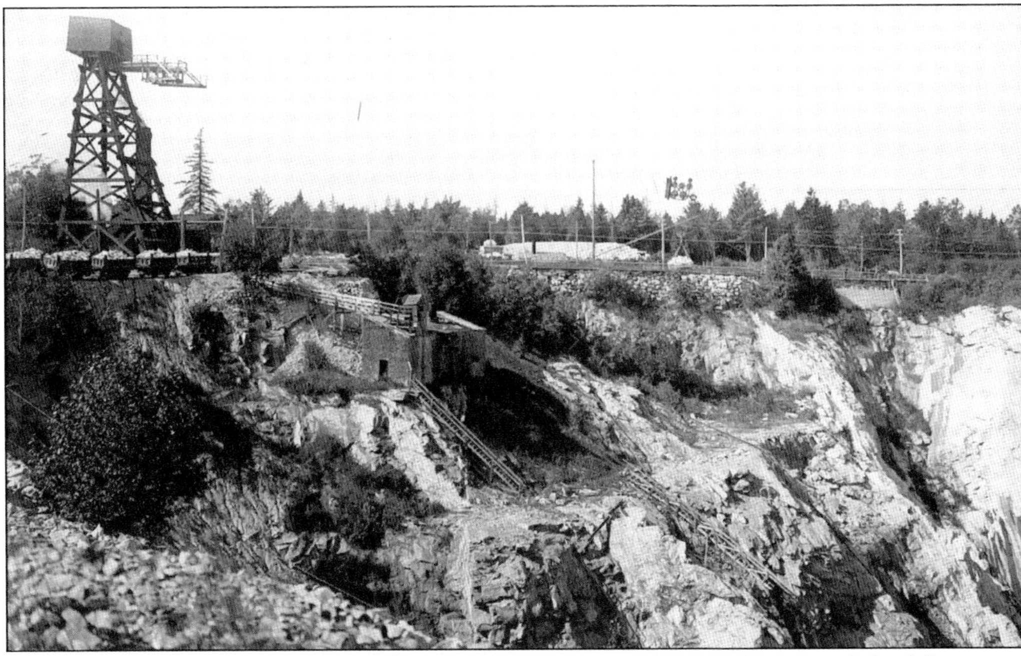

The Jacob's Quarry in Rockport had a tramway tower, seen here in the upper left of the image. Adjacent to the tower are the side-dumping rock cars. The Jacob's Quarry was terraced; note the series of ladders to the lower levels, and the drag filled with rock on the tramway in the middle of the photograph. (CRHS.)

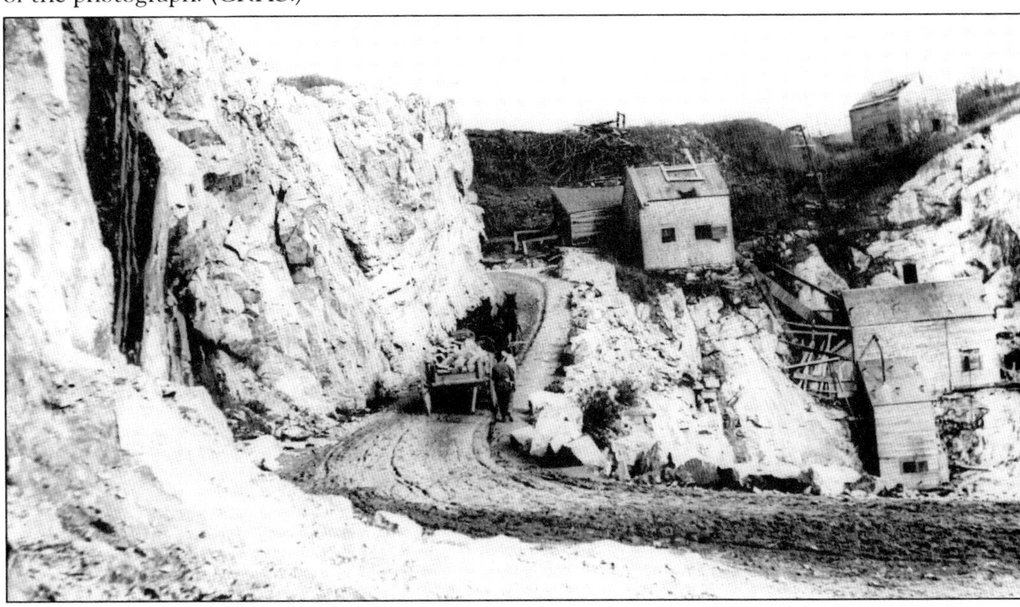

The Jacob's Quarry in Rockport contained some of the purest and whitest lime rock in the area. In 1817, a cargo of 300 casks of Jacob's Quarry Lime was sent to Washington, D.C., for use in the construction of the United States Capitol. This image, taken in the late 1800s, shows a loaded rock wagon being drawn out of the quarry by a four-horse team. The buildings include a pump house (lower level), a field office, and a storage building (upper level). The quarry is now the site of the Camden-Rockport transfer station and dump on Union Street. (CRHS.)

Two

From Quarry to Kiln

Quarry workers loaded lime rock by hand onto rock wagons on the quarry floor. Extra teams were added to pull the wagons up the steep incline to the surface. At the quarry rim, the extra teams were unhitched, and the wagons were pulled by either two or four horses to the kilns. Unpaved roads made travel difficult during mud time in the early spring or after a spell of wet weather, when the heavy wagons became mired in mud. A rock wagon made two or three round-trips a day, depending on the location of the kiln and quarry it was serving.

In 1888, several Rockland companies pooled their resources to build the Lime Rock Railroad to carry the rock to the kilns by train. A standard-gauge line, it had 12.5 miles of track. In 1901, the Lime Rock Railroad carried 298,000 tons of rock and served 39 kilns. It ran on a raised trestle around the rim of the harbor so that it could pull up at the kiln tops and load the lime rock directly into the kilns from side-dumping cars. It created new jobs on the rail line but spelled the end of a livelihood for many teamsters, who, needless to say, did not support it.

Two other local lime railroads were built at about the same time. In 1886, Rockport lime manufacturers Carleton, Norwood Company, and the Shepherd Company laid out the Rockport Railroad, a narrow-gauge line running three miles from Simonton's Corner to the kilns at the Rockport waterfront. The railroad had two Vulcan locomotives; its 35 five-ton cars were built by Knowlton Brothers in Camden. It operated for 14 years, after which it was sold to the Rockland-Rockport Lime Company, a conglomerate managed by William Cobb of Rockland. The Georges Valley Railroad, known as the Doodlebug Railroad, picked up lime at the North Warren and Union quarries and brought it to Warren Depot, where it connected to the regular Rockland branch of the Maine Central Railroad. The eight-mile line with a two-mile spur was built in 1893 by the Rockland firm of McLoon and Stover, whose high-magnesium lime was sold to the pulp paper industry. The Great Northern Paper Company bought the line in 1918 and operated it until 1932, when it was permanently closed.

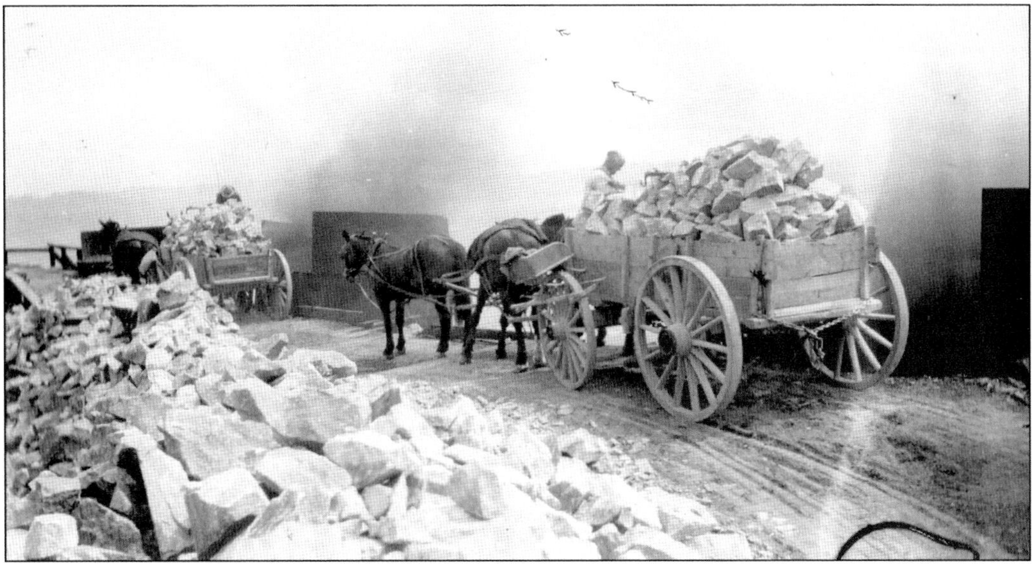

Since the 1830s when the first kilns were built at the harbor, teaming was an important part of the local economy. Even after 1888, when the Lime Rock Railroad began operating, some teaming continued, but eventually in Rockland, 375 horses and 120 teamsters were replaced by a few locomotives and about 35 men. However, teams still hauled rock to the smaller kilns. They also hauled rock from the nearby quarries in Rockport, and they continued to haul waste rock to the dumps and other locations not served by the railroads. (EC.)

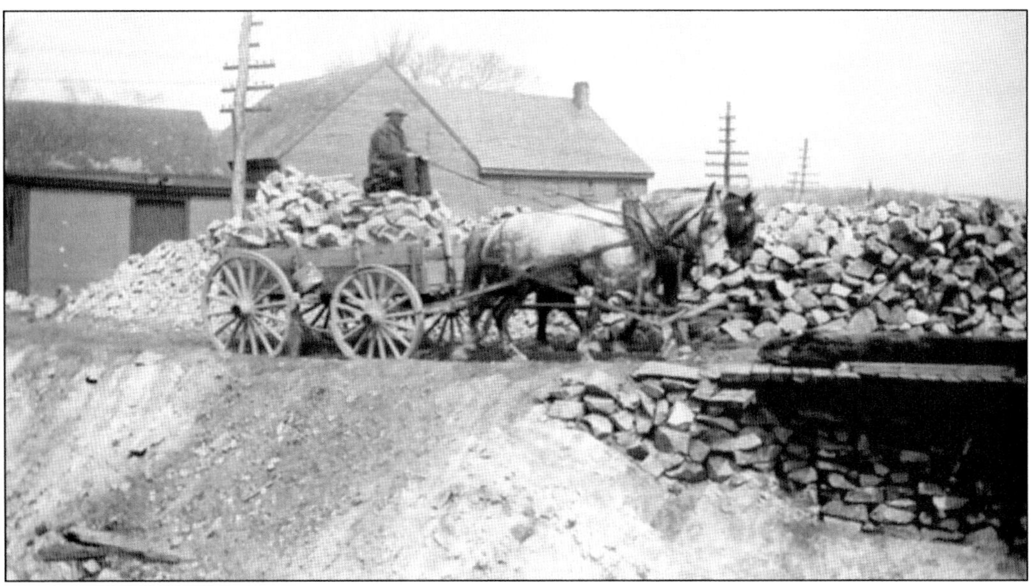

This photograph was taken in 1924, decades after the railroads began operating. The wagon is heading for a waterfront kiln that was not served by the railroad. (DH.)

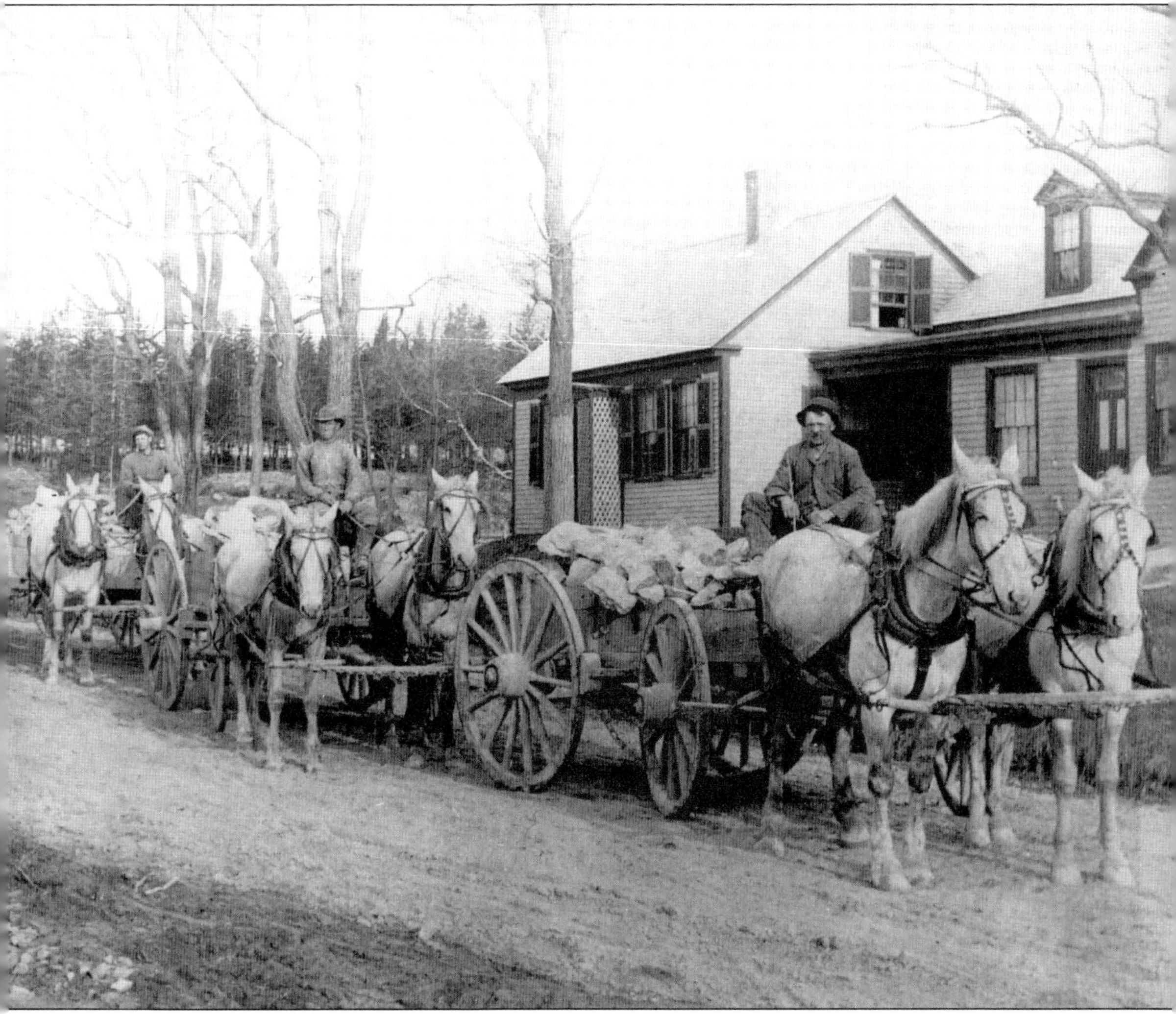

A string of rock wagons heads toward harbor-front kilns in "Lime City," driven by local teamsters. Throughout the 19th century, transporting lime rock was a steady business for many local residents. In all seasons, men could have as much work as they wanted. In winter, teamsters used horse-drawn sleds to haul rock. Here a four-wheeled wagon is seen in front, followed by two two-wheeled carts. (THS.)

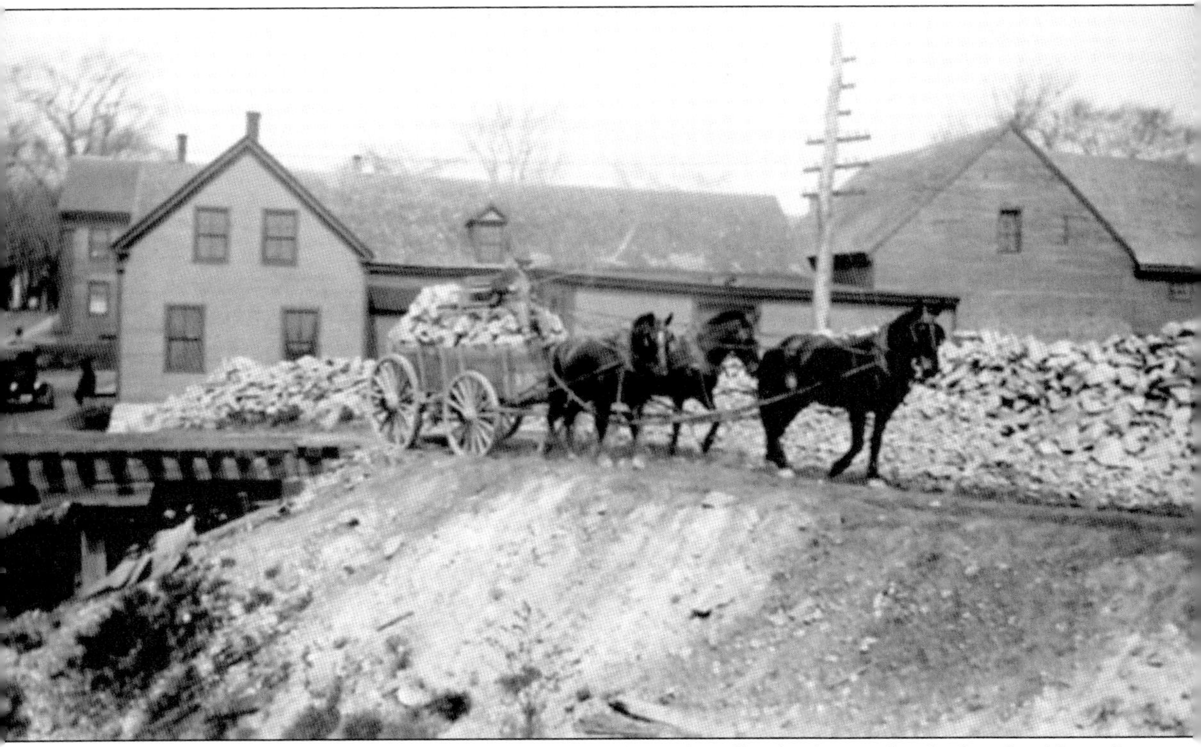

Many rock wagons were built to be extra sturdy to handle the heavy load of rock. Also, the wheels were wide and often had extra spokes for strength. Teaming gave employment not only to team owners and their horses but also to blacksmiths, harness makers, and others. (RHS.)

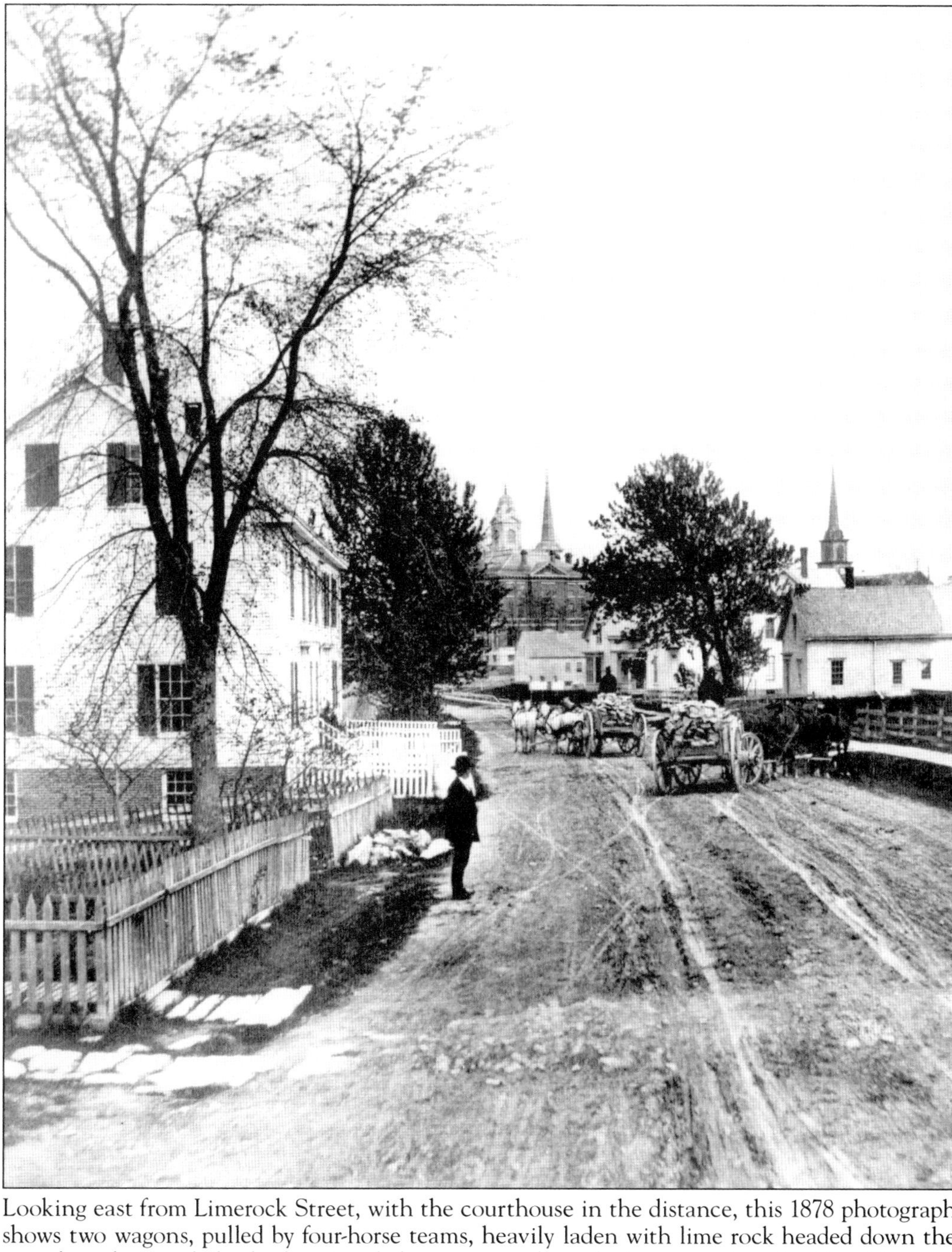

Looking east from Limerock Street, with the courthouse in the distance, this 1878 photograph shows two wagons, pulled by four-horse teams, heavily laden with lime rock headed down the rutted road toward the harbor. Loaded wagons made such deep ruts that Rockland became known for its nearly impassable roads, especially in the spring. Main Street was not paved with cobblestones until 1895 and not paved with granite blocks until 1910. (RHS.)

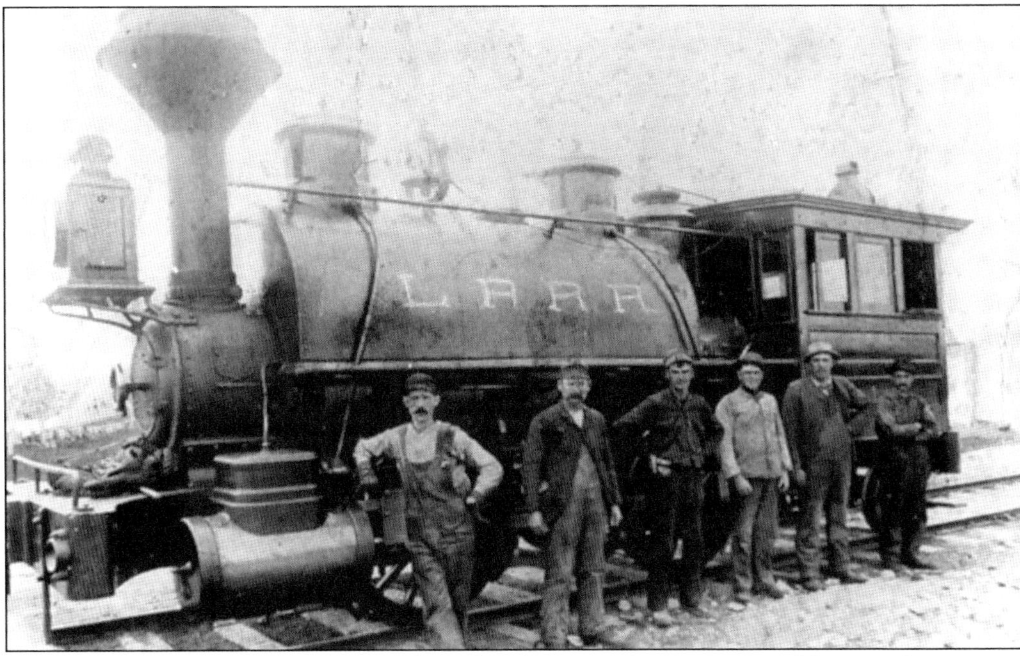

In its original configuration, Lime Rock Railroad engine No. 1 was a wood-burning locomotive. The balloon stack served as a spark arrester, which helped prevent fires along the railroad right-of-ways. These trains not only carried lime rock from the quarries to the kilns, but they also carried coal from the coal tower around the rim of the harbor to the kilns to be burned as fuel. (MH.)

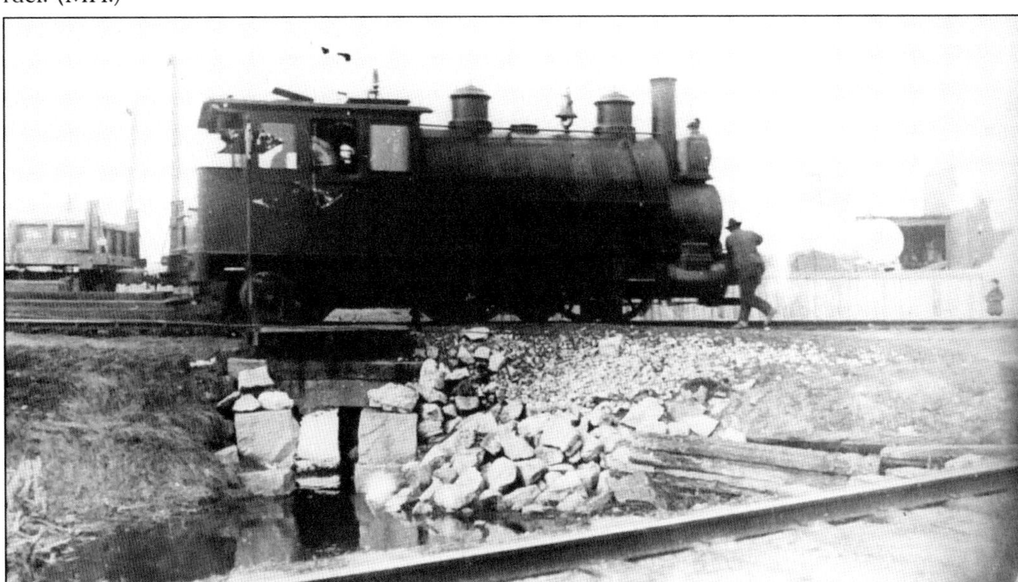

Here is a later image of engine No. 1, the Lime Rock Railroad's first and most enduring steam locomotive. It was built by the Porter Locomotive Company and put in service in 1888 when the railroad began operations. It was still in use in 1941 when the line ceased operations. It is seen here after it was modified into a coal burner with a different stack and a steel cabin that replaced the original wooden one. (MH.)

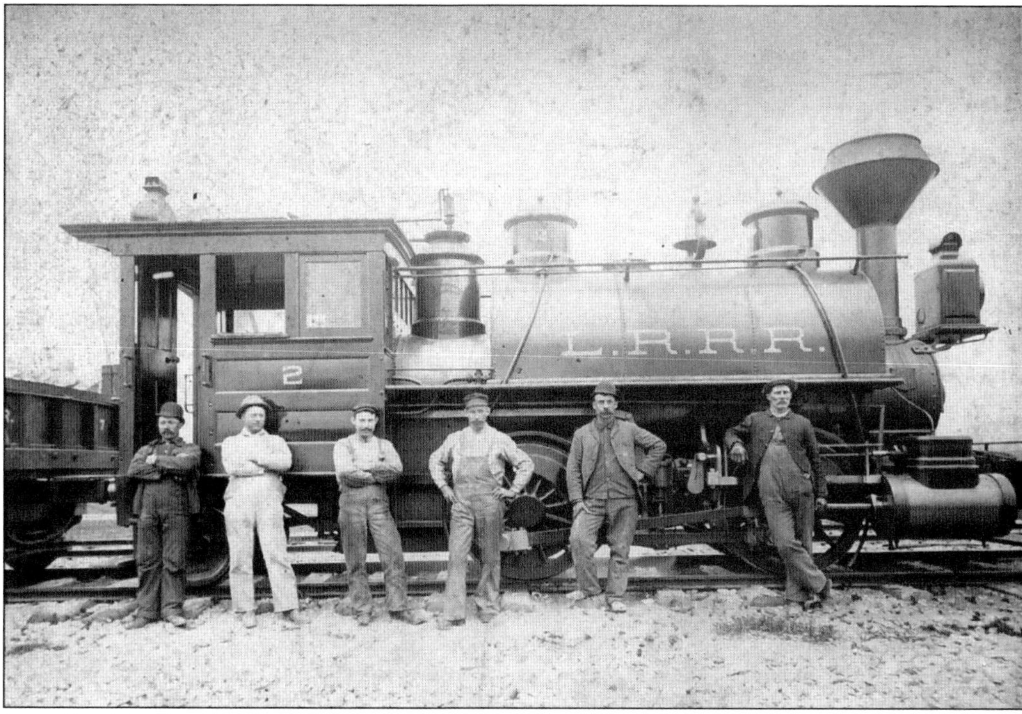

Lime Rock Railroad engine No. 2 is seen here with an unidentified crew. Note the spark catcher smokestack, indicating that when it went into service, it was a wood-burning locomotive. (MH.)

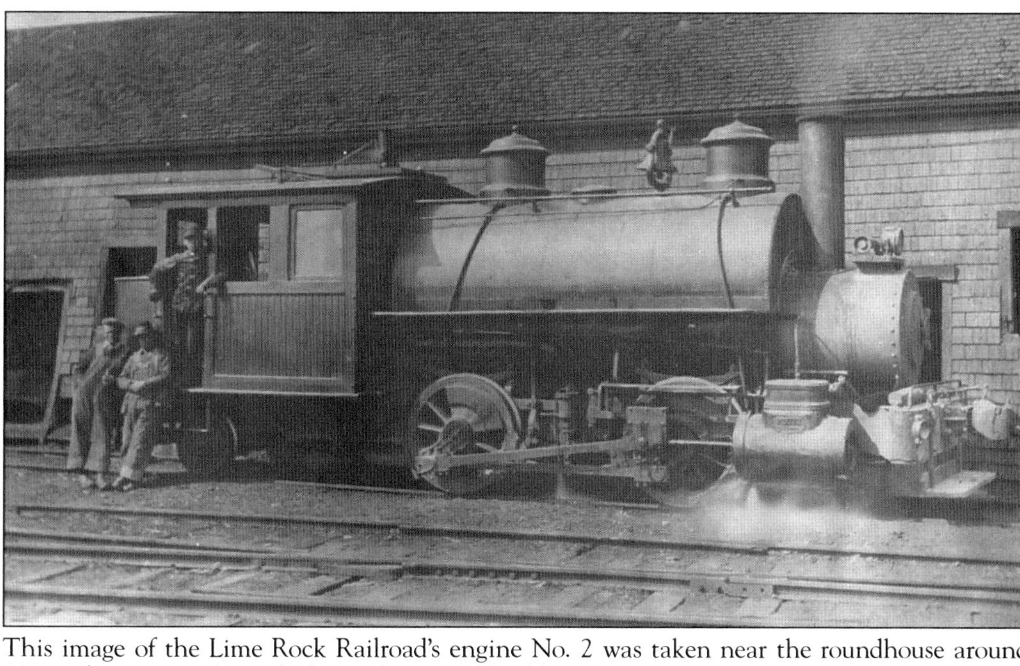

This image of the Lime Rock Railroad's engine No. 2 was taken near the roundhouse around 1920. The new smokestack shows that it too had been modified to burn coal. The cab has also been updated and a coal bunker added to the rear of the cab. In the cab is engineer Fred V. Waltz. On the ground in the cap is conductor Bill Widdecomb. The other man is unidentified. (MH.)

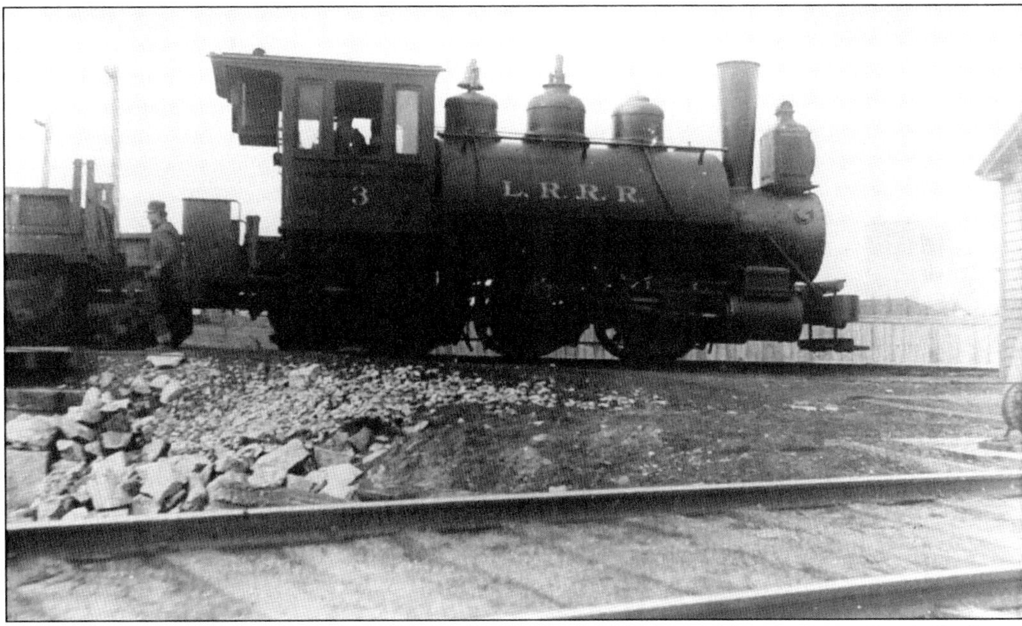

Engine No. 3 was one of five steam locomotives eventually owned by the Lime Rock Railroad. The Baldwin Locomotive Works built it in 1903. In this 1920 photograph, it is seen in Rockland near the Maine Central Railroad and the Lime Rock Railroad crossover. (MH.)

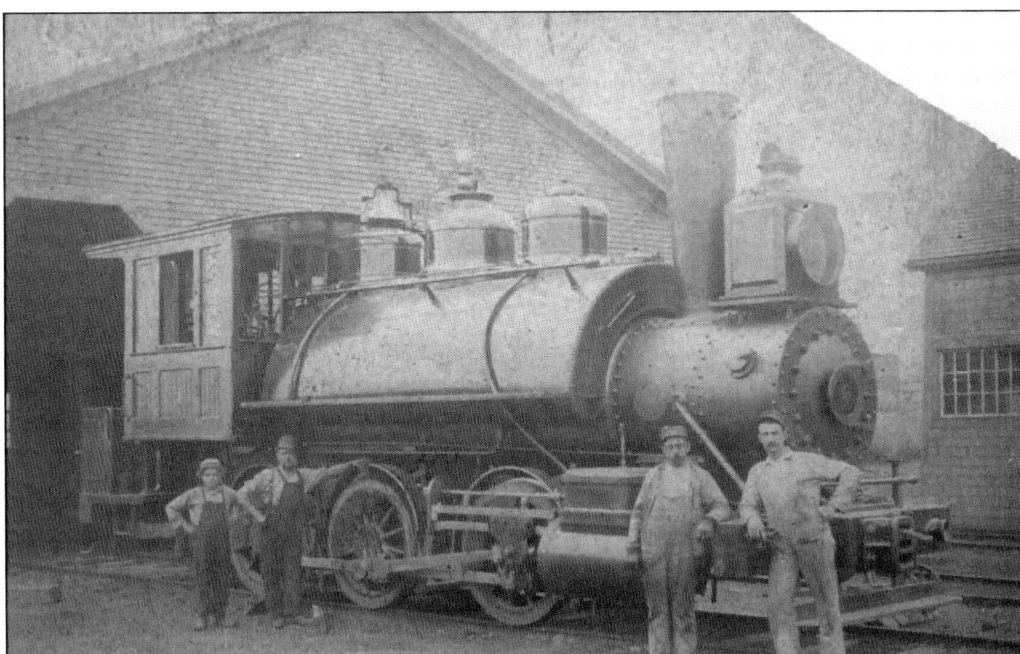

Lime Rock Railroad's engine No. 3 sits near the old Lime Rock Railroad engine house. From left to right are Bill Stears, fireman Erving Gray, an unidentified crew member, and engineer Newell Shuman. This photograph was taken in 1920. (MH.)

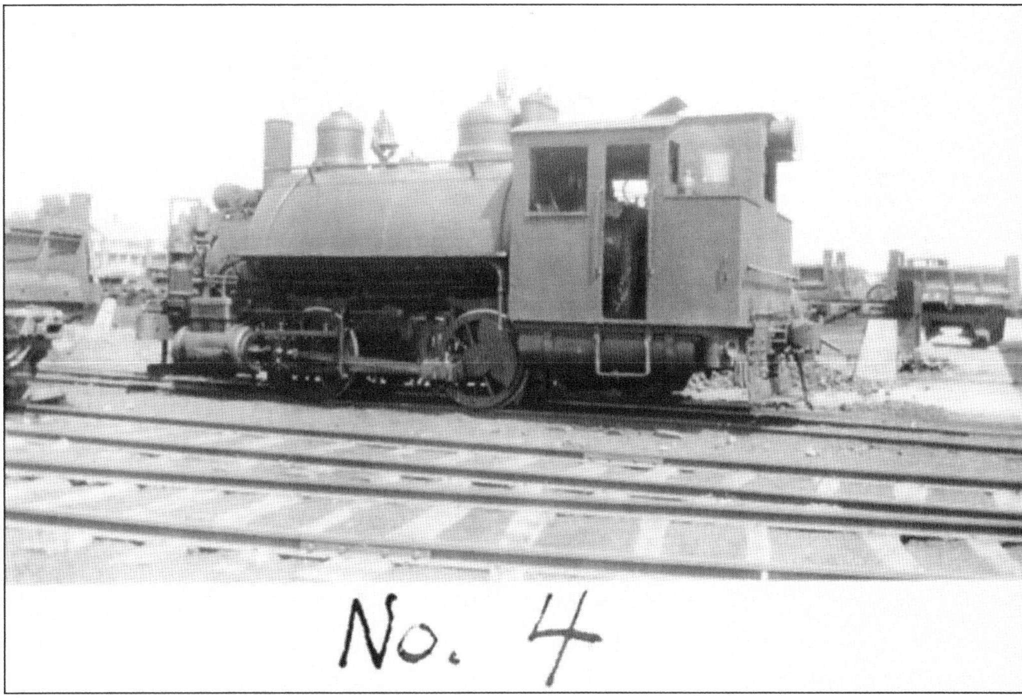

Built in 1905 by the Baldwin Locomotive Works, engine No. 4 operated over 20 years before it became involved in a serious accident. On May 24, 1928, it crashed into a train of rock cars drawn by engine No. 5 at the North End kilns. Engine No. 4 not only lost its wooden cab but also had to be rebuilt. This is how it looked when it came out of the repair shop in June 1931. (MH.)

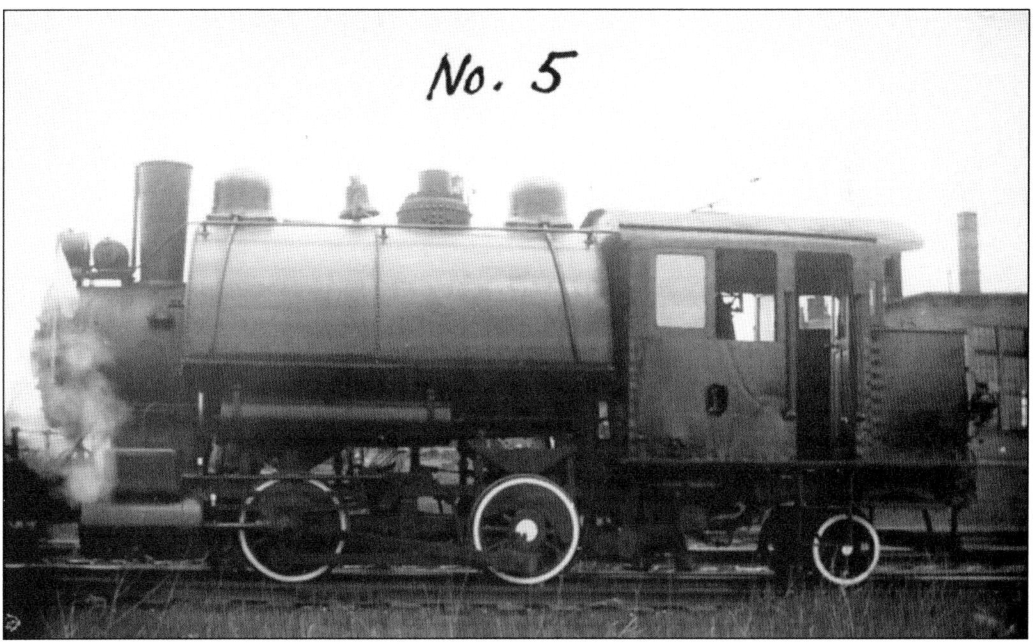

The engine is seen here just out of the shop. This photograph of engine No. 5 was taken on May 21, 1937, in the upper yard of the Maine Central Railroad in Rockland. (MH.)

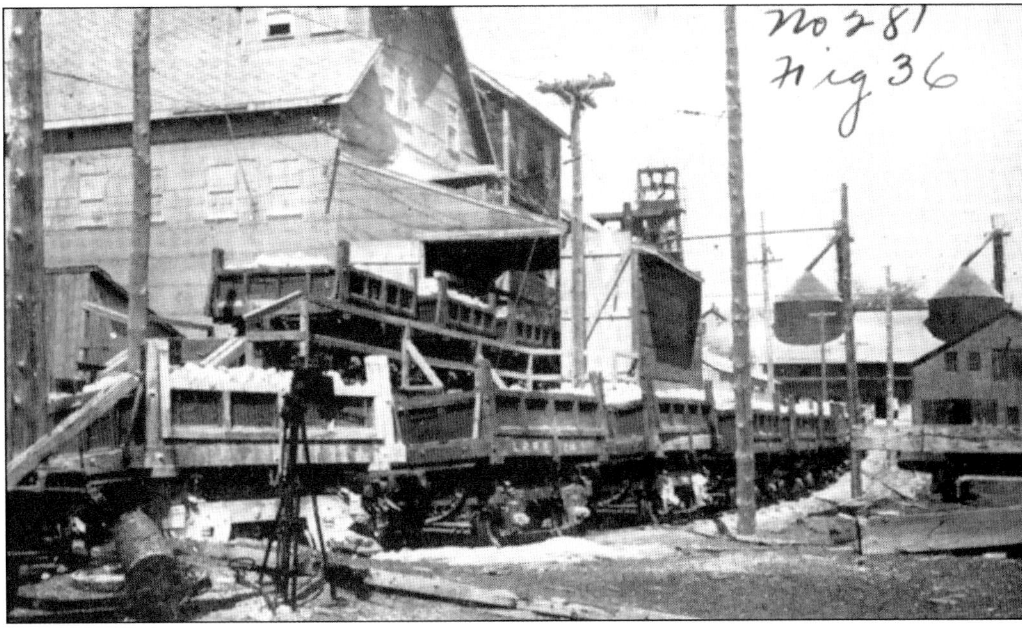

Loaded rock cars are waiting on a track near the Rockland kilns. The Lime Rock Railroad track went three-quarters of the way around the harbor. (DH.)

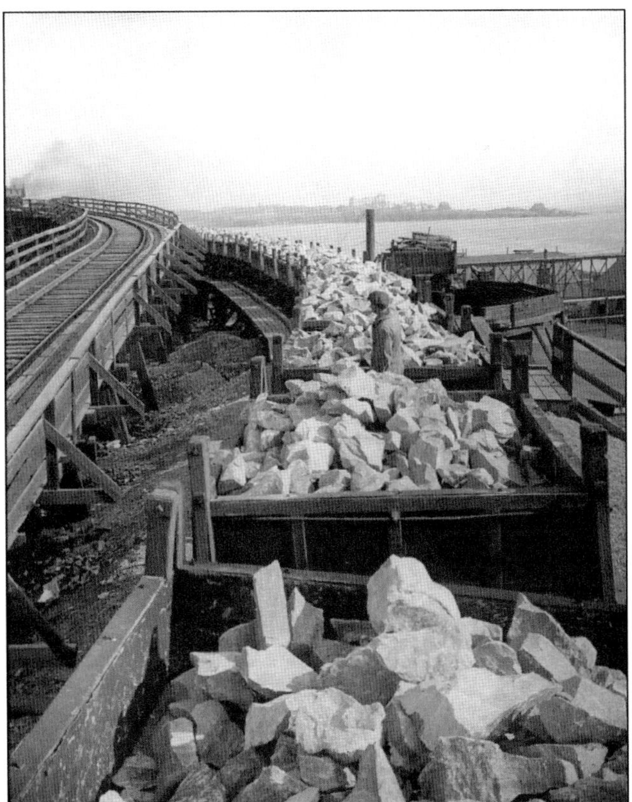

This 1920 photograph shows a string of Lime Rock Railroad cars hauling stone from the quarries. A full train is crossing the trestles in the North End of Rockland. The Samoset Hotel is in the background on the far side of the harbor. (DH.)

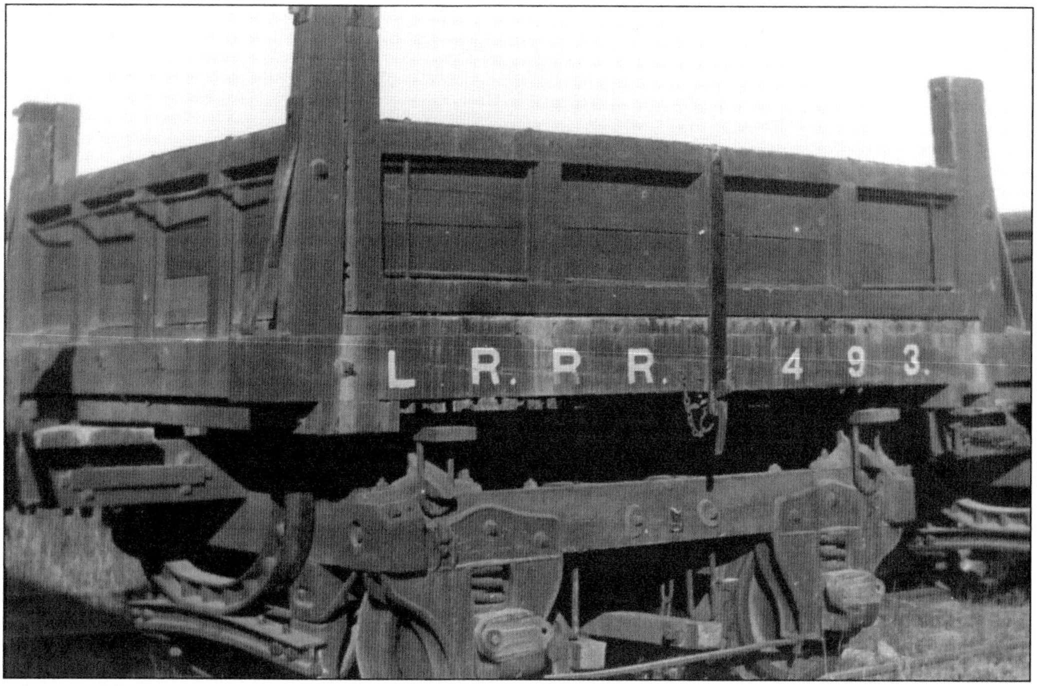

The Rockland-Rockport Lime Company purchased 500 of these rock cars. This is rock car No. 493. They were built so that their sides opened when they tipped sideways, allowing them to draw up alongside the kiln and discharge directly into the kiln top. This was a great convenience, except for the fact that the cars had to be tipped by hand. Later the company bought larger side-dump cars that were operated hydraulically. This photograph was taken in the summer of 1932. (MH.)

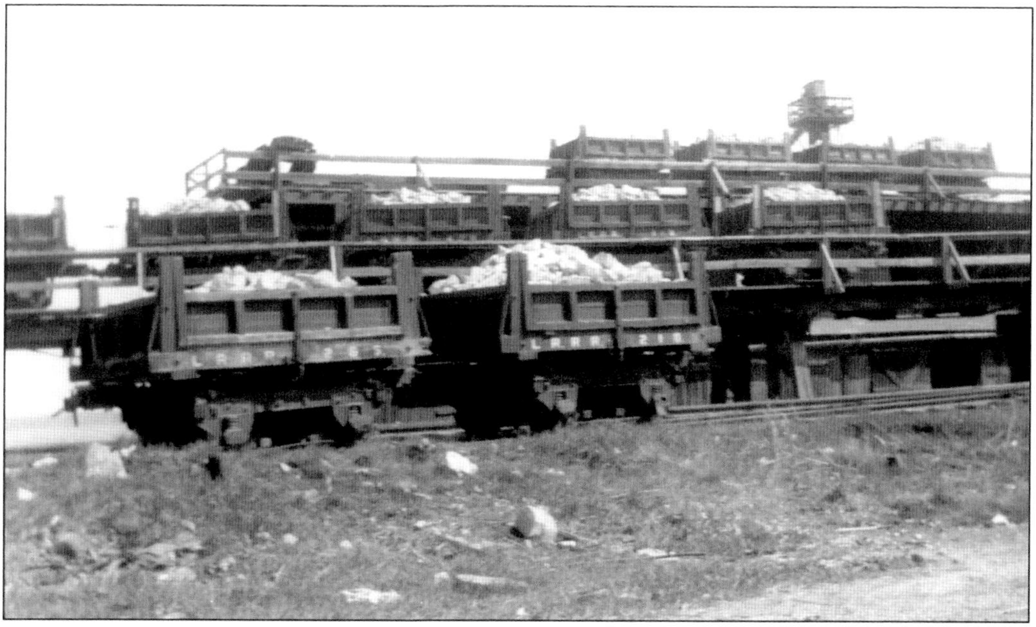

In some places near the harbor, the track system became quite intricate. Here the rock cars appear to be stacked up on three levels of track. (DH.)

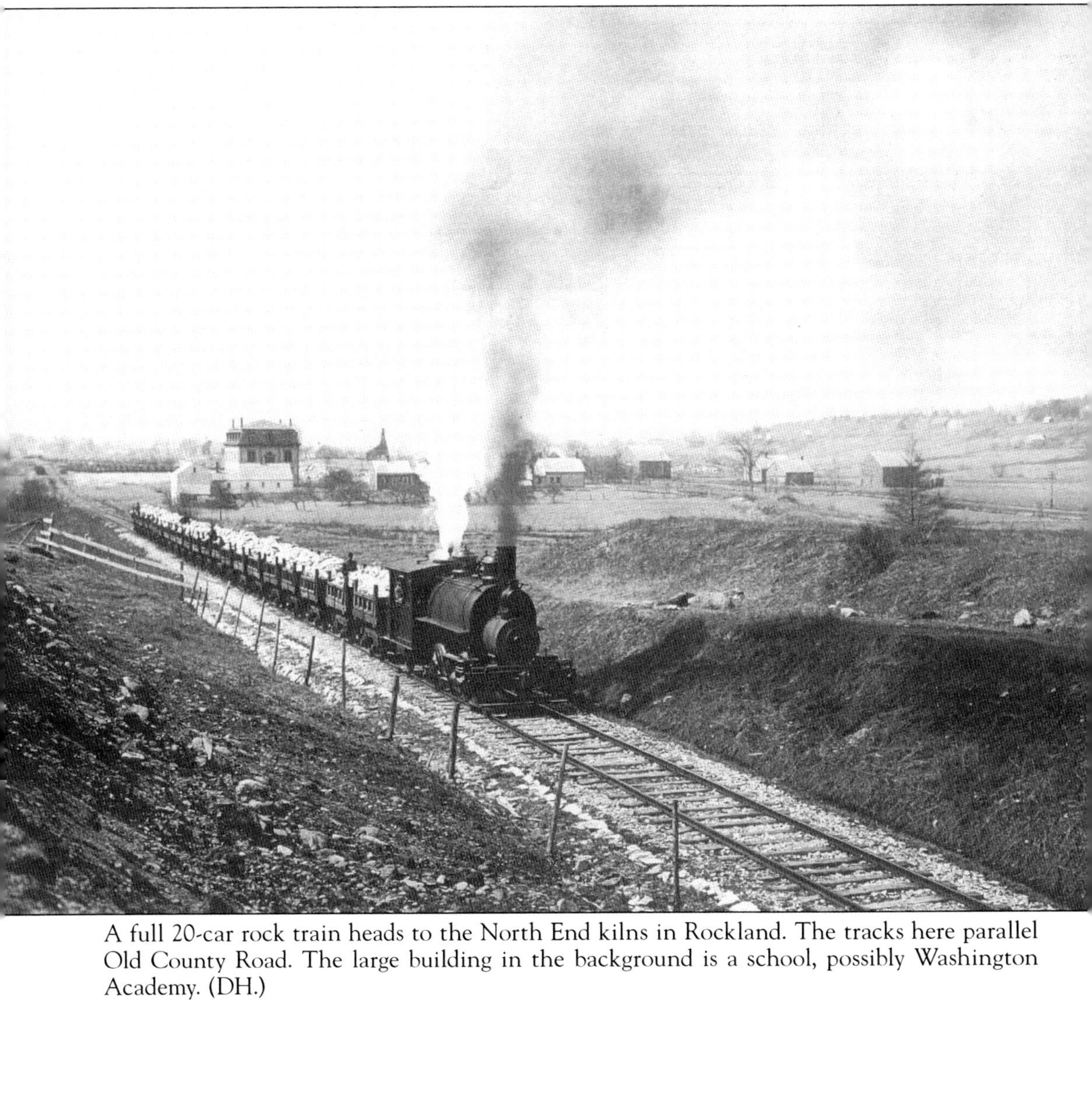

A full 20-car rock train heads to the North End kilns in Rockland. The tracks here parallel Old County Road. The large building in the background is a school, possibly Washington Academy. (DH.)

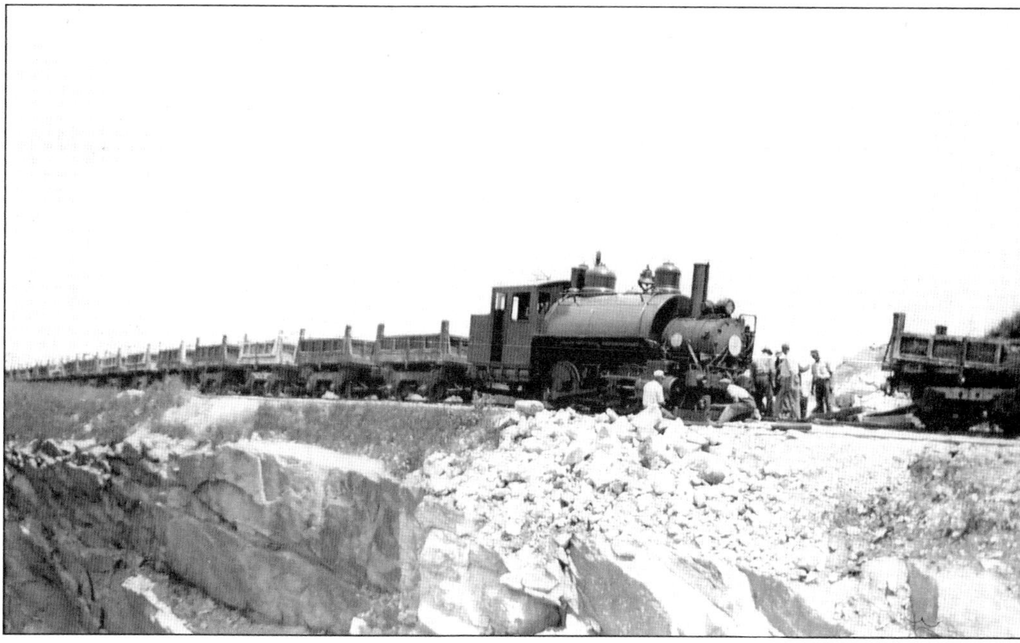

Railroad workers are dealing with a problem on the tracks out by the quarries. The rock car on the far right of the picture may have lost part of its load. (DH.)

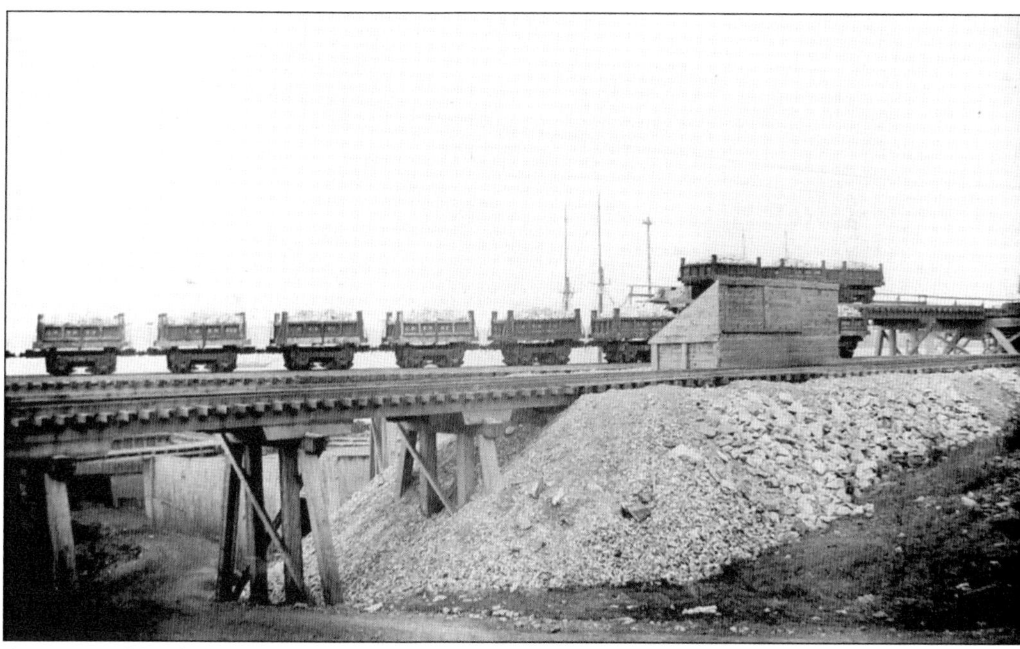

A string of loaded rock cars sits on the trestle, waiting to be discharged into the kilns at Rockland's North End. On the trestle was a scale house with a rail pass-through to weigh the rock-filled cars. The slant-roofed building in this picture may have contained coal or sand for the trains. (DH.)

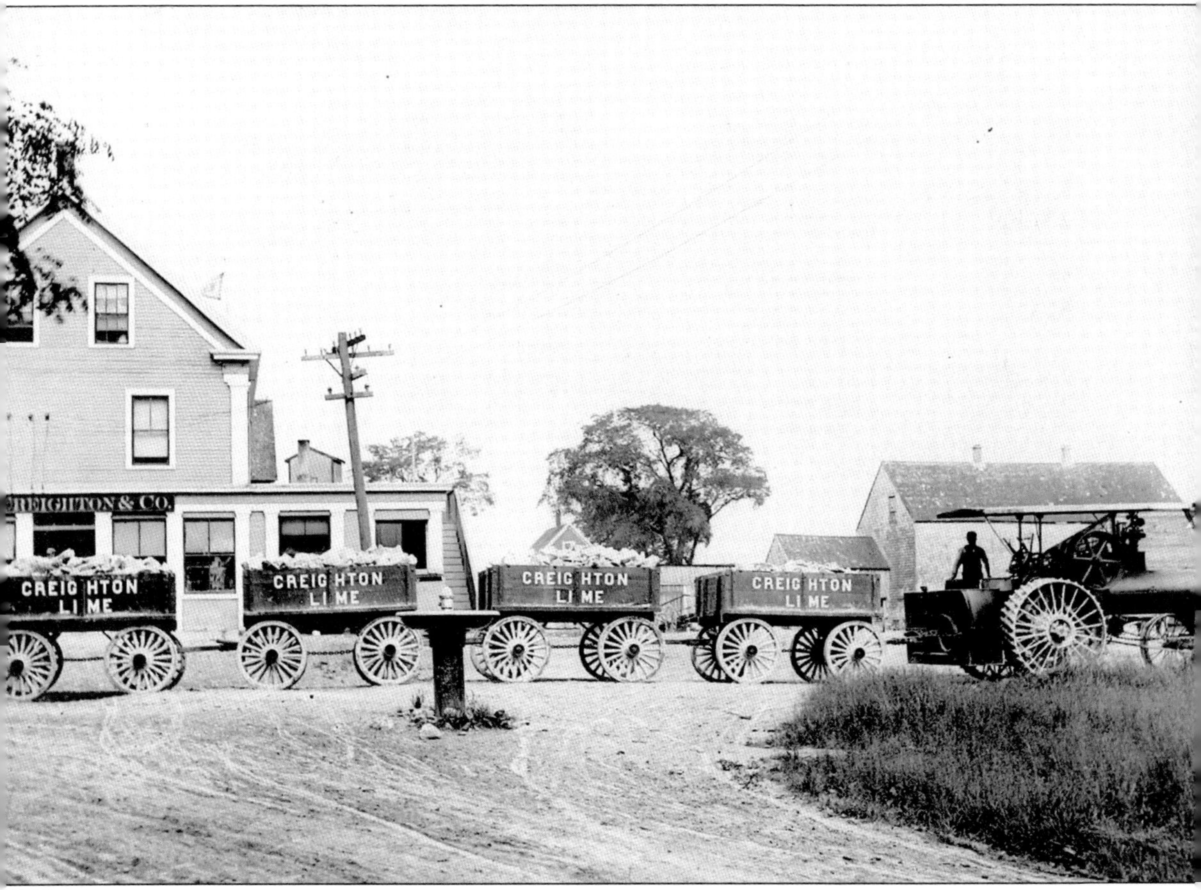

Thomaston did not build a railroad system the way Rockland and Rockport did. They continued to use wagons on the local roads, but they mechanized it to some degree. This string of Creighton Company wagons on lower Knox Street is being pulled to the kilns by a steam tractor with wide wheels for road travel. The Creighton Company was Thomaston's largest producer of lime for years. (THS.)

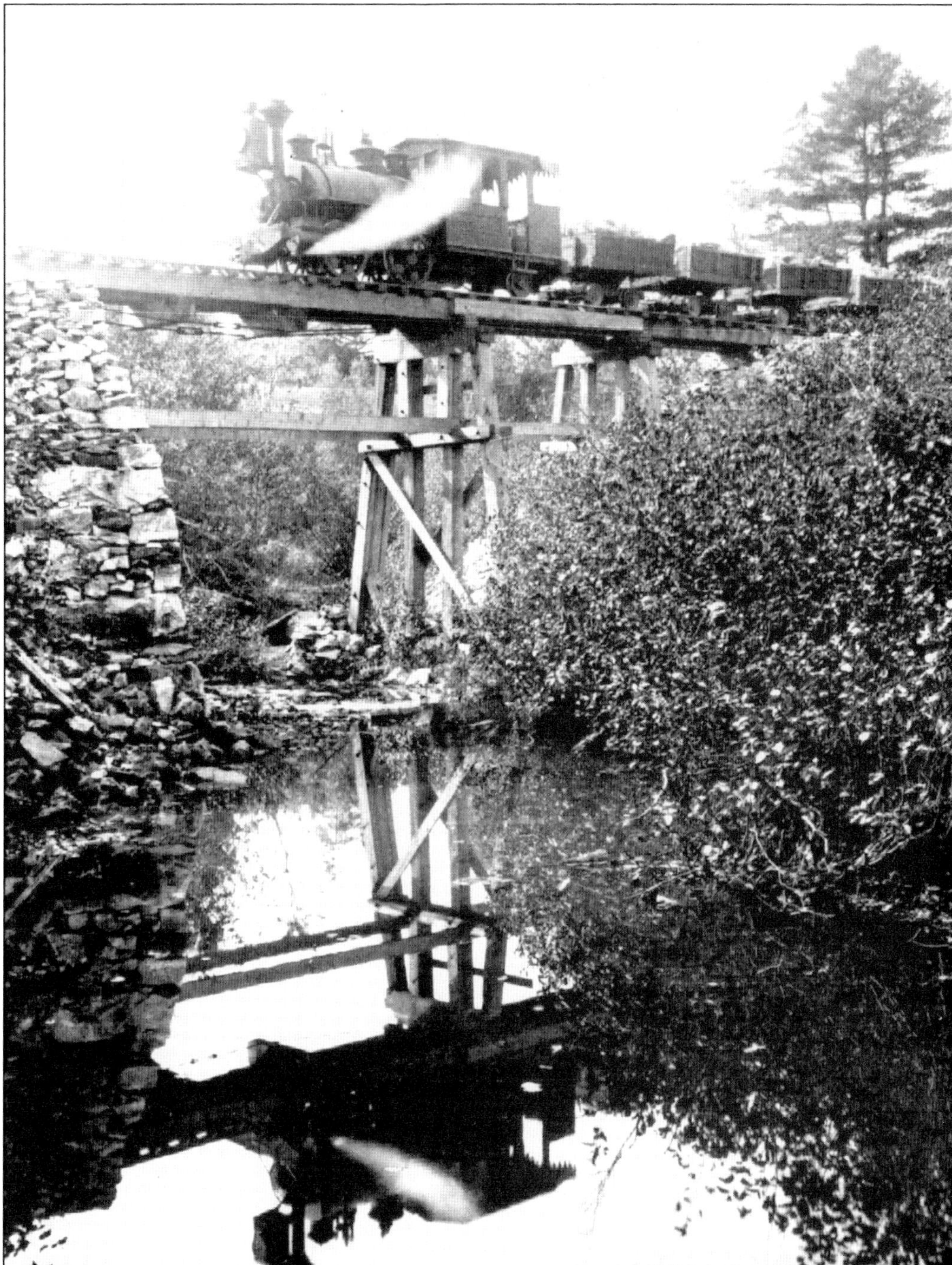

A Rockport Railroad locomotive pulls a string of loaded rock cars. It is crossing the Goose River, probably heading to the harborside kilns from Simonton's Corner. The Rockport Railroad ran over a three-mile stretch of narrow-gauge track that had short, steep grades. It crossed the Goose Rive five times. The train made three round-trips each workday from Limestone Corner (Simonton's Corner) to the kilns. (CRHS.)

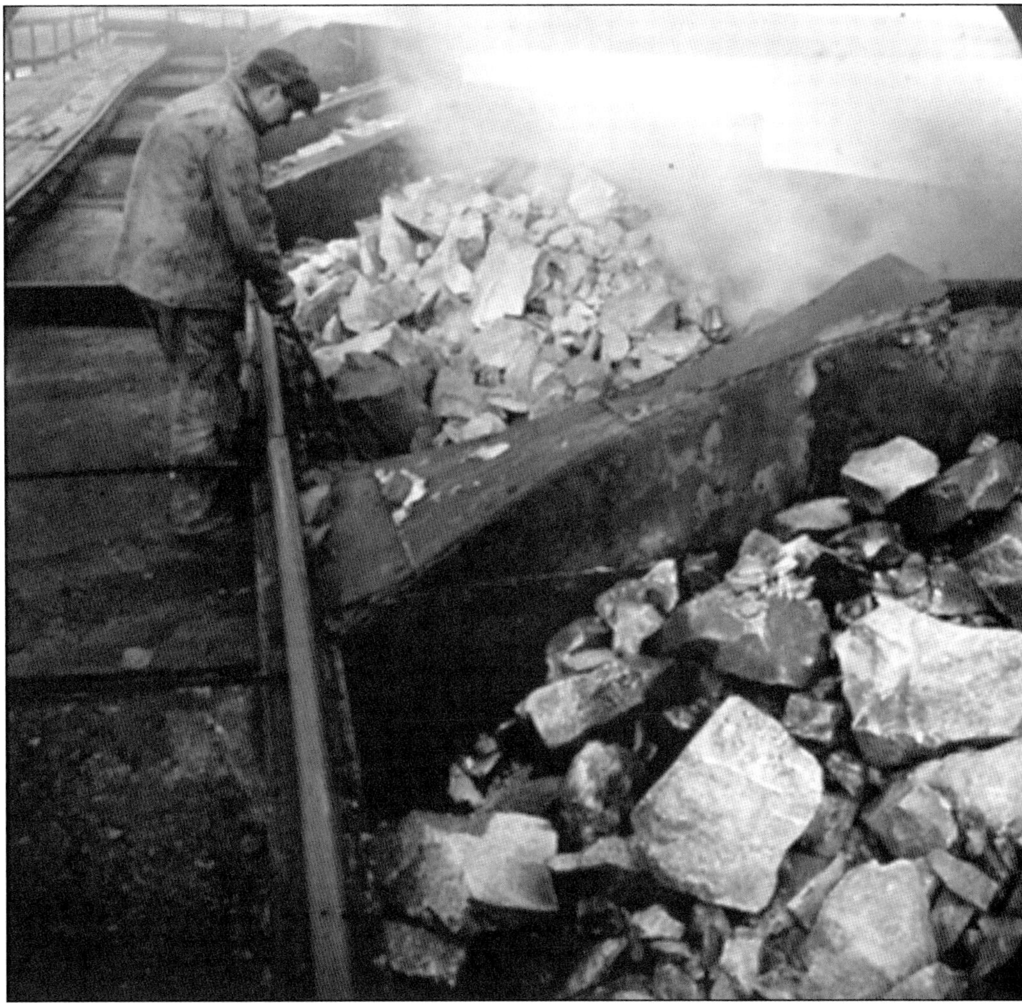

A lime worker at the kiln tops is checking to see which kilns are ready for more rock. If the discharged rock gets jammed or plugged, he will poke and prod it until it falls into the kiln properly. (DH.)

Three

LIME BURNING

Lime rock is not actually burned. It is more accurate to say that the fuel is burned and the lime rock is cooked. The burn is controlled so that it heats the lime rock to 1,000–1,100 degrees and holds it at that temperature until the rock, heated to red-hot, undergoes a chemical change and gives off one of its main components in the form of carbon dioxide gas. The remainder is calcium oxide (CaO), a white substance called quicklime. Quicklime, or lime, has a strong affinity for water. When mixed with water, it expands quickly and gives off great heat. It is this quality that makes lime both dangerous and valuable. It is dangerous if it accidentally mixes with too much water too fast. It is valuable to the building trades when it is mixed with a controlled amount of water, which makes it malleable. Since it has a tendency to return to its original rocklike form, it hardens in the shape that the mason or plasterer requires.

Field kilns and their successors, pot kilns, were the earliest lime-burning kilns in the area. Fueled with wood, these inefficient kilns were intermittent. The farmer burned the lime steadily for several days and nights. Then he let the fire go out, drew out the hot lime, and sorted it. Another load of lime meant another separate burning cycle. Often the farmer burned lime only three or four times a year.

In the 1850s, patent kilns were introduced. Forty feet tall and built along the waterfront out of granite, they were far more efficient because the fire never needed to go out. The patent kiln consisted of three levels: the top level, where lime rock was loaded to be burned; the middle level called the firing floor, which held the fireboxes or arches, built into the walls of the kiln, one on each side; and the bottom level, or draw pit, from which the burned lime was taken. (See the diagram on page 50.)

Lime burning followed an annual burn cycle. January and early February found the kilns hibernating because building contracts in the cities were not made until the first of the year. By late February, lime manufacturers fired the first kilns, and railroad crews cleared the tracks for the start of regular runs. By April, the spring rush was in full swing. This continued through the summer until August, by which time most of the orders were filled. A lull known as the August layoff was followed by a smaller burst of activity in the fall.

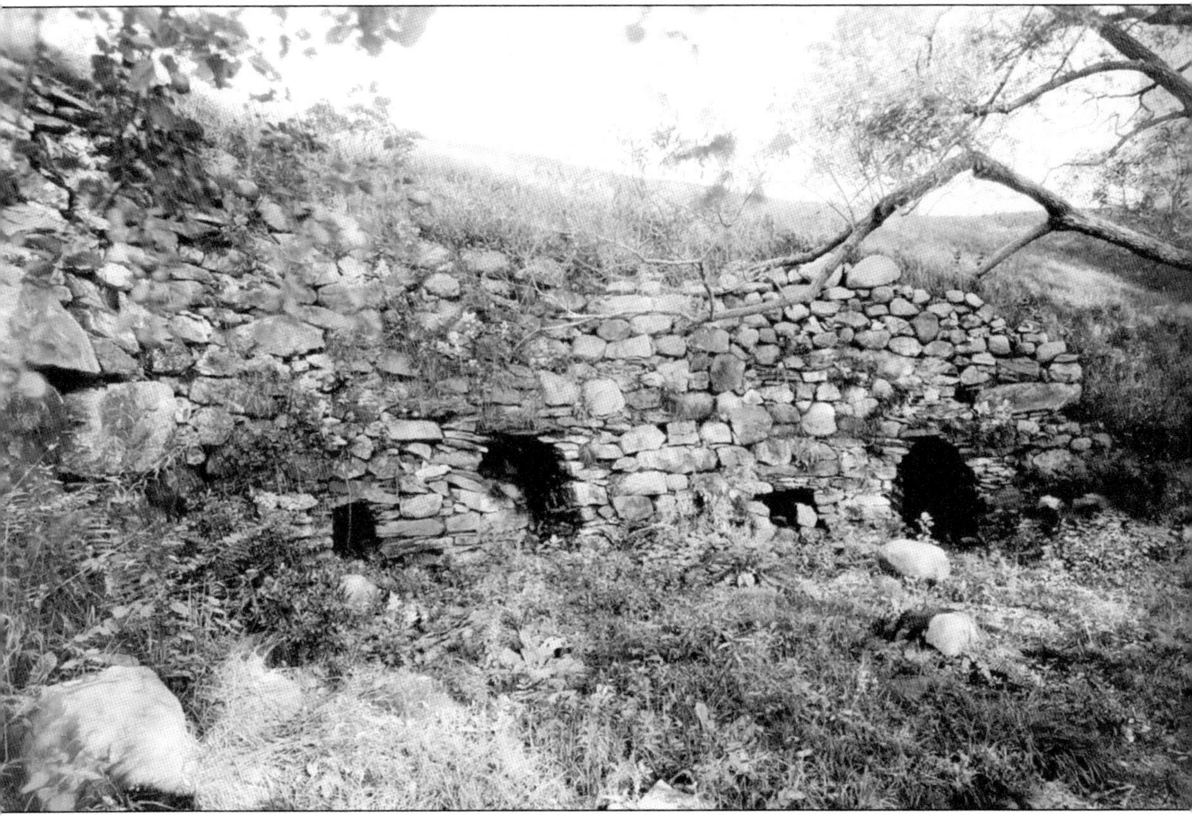

These two early field kilns were built into a hillside in Rockport. Kilns like this were built from local fieldstone. They were intermittent wood-burning kilns, meaning that they went through the whole burn cycle. The fire was allowed to die out before the lime was drawn out. (DH.)

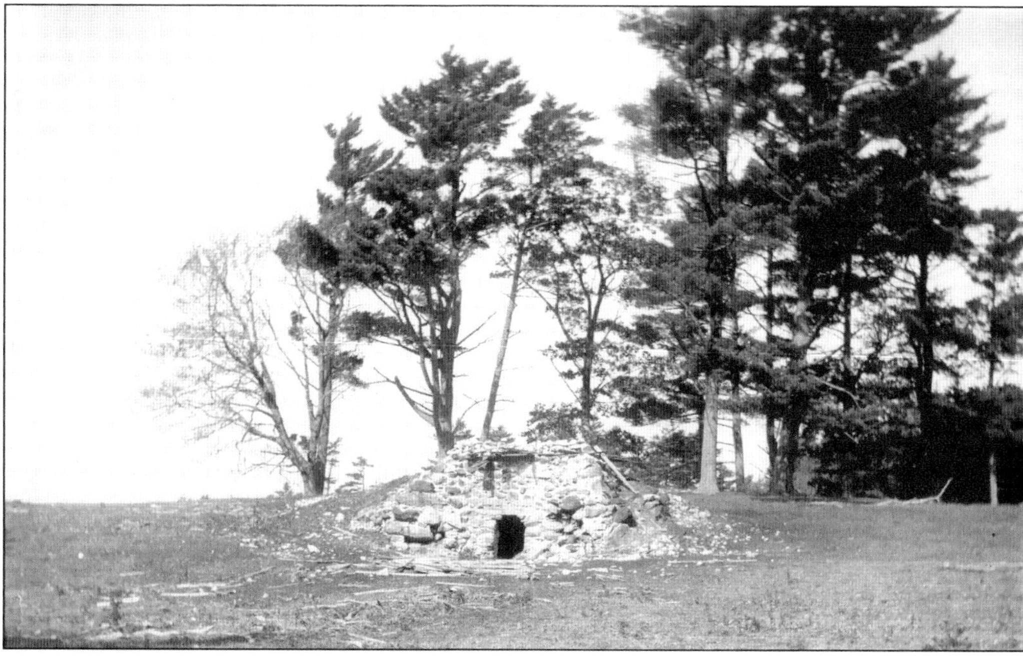

Small field kilns like this one in Warren were scattered throughout the area. As farmers became more proficient in lime burning, they devised a more sophisticated version of the field kiln, called the pot kiln. Taller and lined with clay, it held the heat better. Similar to the field kiln, however, it was intermittent. The lime burner lost a lot of time allowing the kiln to cool down completely and then heating it up again to the required temperature. (WHS.)

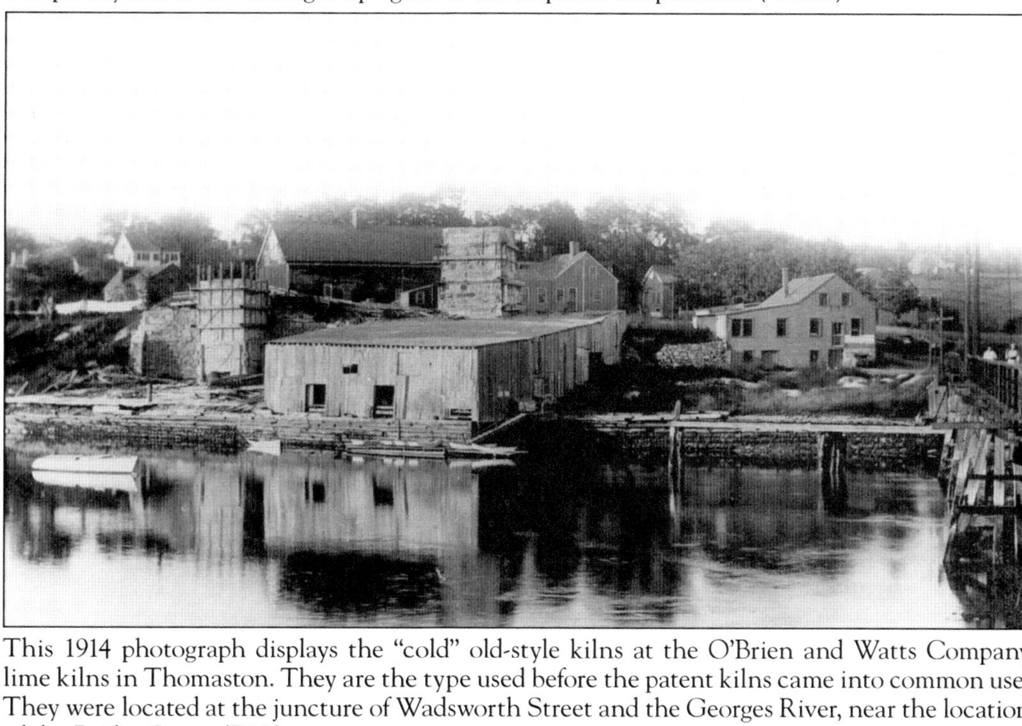

This 1914 photograph displays the "cold" old-style kilns at the O'Brien and Watts Company lime kilns in Thomaston. They are the type used before the patent kilns came into common use. They were located at the juncture of Wadsworth Street and the Georges River, near the location of the Bridge Store. (DH.)

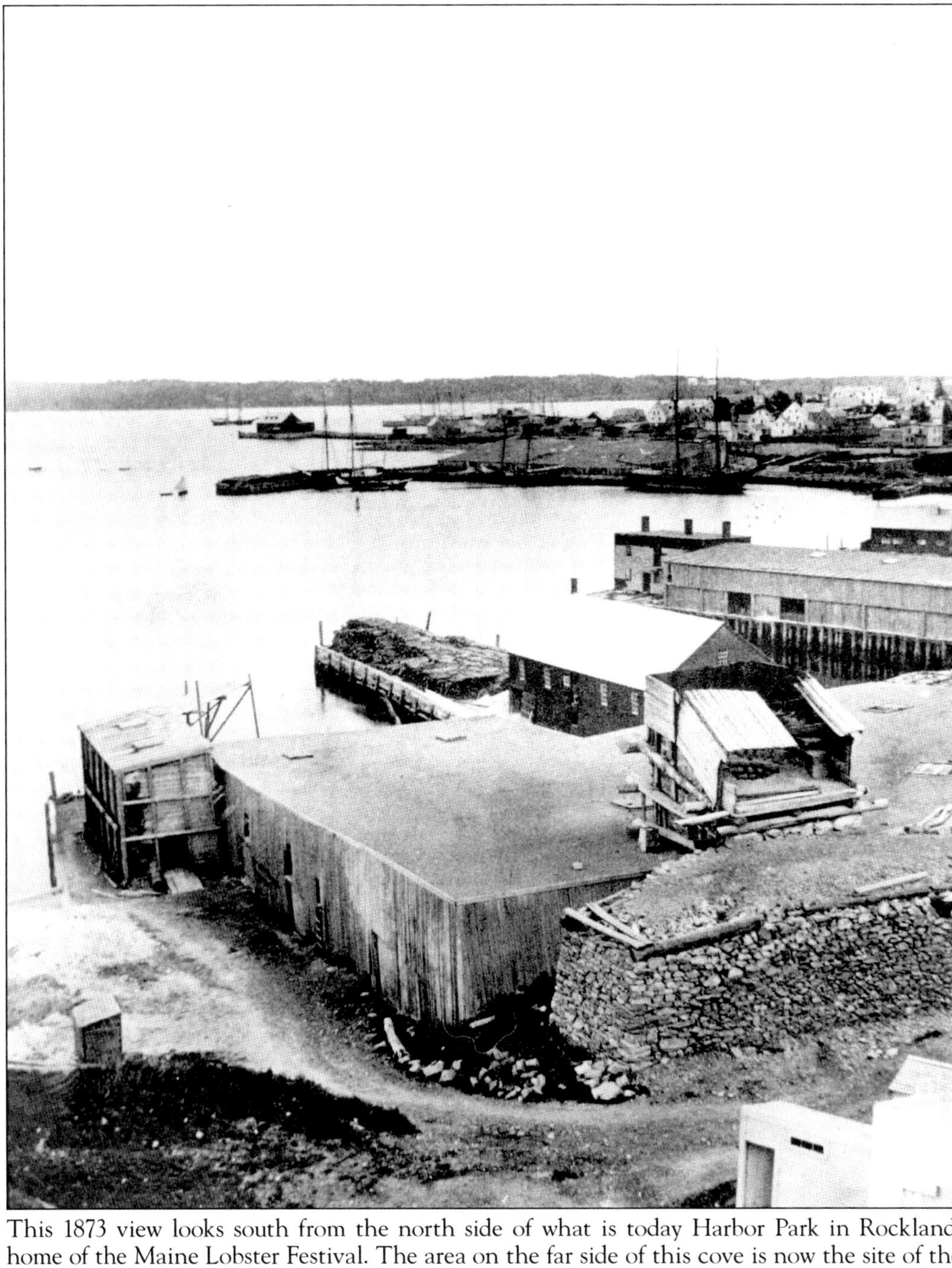

This 1873 view looks south from the north side of what is today Harbor Park in Rockland, home of the Maine Lobster Festival. The area on the far side of this cove is now the site of the former MBNA facilities in the South End. It was known as the Five Kilns. In the foreground, a stone ramp leads to the top of the kiln, where teamsters drew up wagons to discharge the raw limestone. On the left is the lime shed where barrels of burned lime await shipment. (RHS.)

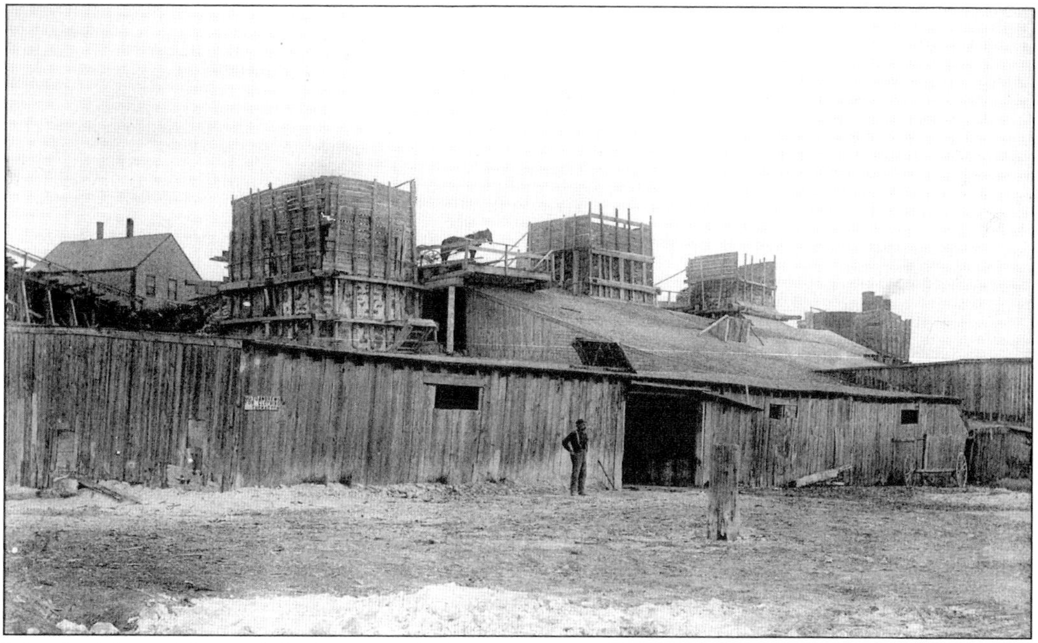

The Creighton kilns and sheds covered almost an acre of land in Thomaston and produced large annual outputs for years. The J. A. Creighton Company was formed in 1880 to manufacture lime and deal in coal, cornmeal, flour, and groceries. Notice the horse and wagon on the loading ramp. The kilns were built in a straight line for more efficient delivery of the raw lime rock. This photograph was taken in 1900. (THS.)

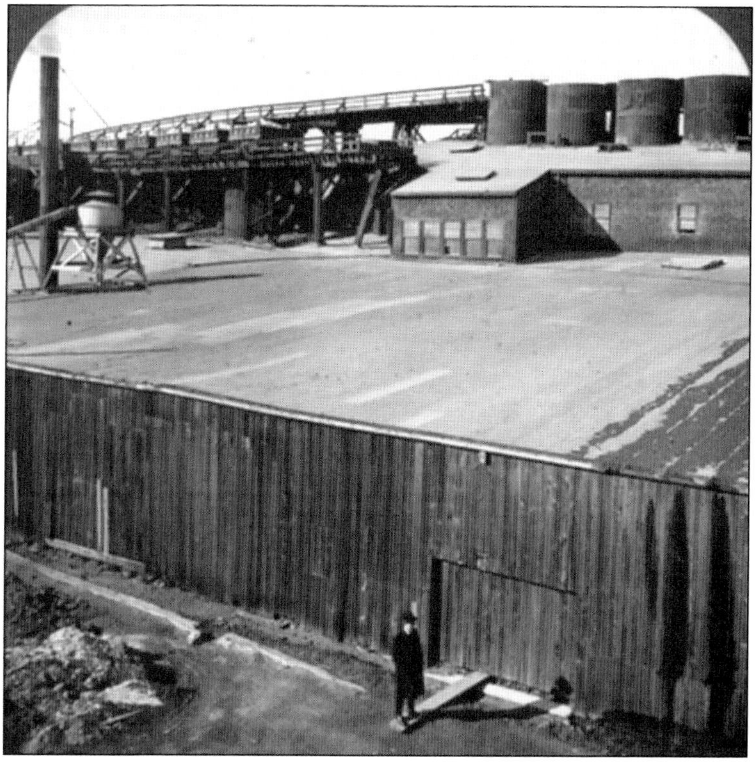

Extensive lime sheds, which covered part of the kilns, the kiln floor, and the fuel for the kilns, were conspicuous everywhere along the harbor. For several kilns, the accompanying sheds cover about 17,000 square feet. (DH.)

This is a winter view of the kiln shed roof and the smoking kiln stacks taken from the trestle track 30 feet above the rim of the harbor. From this vantage point, the trainmen discharged lime into the top of the kilns. The stack on the left is connected to a steam bellow, which helped to increase the temperature of the fires. (DH.)

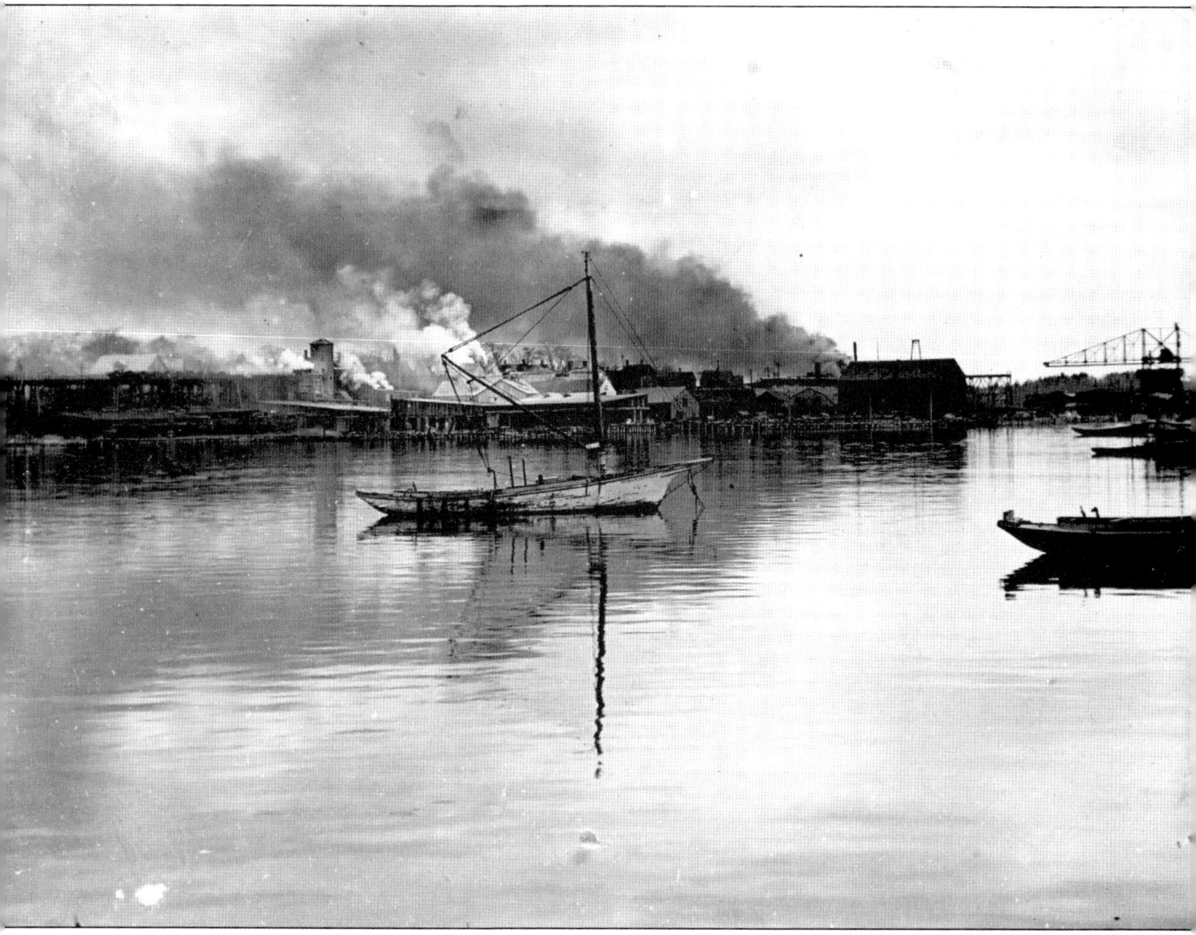

Dust, steam, and smoke from the kilns and the hydrate plant were an everyday experience along Rockland's waterfront. Sometimes the whole town was covered with smoke and dust from the kilns. When the wind blew from the east, as it is in this picture, housewives rushed to bring in their clean laundry drying on the line so that it would not be covered with soot. This image, an Alton Hall Blackington photograph, shows the Rockland-Rockport Lime Company's operation around 1920. (FM.)

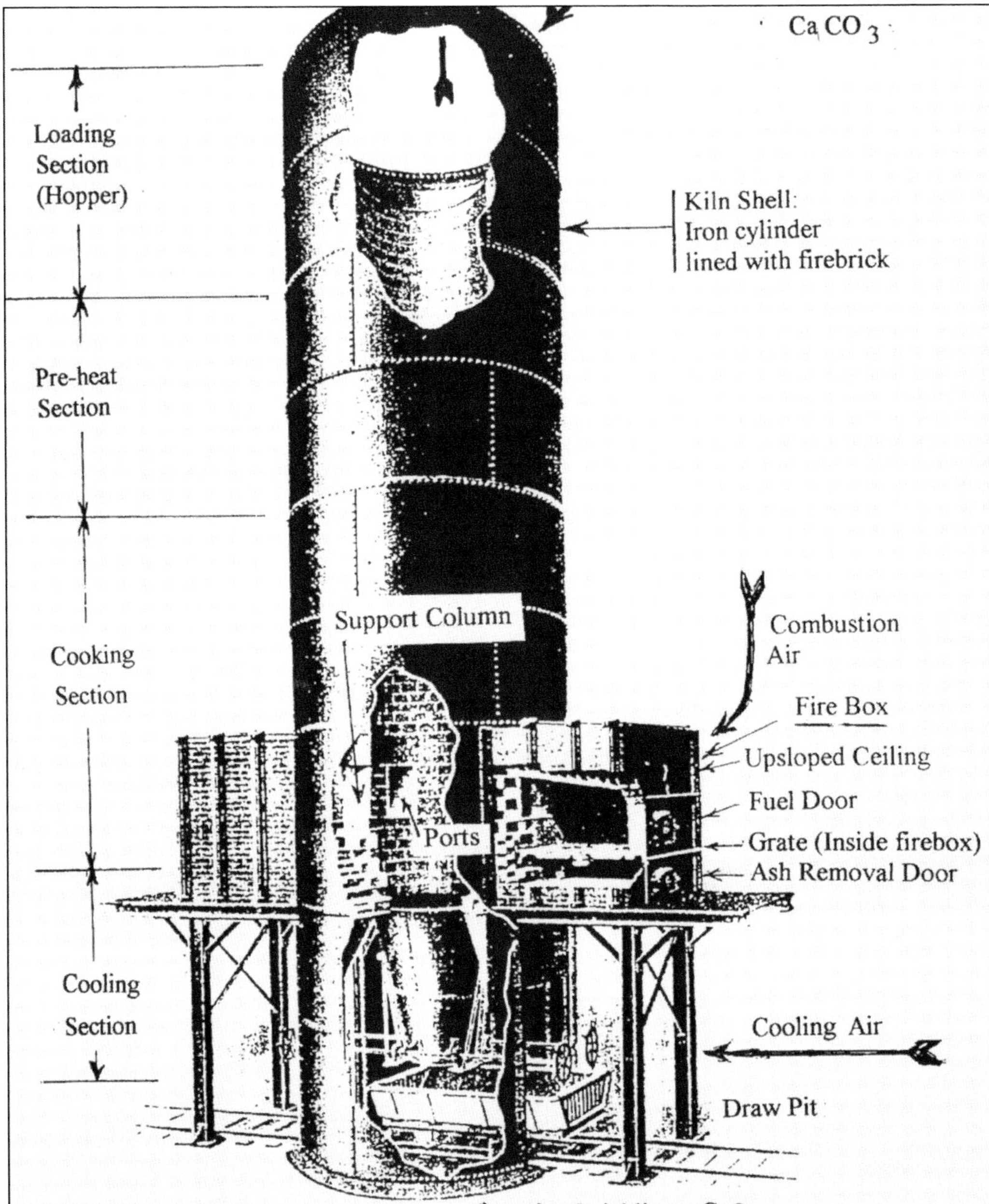

A cutaway view of a patent kiln shows the process of burning lime. Rock was loaded and drawn out continually, and the fires burned nonstop in this three-level furnace. The kiln held from 150 to 200 casks of lime. The time required for burning the lime was seven to eight hours. (DH.)

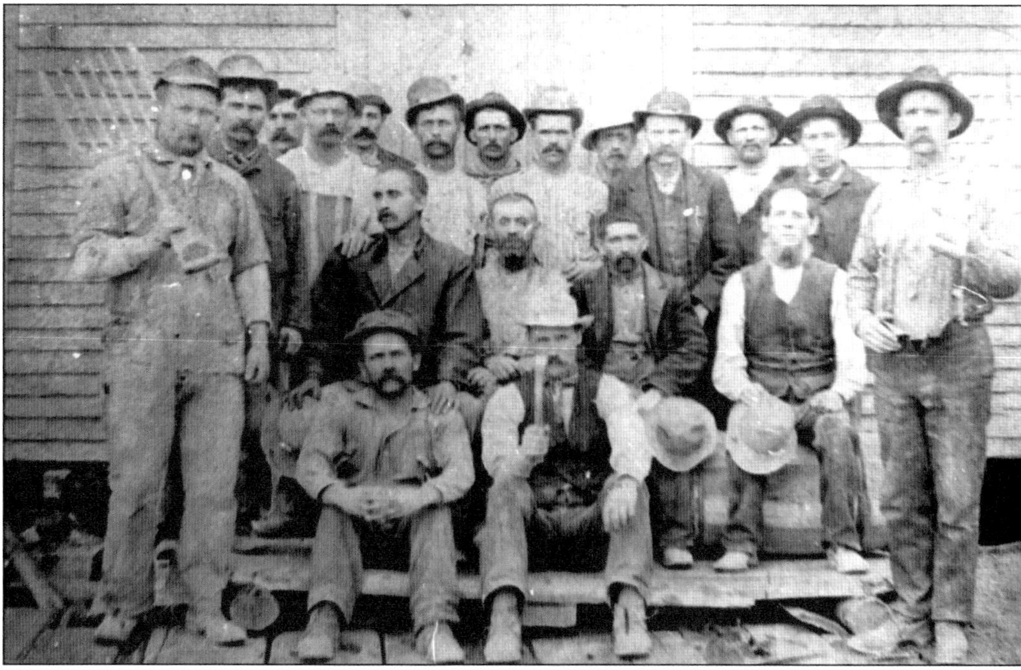

This is an undated photograph of the crew of Atwood Levensaler's kiln in Thomaston. The man standing on the left holds a seven-tine, short-handled pitchfork for shoveling lime. Workers at the lime kilns earned about $1.75 a day in 1908, compared to $2.50 a day for carpenters and $3.50 a day for masons. Nine hours constituted a full day's work for all trades. (THS.)

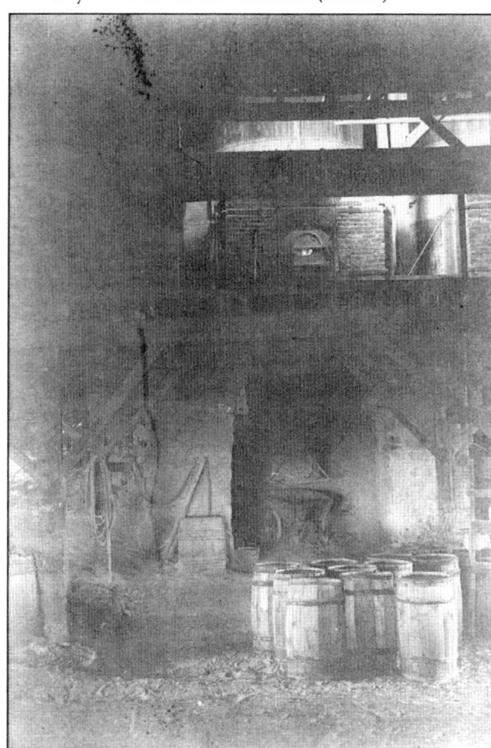

In this rare photograph, the two levels of the interior of a patent kiln can be seen. The middle level, on top in this picture, was called the firing floor. Fires were maintained continually during a burn. They were allowed to cool down just before a draw, but they were not put out. The cooling caused the lime to contract. When the burned lime collapsed, or settled onto the draw pit floor, hot gas and coals blew out through the fireboxes, and sparks shot up the chimneys. Kiln tenders made sure to stand out of the way. This is a Creighton Company kiln in 1900. (THS.)

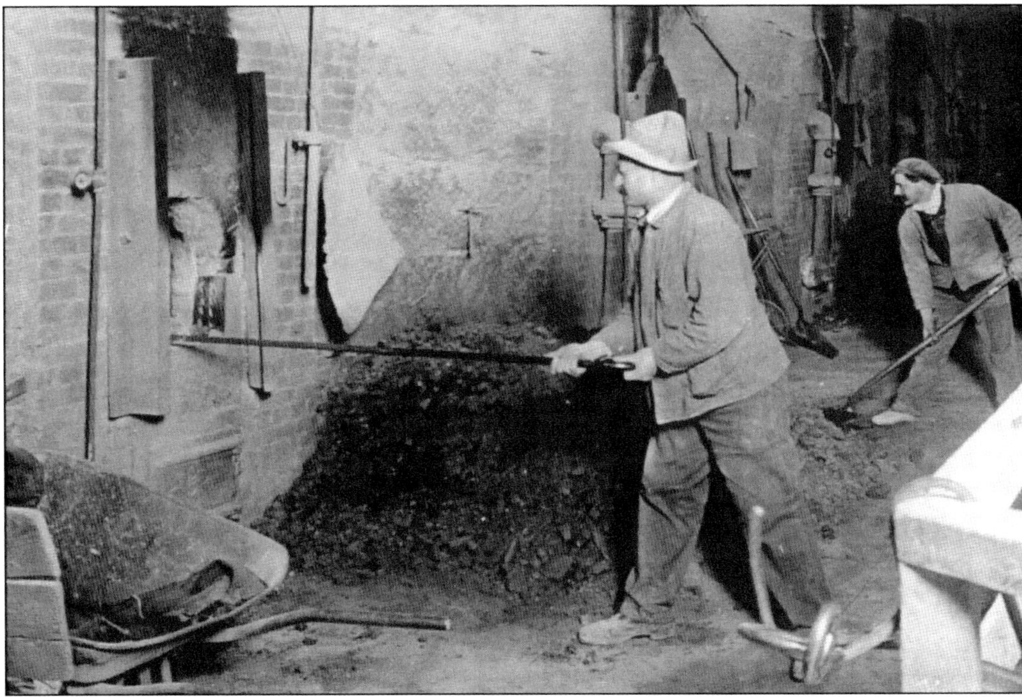

Stokers were responsible for maintaining a steady heat of 1,000 to 1,100 degrees at all times, except draw time when the cooked lime was removed. Kiln work was hot and physically demanding but much safer than work in the quarries. (DH.)

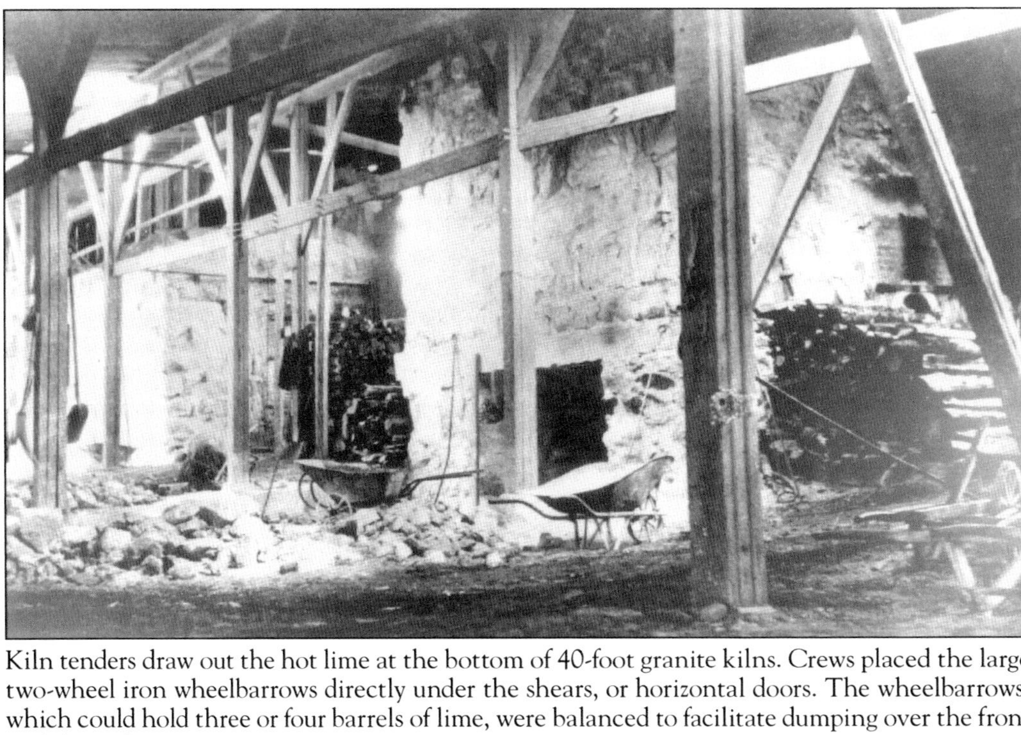

Kiln tenders draw out the hot lime at the bottom of 40-foot granite kilns. Crews placed the large two-wheel iron wheelbarrows directly under the shears, or horizontal doors. The wheelbarrows, which could hold three or four barrels of lime, were balanced to facilitate dumping over the front end. (RHS.)

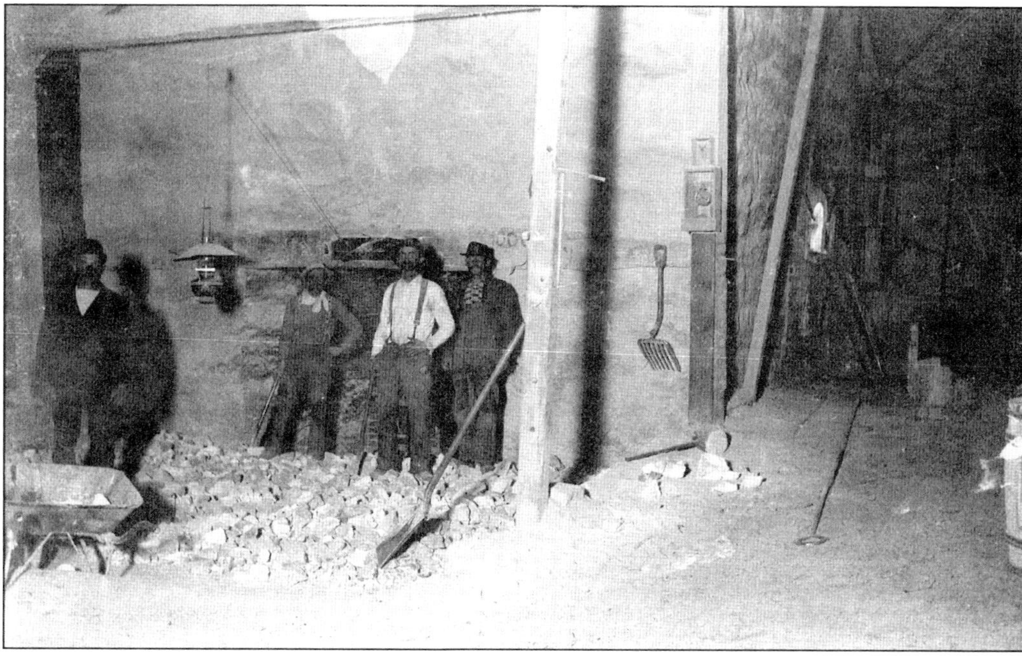

Kiln tenders stand at the draw pit of a Creighton Company lime kiln in Thomaston around 1900. Workers have shoveled out the calcined lime from the hopper with the long-handled shovel leaning against the upright. The hot lime on the hearth is ready to be sorted and packed. (THS.)

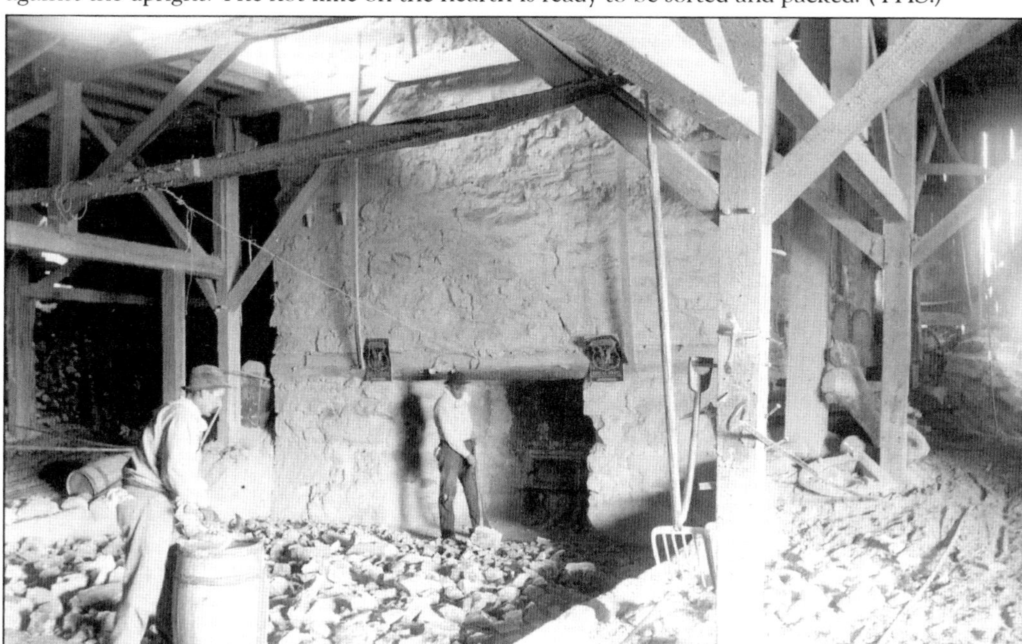

Here at the kiln base of a Creighton Company kiln in Thomaston, the burned lime is being picked over and the uncooked core removed to be dumped. One kiln worker is breaking up the hot lime while the lime trimmer is filling the barrel. In the 1890s, kiln tenders earned $13.51 for a seven-day work week, and rock breakers earned about $10.85 a week. (THS.)

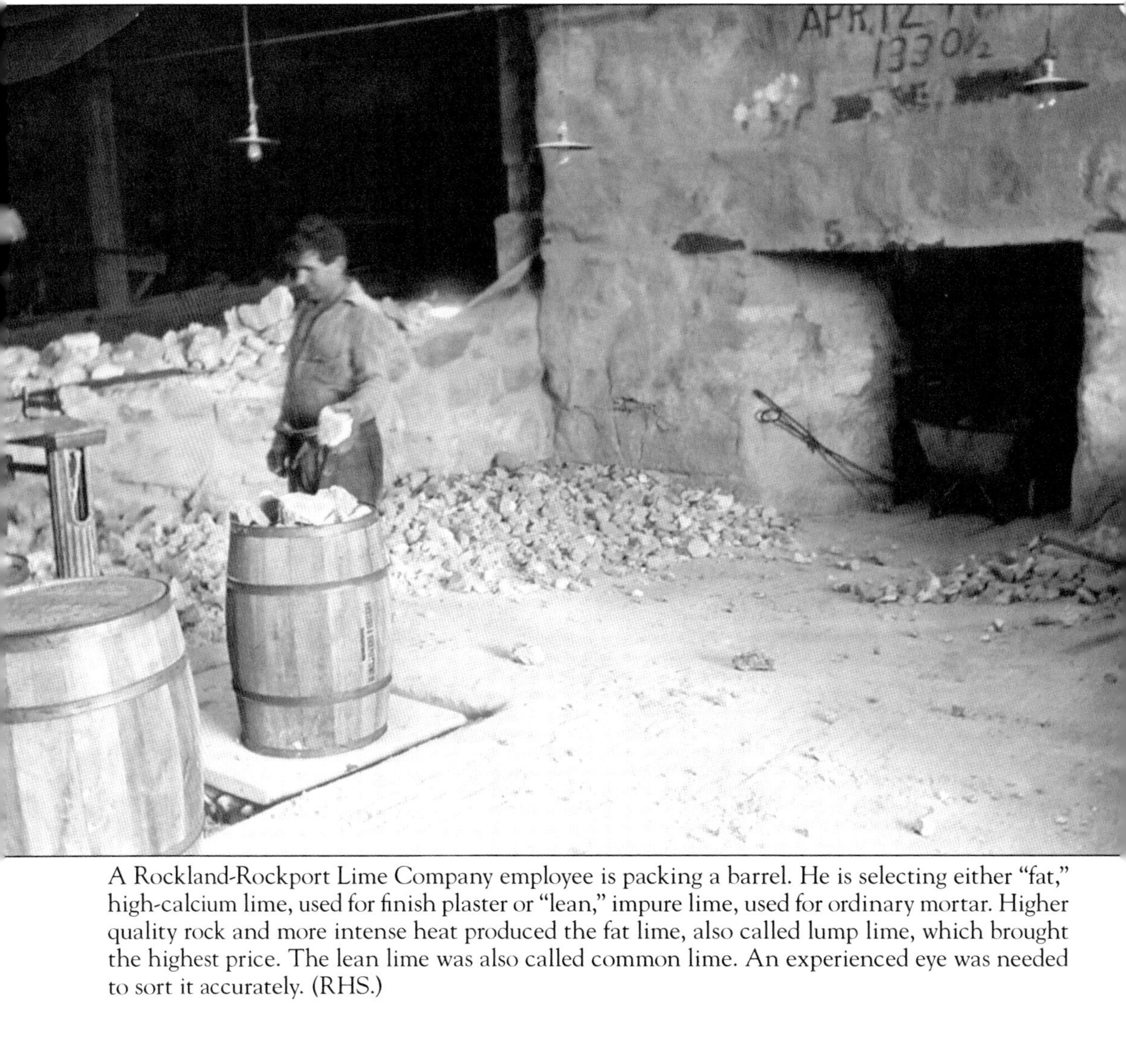

A Rockland-Rockport Lime Company employee is packing a barrel. He is selecting either "fat," high-calcium lime, used for finish plaster or "lean," impure lime, used for ordinary mortar. Higher quality rock and more intense heat produced the fat lime, also called lump lime, which brought the highest price. The lean lime was also called common lime. An experienced eye was needed to sort it accurately. (RHS.)

In this sample of uncooked core, the darker center of the lime rock is uncooked; only the outer edge is burned white. If it had been cooked correctly, the whole rock would be white throughout. Rock like this was thrown away. It was too time-consuming for the lime sorter to try to separate the uncooked section from the cooked section of rock and send it up to kiln top to be recooked. (DH.)

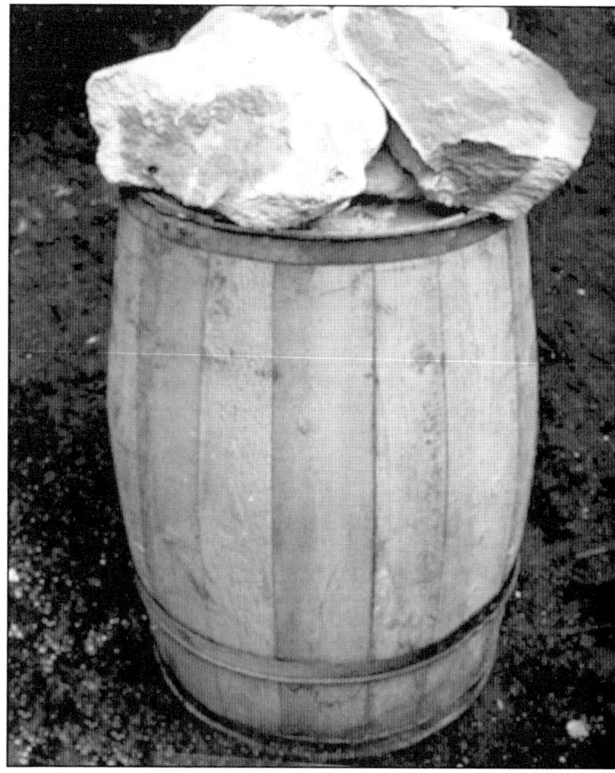

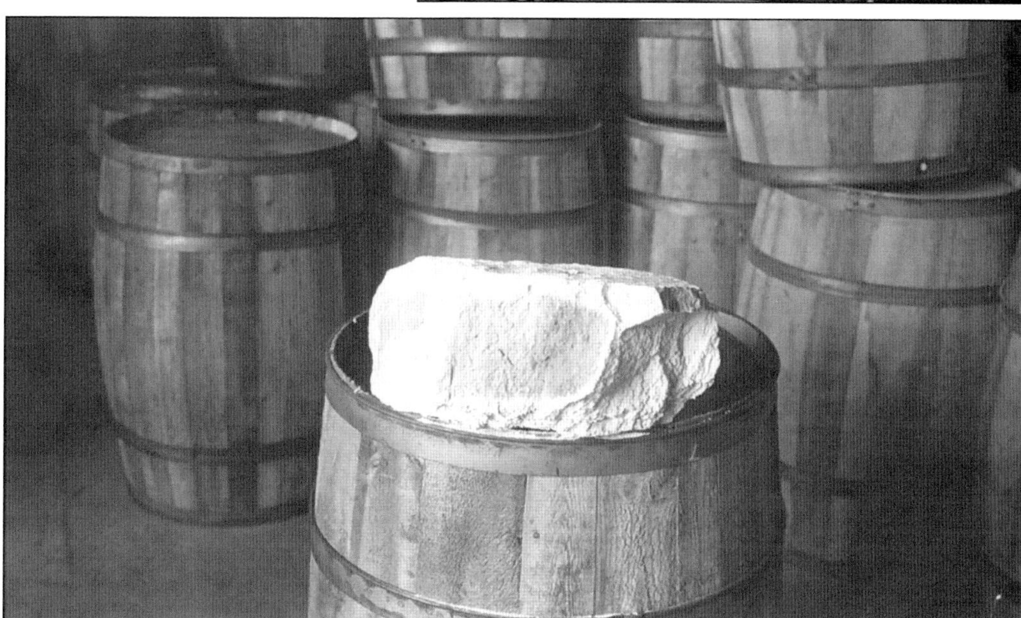

Here is a large piece of uncooked core. When limestone is over-burned, lime from it slakes slowly and incompletely. On the other hand, if the temperature gets too low, the larger pieces may not be thoroughly cooked, which makes the lime lean. To avoid this, the pieces of rock that go into the kiln must not be too large. That is the major reason the rock needs to be head size when it is put into the kiln. (DH.)

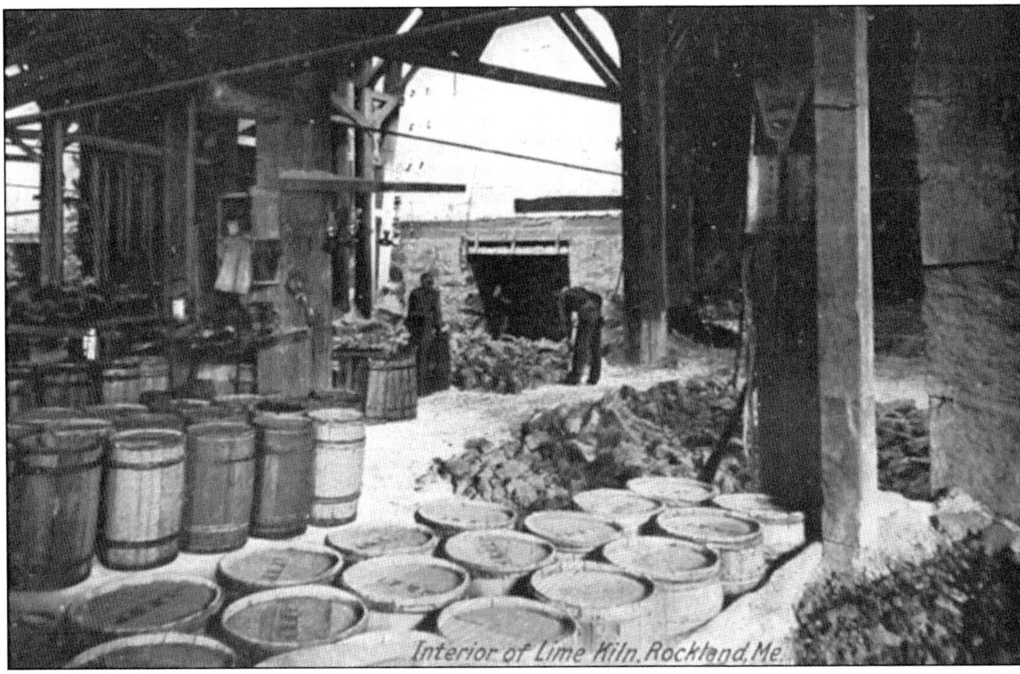

At the bottom level of a patent kiln is the kiln floor, the hearth, and the opening in the kiln where burned limestone is drawn out. On the left foreground are empty barrels awaiting the cooled lime, and on the right foreground are filled barrels with their heads set in tightly. (DH.)

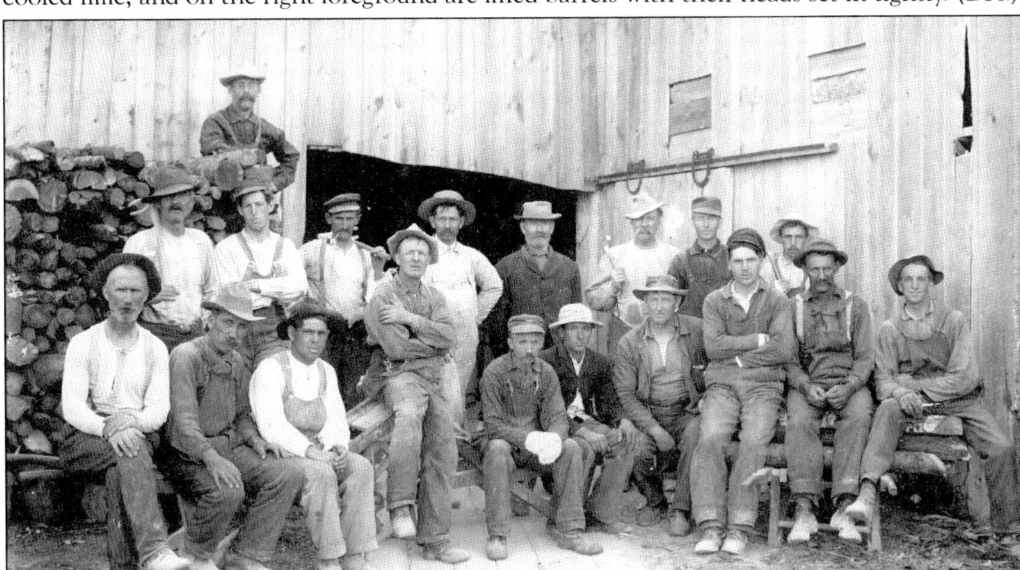

The crew of the Eells Lime Company of Rockport, one of the last companies to remain independent of the growing Rockland-Rockport Lime Company, poses in front of the camera in 1905 or 1906. From left to right are (first row) John Ott, George McKinney, Ralph Snowman, Will Clough, Harry Dow, Eugene McFarland, Cliff Rackliff, John Carver, Aurelius Rollins, and Eugene Kneeland; (second row) Mr. Merservey, Stanley Wall, George Thomas, Gus Carroll, Mr. Robbins, Del Cook, Charlie Carver, and Ray Wasgatt; (third row) Lewis Butler. (THS.)

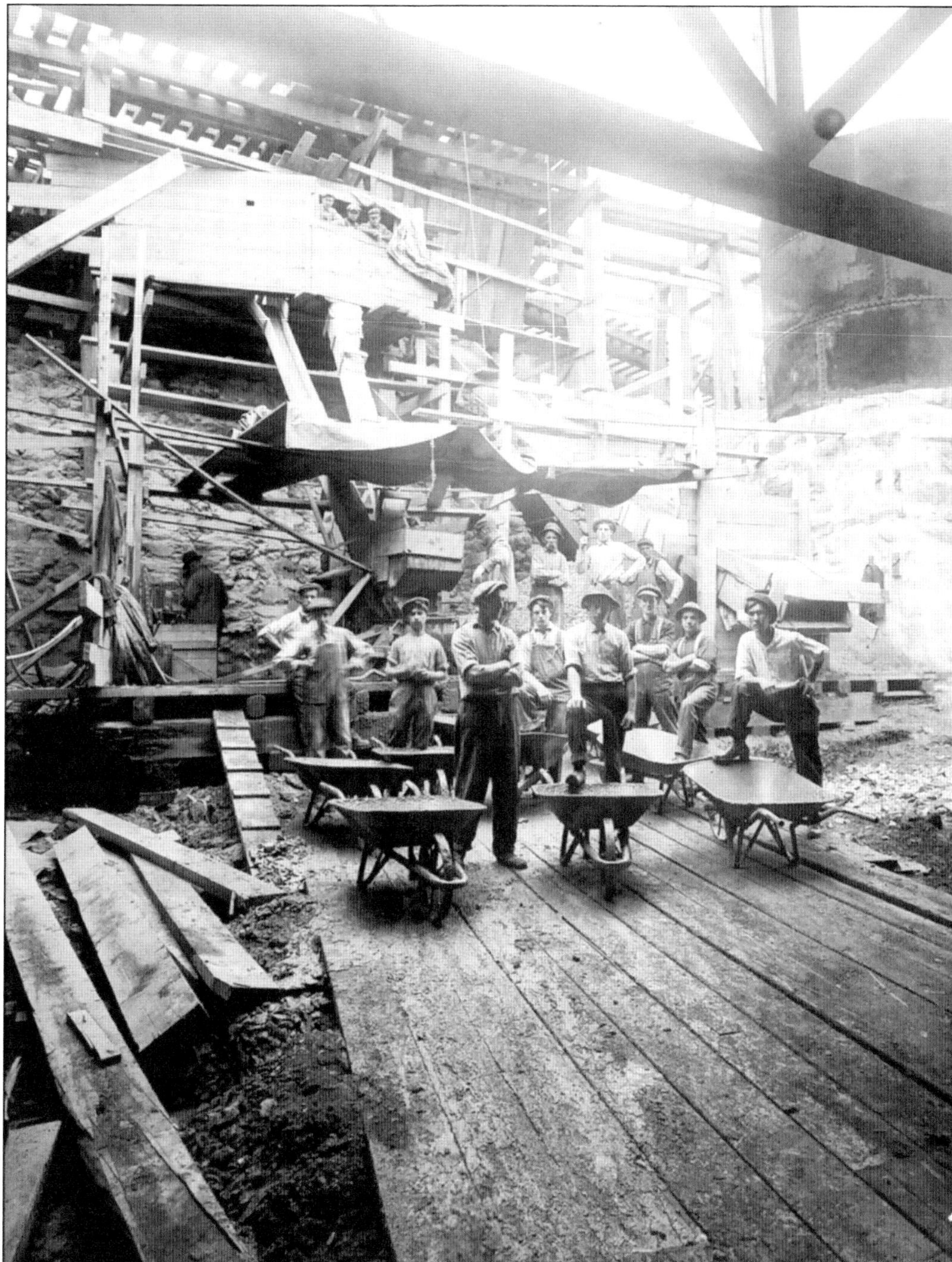

The constant intense heat of a lime kiln meant that it needed periodic repairs. Here a crew is posing with its wheelbarrows. They have been removing rubble in preparation for repairing the understructure of a kiln. Timing was important in repairing kilns because the kiln needed to be fully operative in time for the annual spring rush. (DH.)

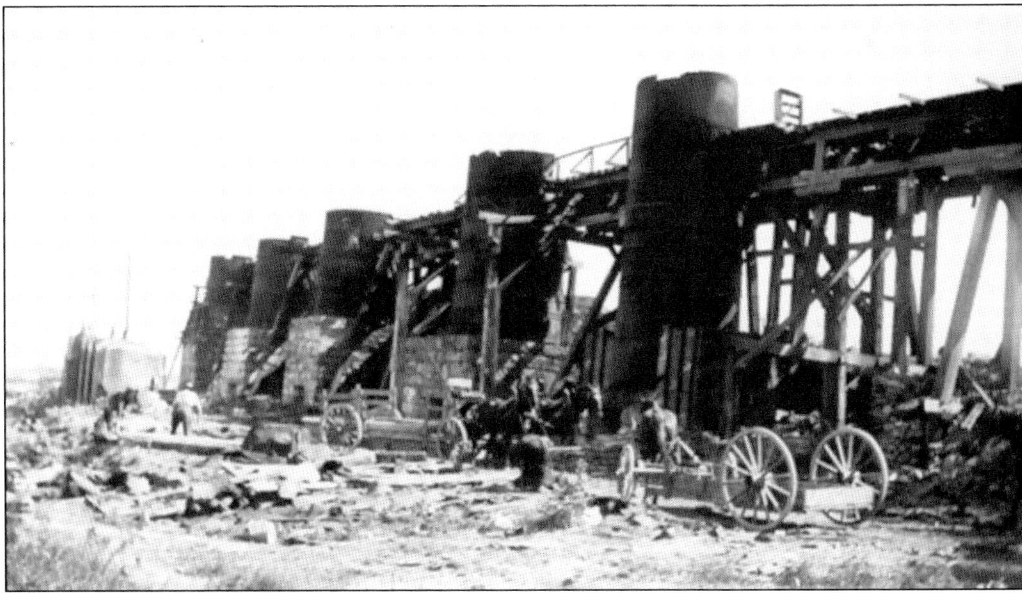

The dismantling of kilns and their support structures was a big job that occurred when kilns had outlived their usefulness. Here are two 1932 images of the old Five Kilns in Rockland's South End in their last days of existence. Above, horses and wagons are being used to haul rubble, but the kiln stacks and trestle are still in place. Below is the trestle bridge to the kiln stacks. When it was taken down, the Rockland-Rockport Lime Company donated it to the City of Rockland as part of a pier at the public landing. It is still in use today. (DH.)

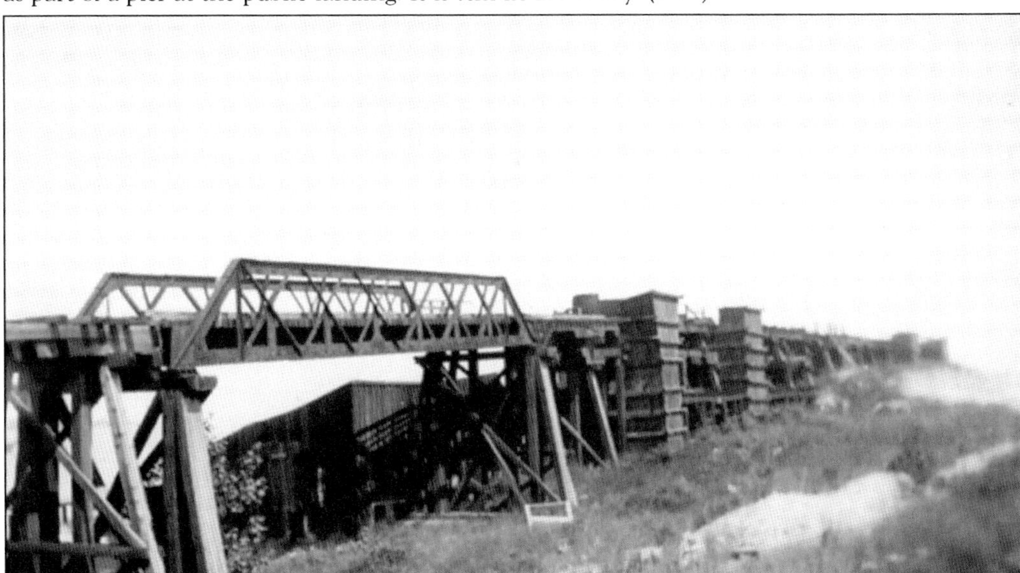

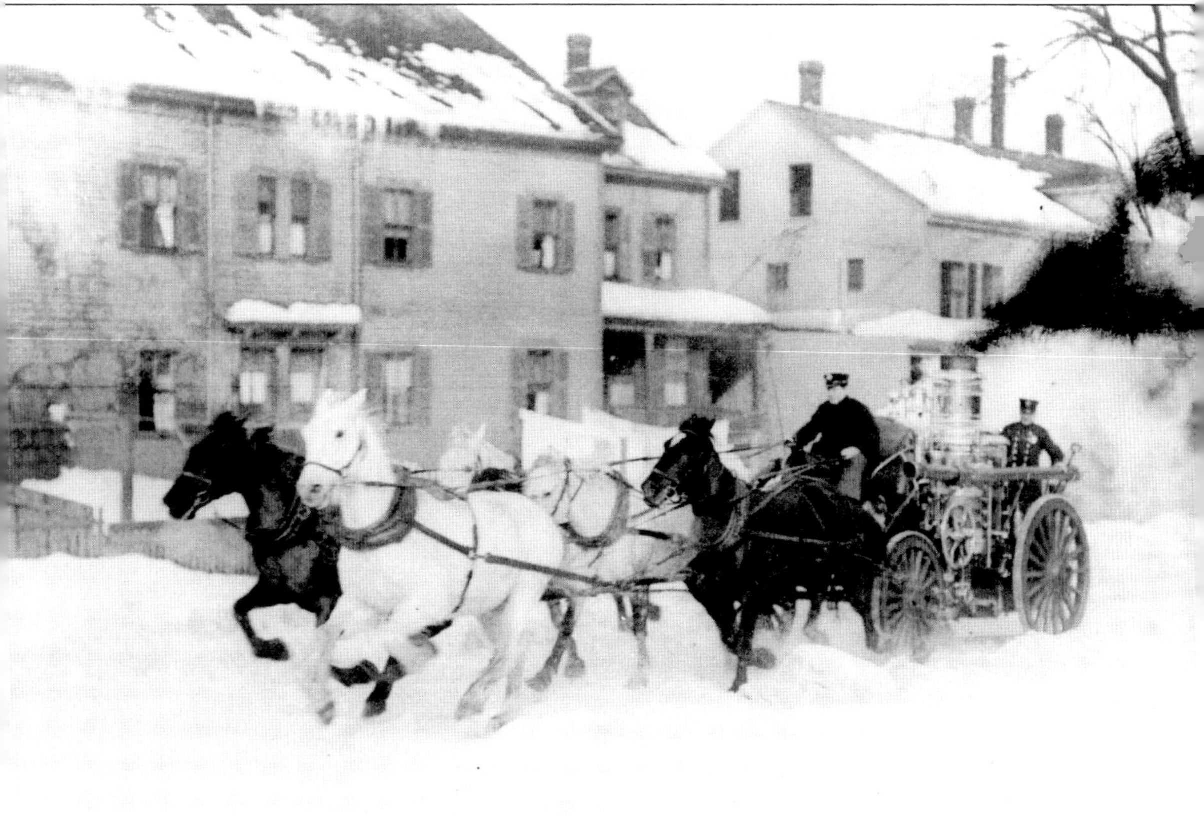

The Rockland Fire Department was busier than most. House fires in winter from heating problems were common everywhere, but Rockland had the additional threat of fire at the kilns. The burning lime itself could not be put out by water. However, wooden lime sheds and adjacent wooden buildings that had caught fire could be handled with regular firefighting apparatus, so the fire department was called regularly to deal with fires at the waterfront. Rockland had a number of small stations placed strategically throughout the city. (RHS.)

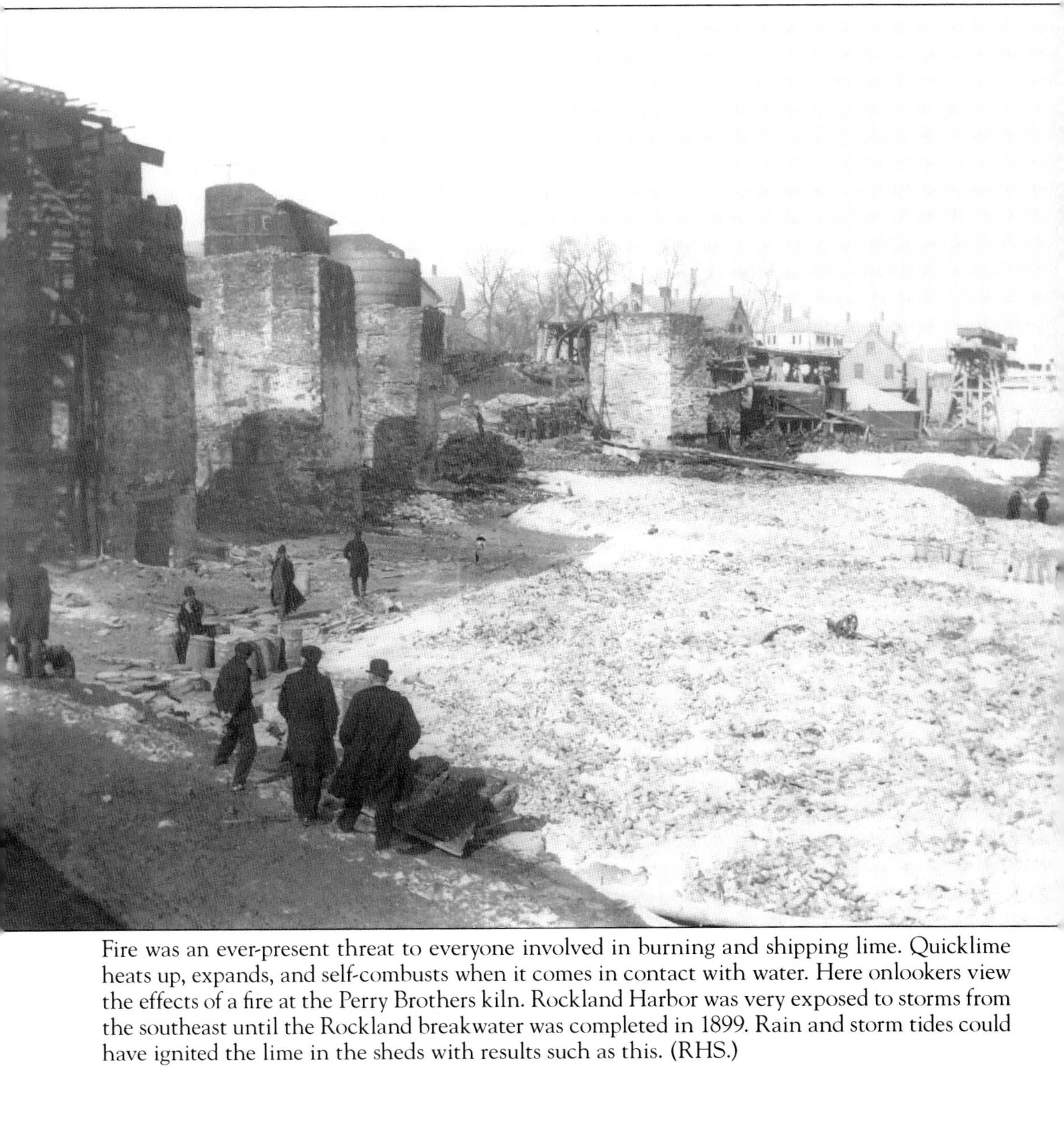

Fire was an ever-present threat to everyone involved in burning and shipping lime. Quicklime heats up, expands, and self-combusts when it comes in contact with water. Here onlookers view the effects of a fire at the Perry Brothers kiln. Rockland Harbor was very exposed to storms from the southeast until the Rockland breakwater was completed in 1899. Rain and storm tides could have ignited the lime in the sheds with results such as this. (RHS.)

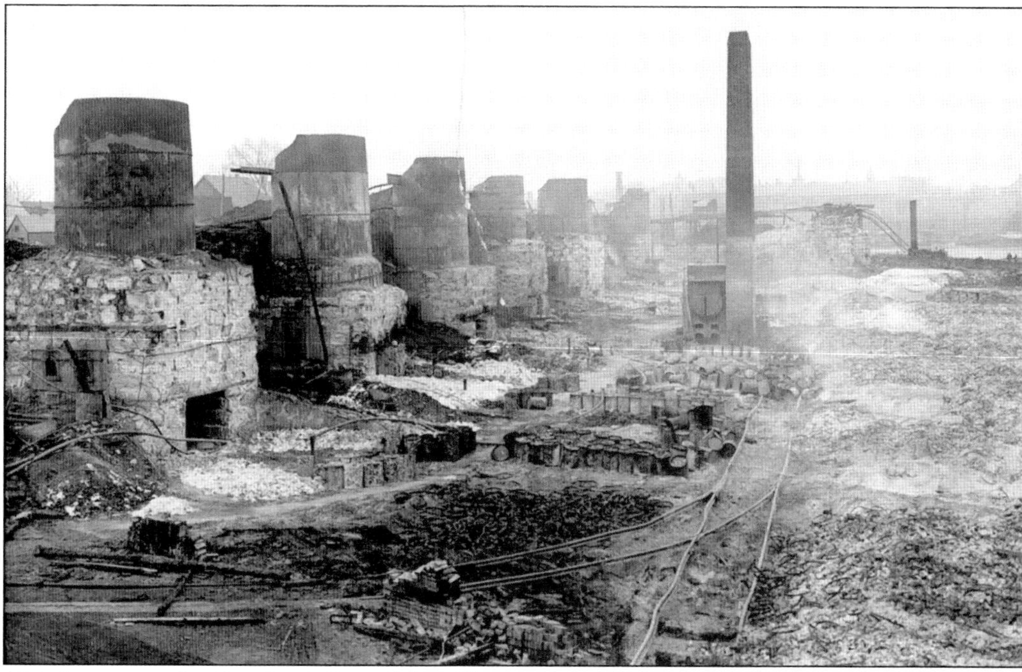

This fire was at the Crockett's Point kilns. The single smokestack was for the steam boiler, which injected steam into the firebox to increase the temperature during a burn. On the site of these ruins, the Algin Corporation (now FMC BioPolymer) developed after 1939. (DH.)

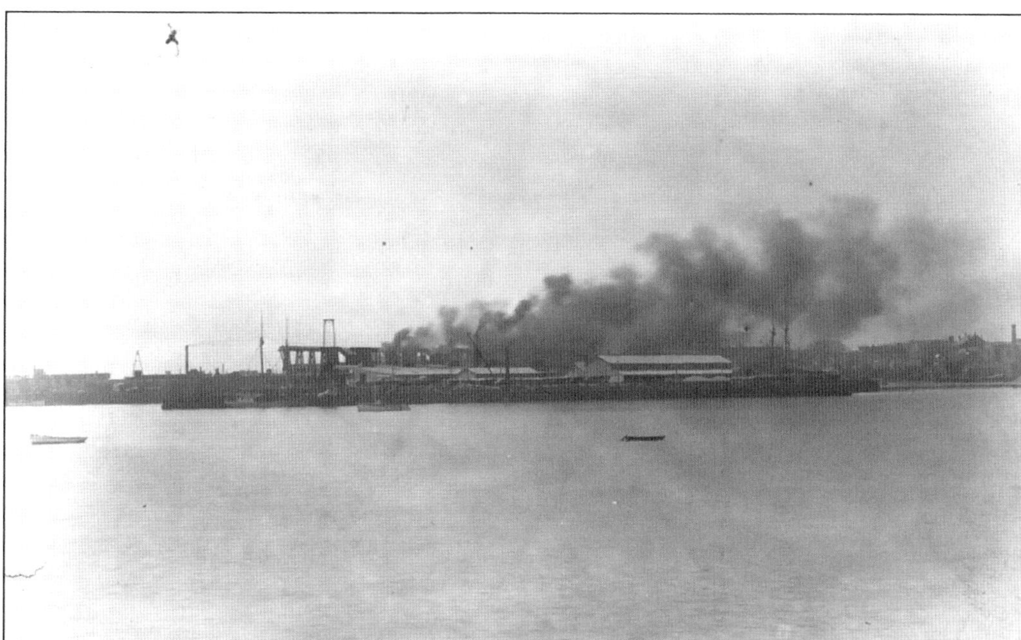

This photograph shows the billows of black smoke coming from the burning kilns. In both its quarrying and its burning aspects, lime manufacturing was a very polluting industry.

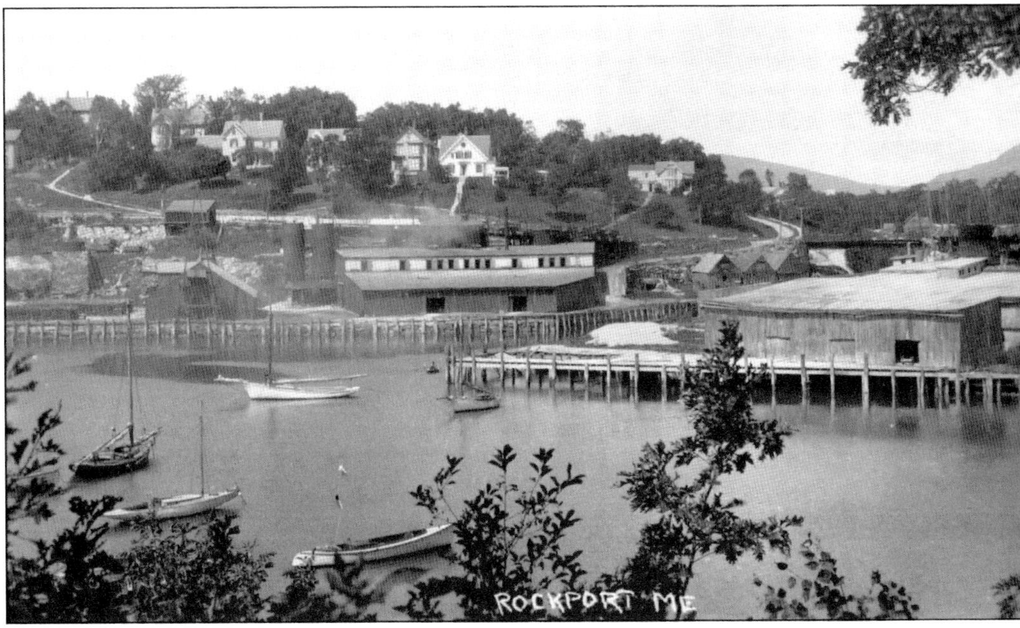

This peaceful picture of Rockport's inner harbor shows the kilns, sheds, and wharves in good working order. Kiln sheds served the duel purpose of protecting the barreled lime from the elements and also keeping the cordwood dry. On the right, the railroad track winds off toward the piles of waste lime rock, which can still be seen from the Goose River bridge. (CRHS.)

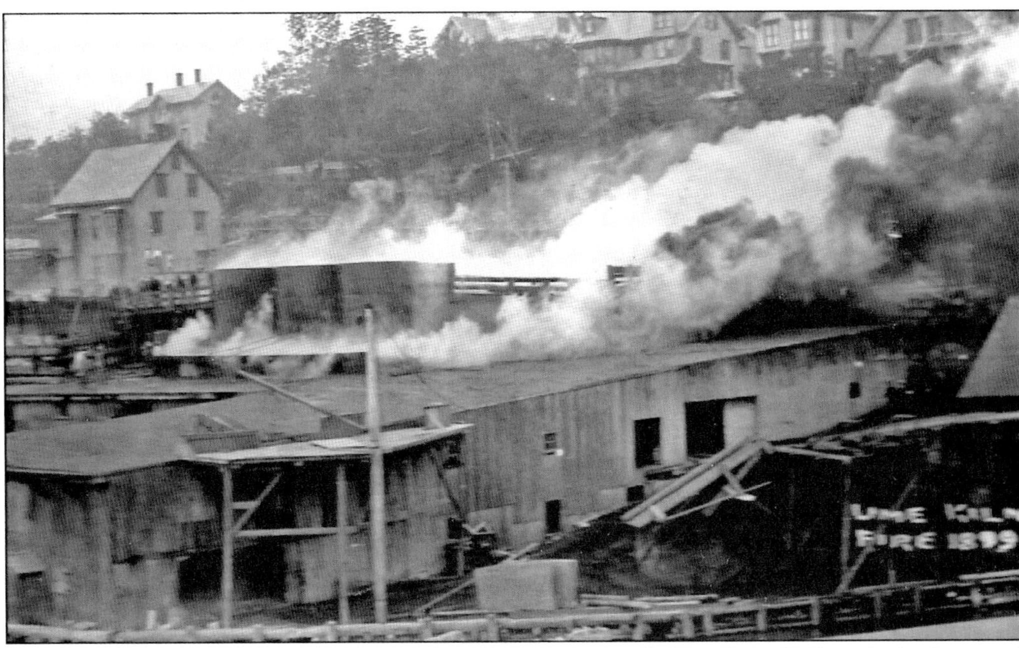

Here is the same harbor in the midst of a lime fire in 1899, with Amesbury Hill in the background. Many kiln sheds burned over the years. Rain or storm tides could cause the blaze. Also, fire was often caused by the heat of the kiln itself igniting the shed yokes, or frames, which surrounded the kiln. Most were rebuilt if the kiln was still active. (CRHS.)

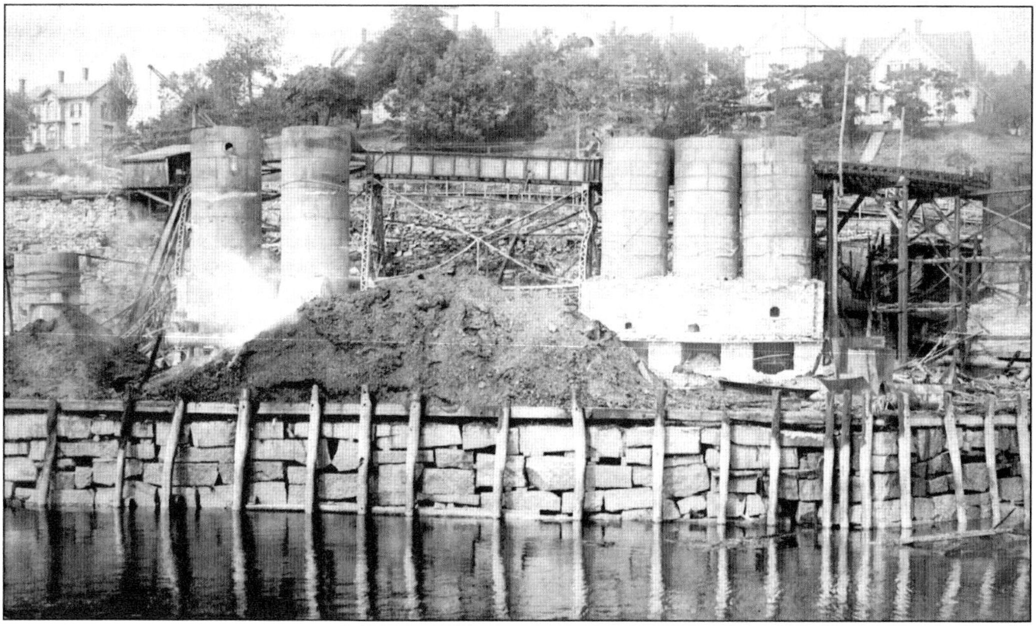

This is how Rockport harbor looked in the aftermath of the big kiln fire, with rubble everywhere and kilns looking naked with their sheds gone. In 1875, the kilns on the left were owned by the Carleton Company, and those on the right were Shepherd Company kilns. When they burned, they belonged to the Rockland-Rockport Lime Company. One can see the high train trestle behind the kiln tops. Remains of several of these kilns on the west side of the harbor have been preserved as part of a waterfront park, but remnants of the Rockport Railroad have disappeared. (CRHS.)

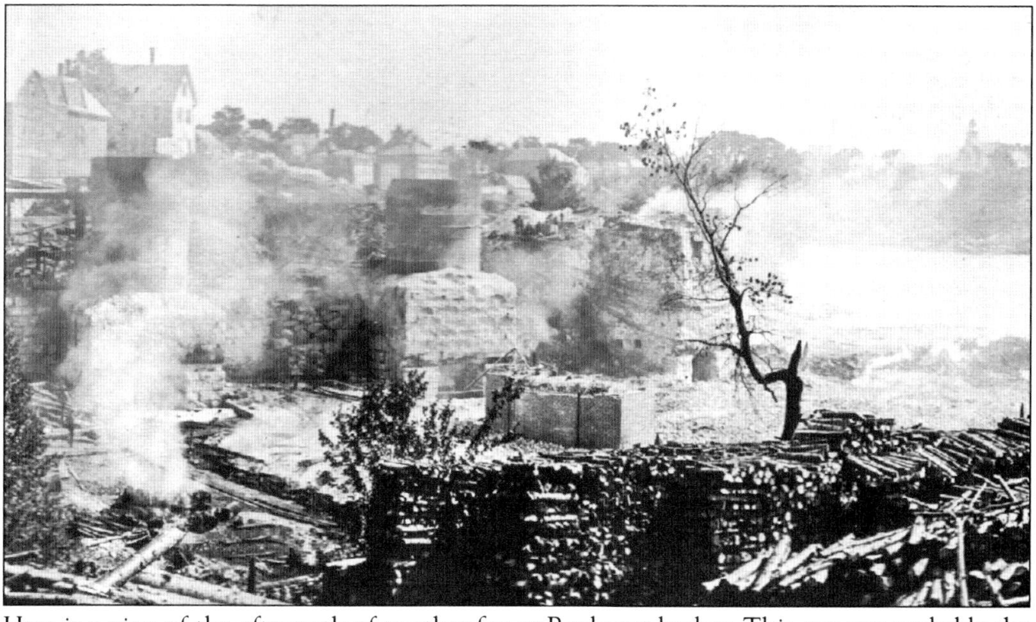

Here is a view of the aftermath of another fire at Rockport harbor. This one was probably the fire at the Eells Kilns on the west side of the harbor in 1907. In the foreground are piles of kiln wood that survived the heat. (CRHS.)

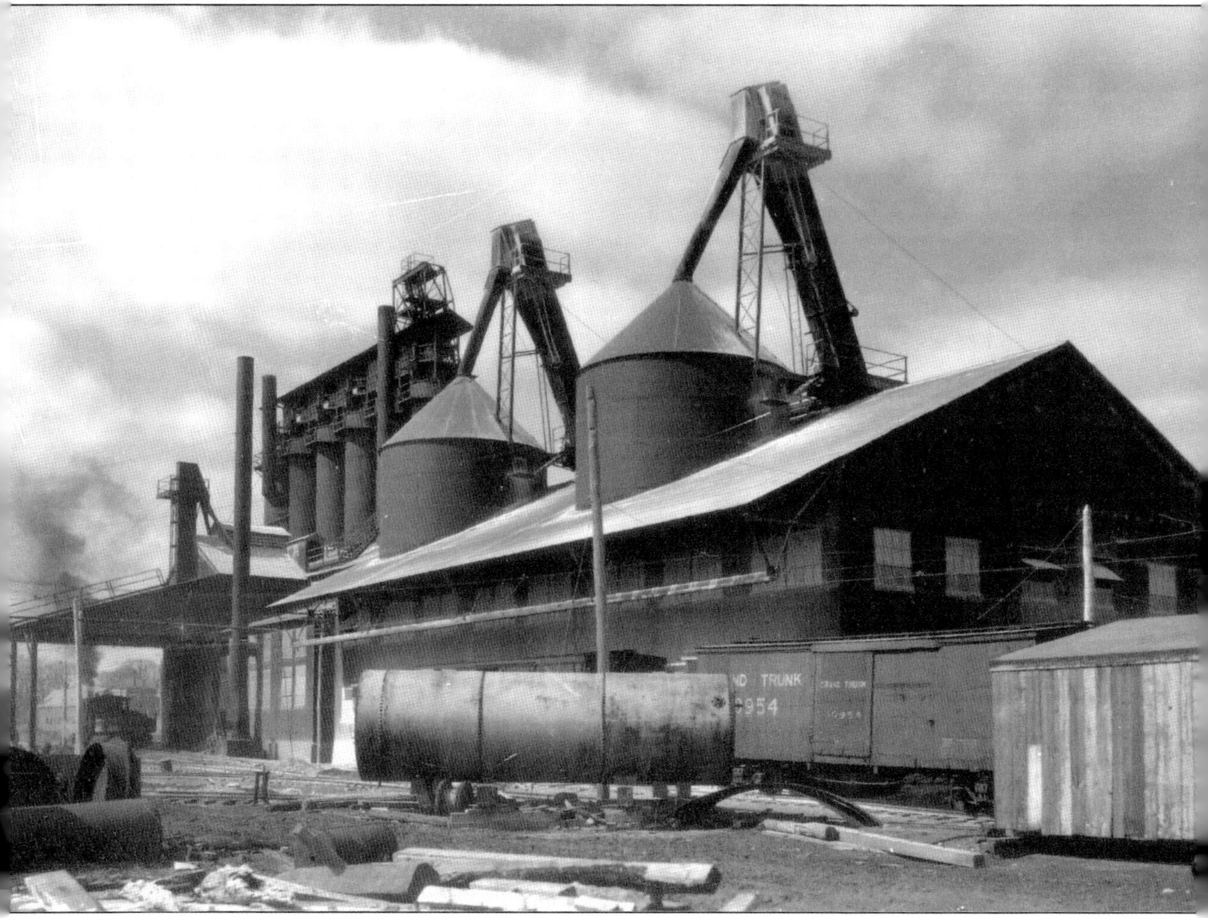

In the 1920s, the owners of the Rockland-Rockport Lime Company invested approximately $1 million in a new plant to burn lime using coal gas for fuel. It included its own gas manufacturing facility. The kilns exuding smoke are the gas plant, built from a German design. Although promising, the project was eventually abandoned because local limestone was different chemically from German limestone and did not burn well using this new method. (RHS.)

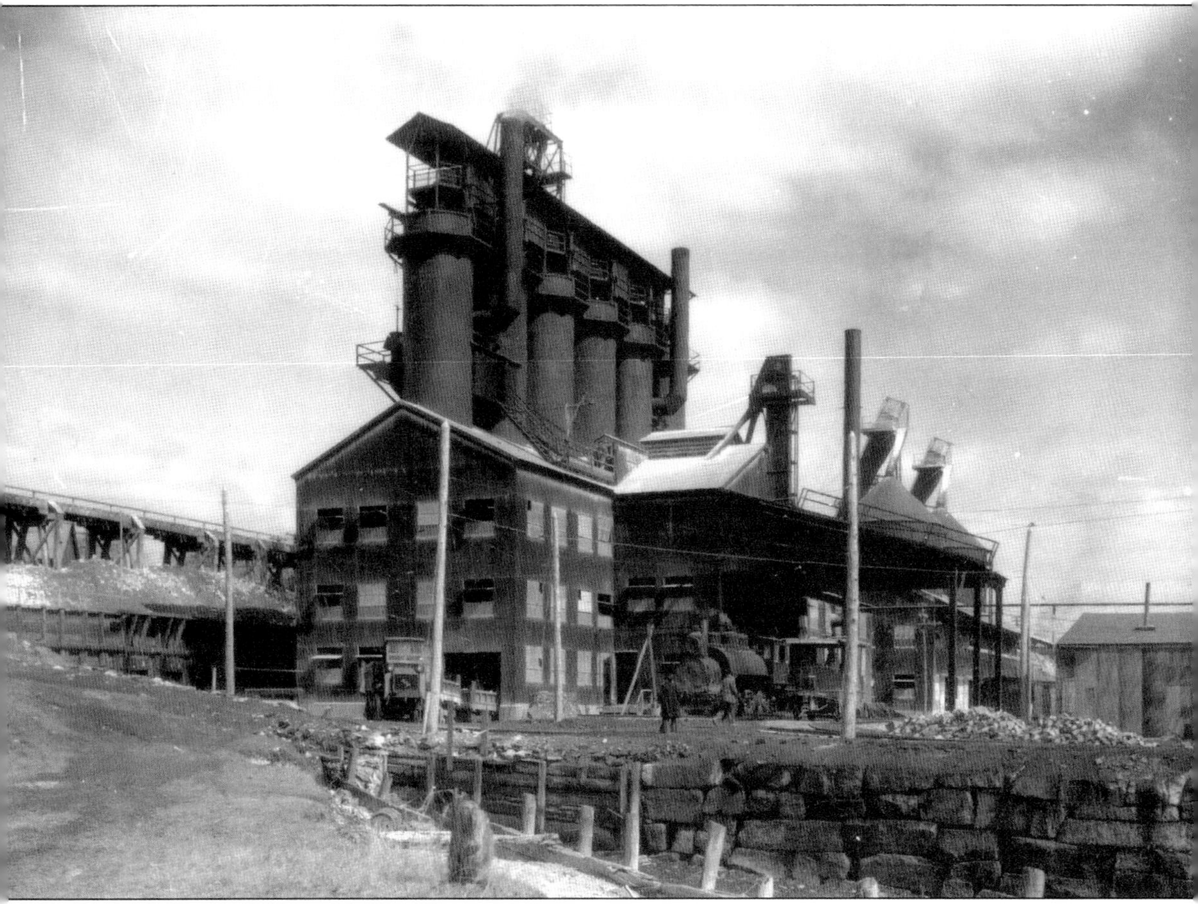

The Rockland-Rockport Lime Company gas kilns were under construction from 1921 to 1923. About 90 feet high, they dominated the Rockland waterfront, dwarfing the storage sheds at the right of the picture. They were a radical departure from the older familiar-looking kilns. (DH.)

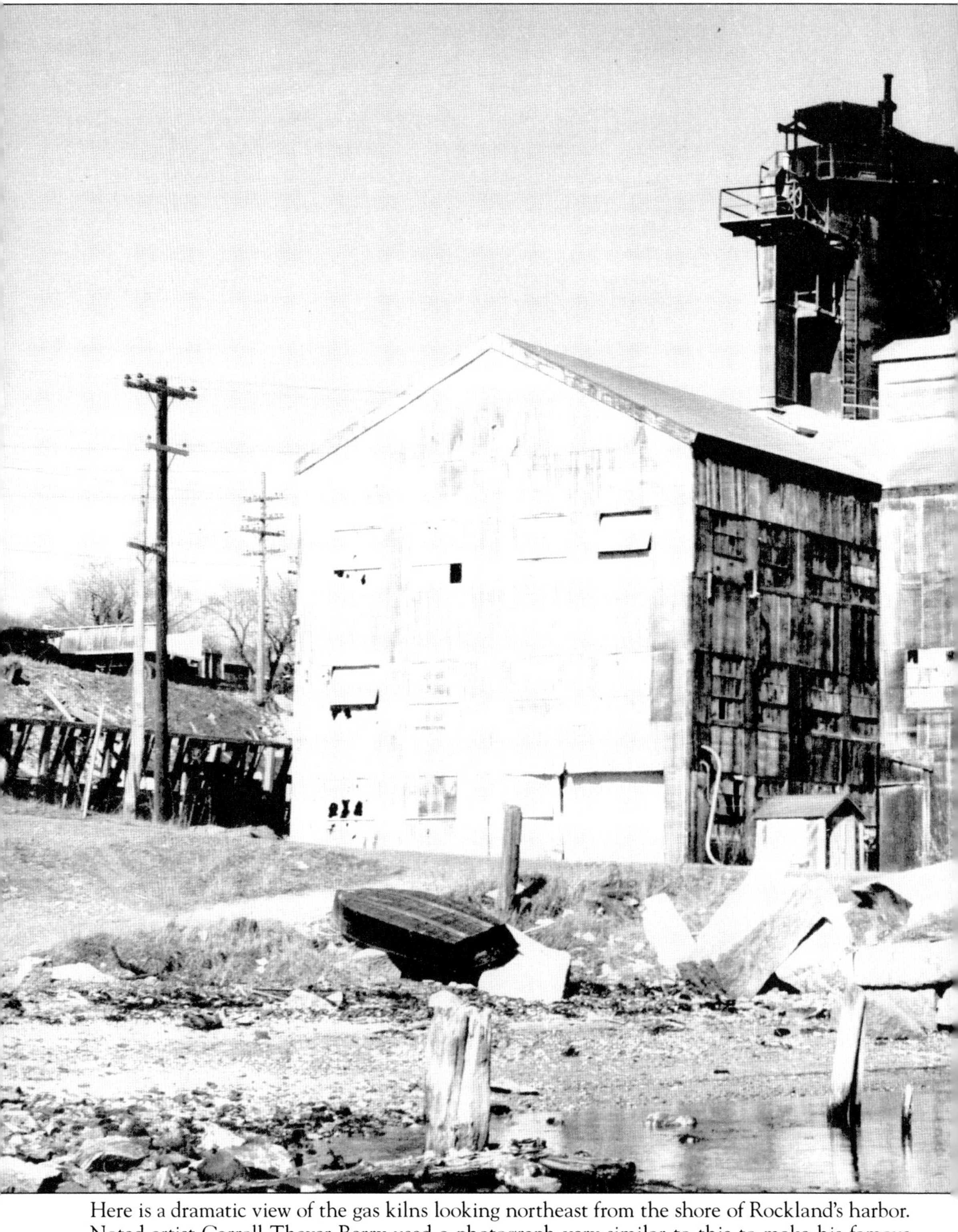

Here is a dramatic view of the gas kilns looking northeast from the shore of Rockland's harbor. Noted artist Carroll Thayer Berry used a photograph very similar to this to make his famous

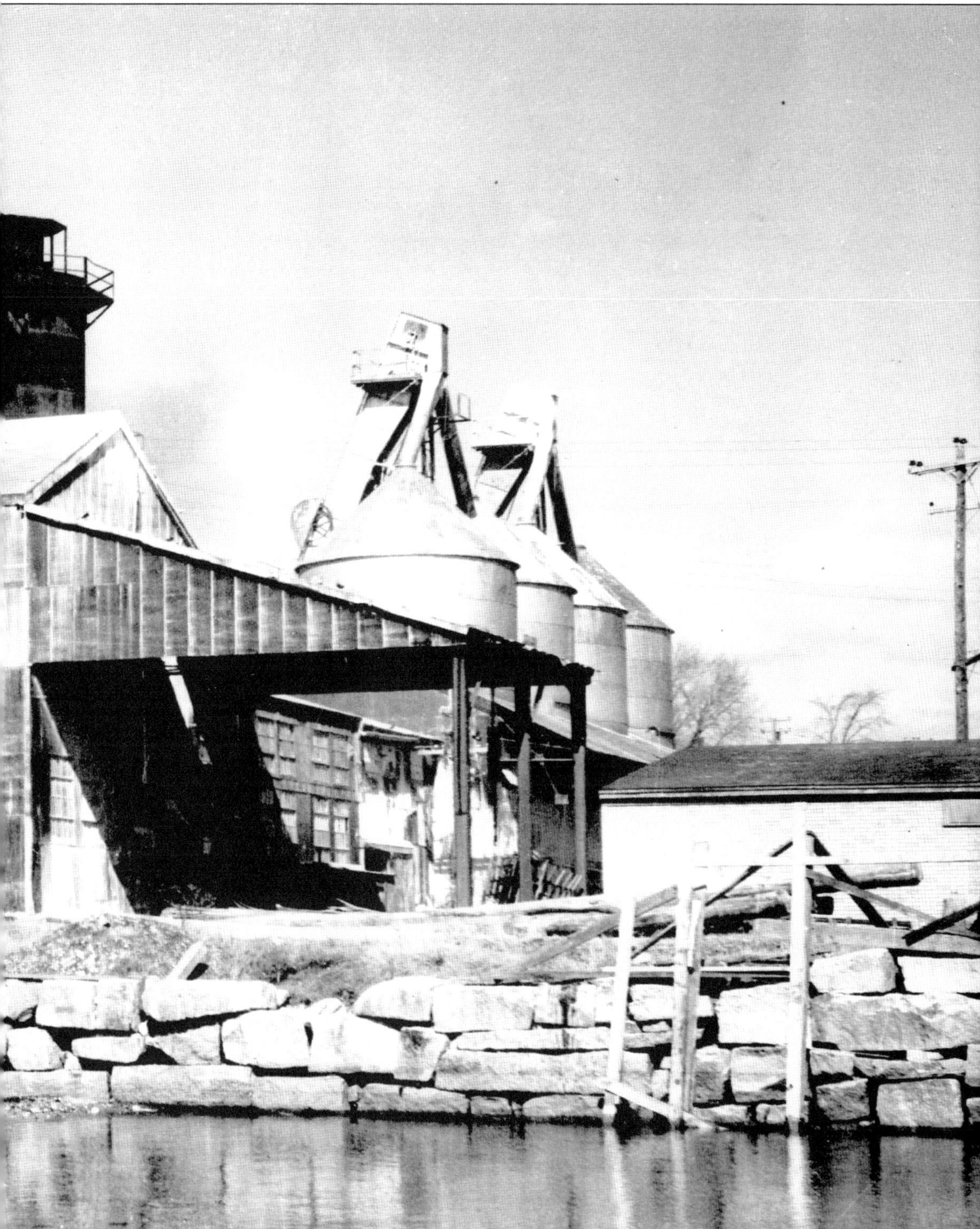

woodcut titled *Limestone and Sail*, in Elwyn Dearborn's *The Down East Printmaker*. It was a tribute to the area's limestone and shipbuilding industries, which are a glory of the past. (DH.)

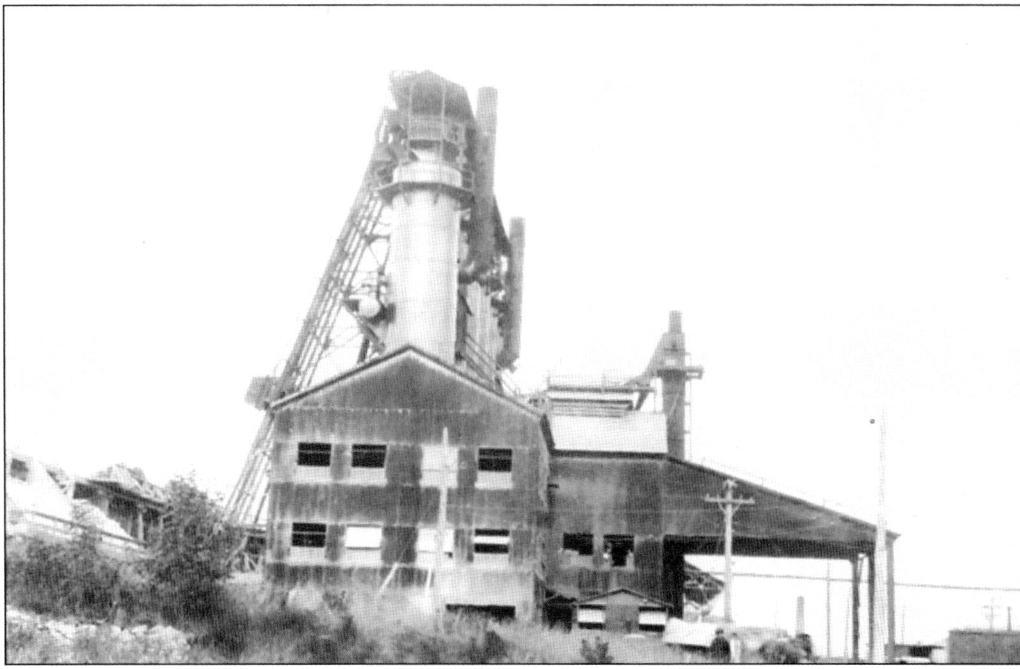

This is a side view of the gas kilns at the Perry Wharf in Rockland's North End. The building was constructed wholly of steel and had a cement foundation, very different from the traditional materials of granite, fieldstone, and wood. (DH.)

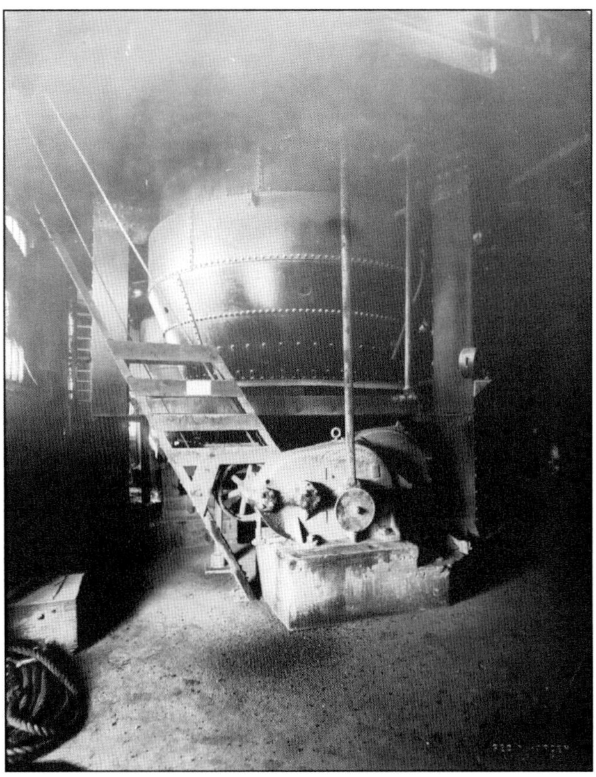

Here is a view of the interior of the gas plant. When the soft coal was burned, it produced coke and coal gas. The company sold the coke and used the coal gas to fire the kilns. (DH.)

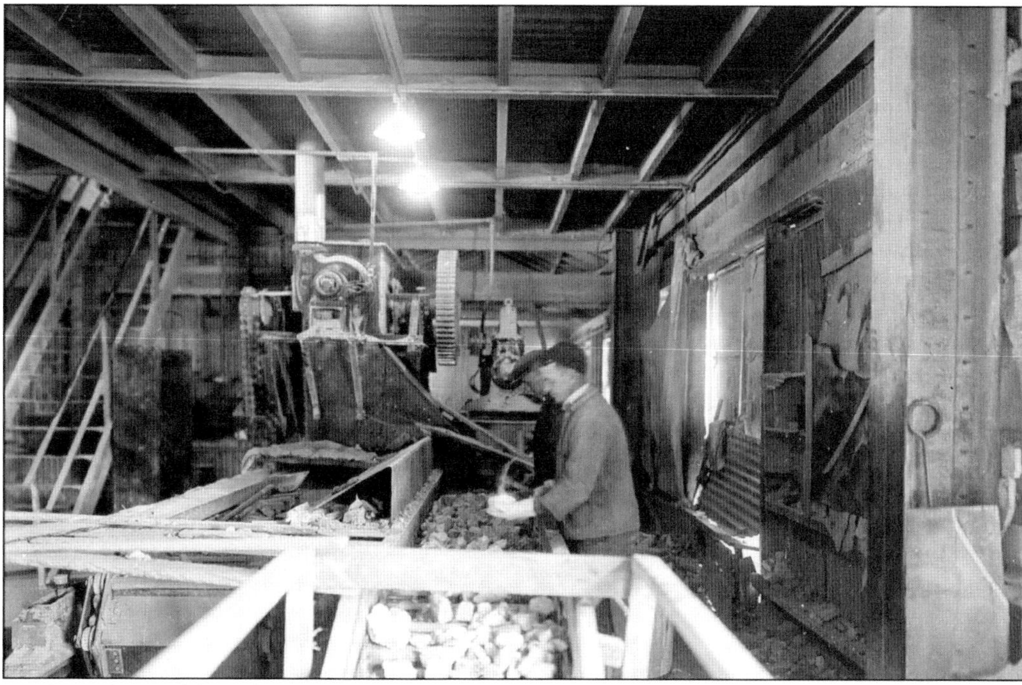

At the picking table at the gas kilns, the quicklime moves along a conveyor belt as the worker picks out the uncooked core and removes it. This image was taken sometime during the 1920s. (DH.)

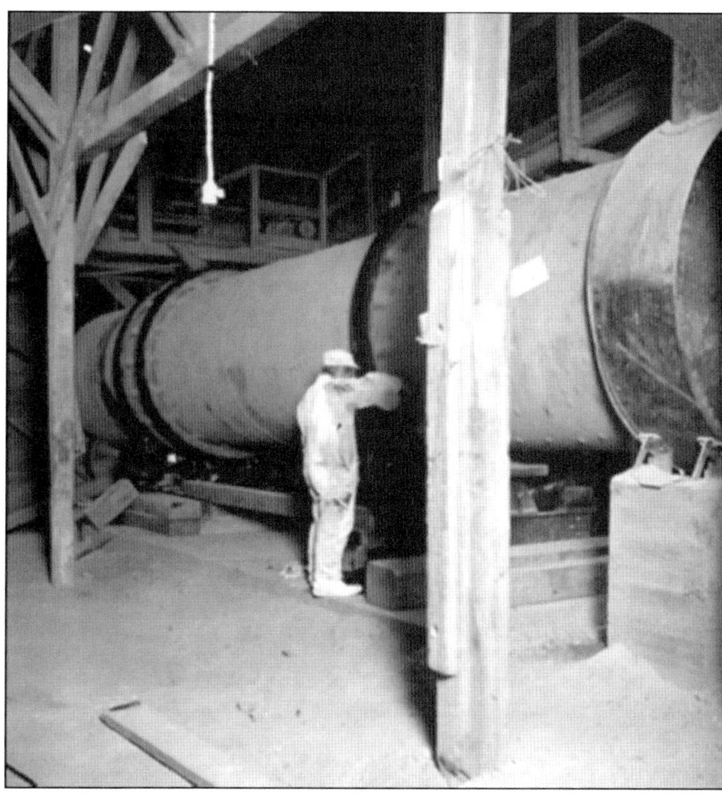

In 1943, after it was determined that the gas process did not burn limestone as well as it had hoped, the Rockland-Rockport Lime Company converted the kilns into facilities for producing agricultural limestone. This machine is the rotating dryer from mill No. 3 at the gas kilns. Here the agricultural limestone was pulverized to a specific degree of fineness, and all traces of moisture were removed before it was bagged. The plant operated in this capacity until 1975, when, having outlived its usefulness, it was demolished. (DH.)

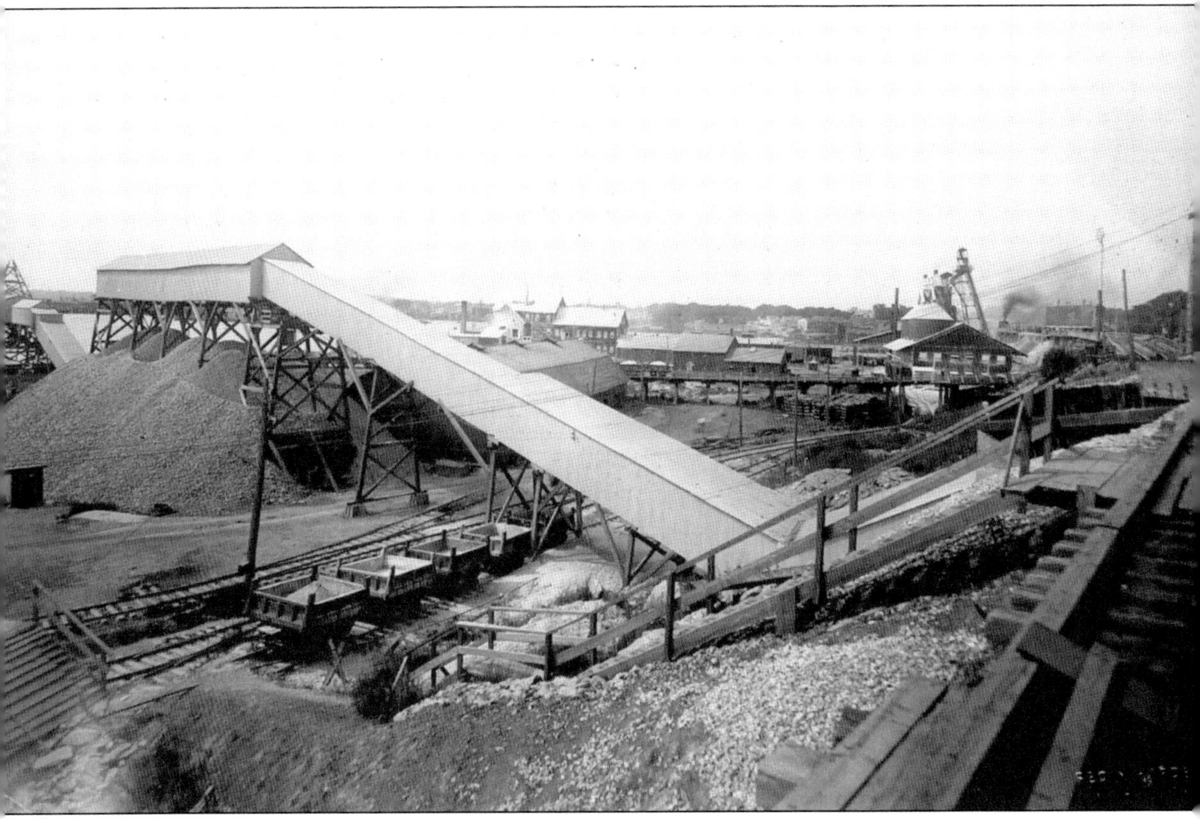

This 1926 photograph and the following two photographs show the flux stone facility at the harbor. Flux stone is not burned lime rock. It is crushed lime rock that is used to clear out impurities such as silica, phosphorus, and sulphur in steel refining. Here is a broad view that shows the total conveying and screening system for the flux stone plant with stockpiles of crushed stone below. At the far left is the final loading conveyor to load the barges for Boston. (DH.)

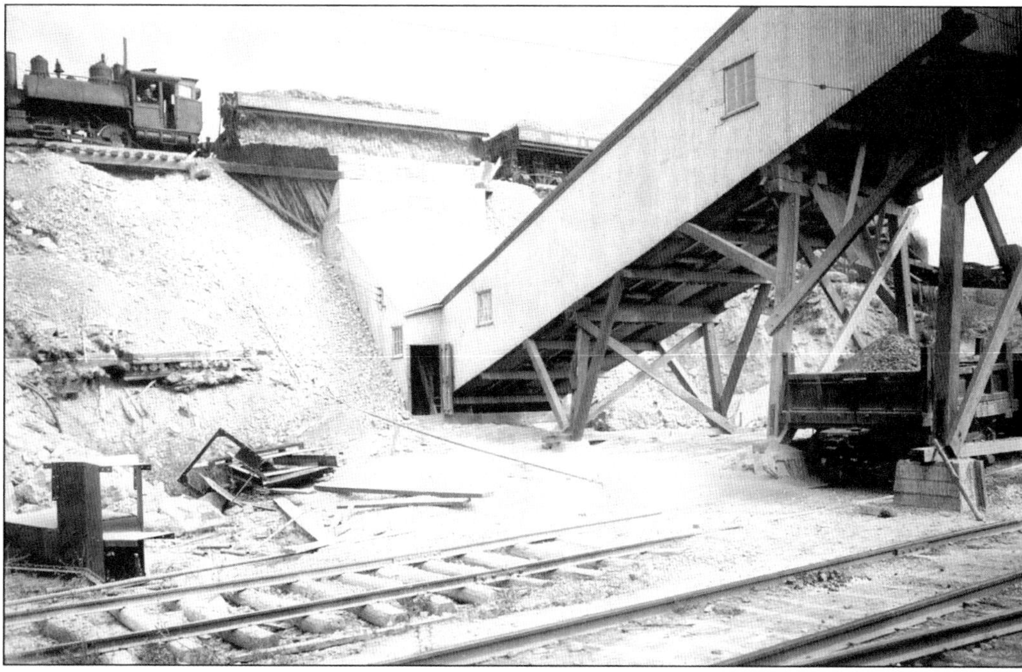

The flux stone came down to the North End from the crushing plant at the quarry on the Lime Rock Railroad. The large hydraulic rock car is side-dumping into the hopper, which still exists, and onto a conveyor system. (DH.)

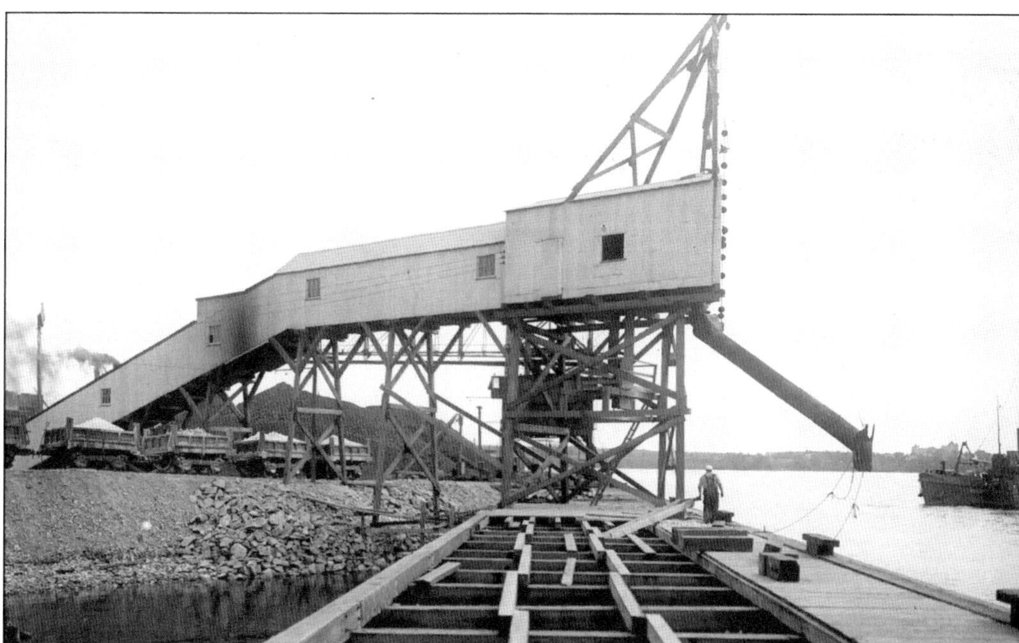

This conveyor belt loaded the barges. The flux stone traveled up the conveyor belt and then out through the spout into the hold of the barge. No barge was docked when the photograph was taken, but a tug can be seen on the far right. (DH.)

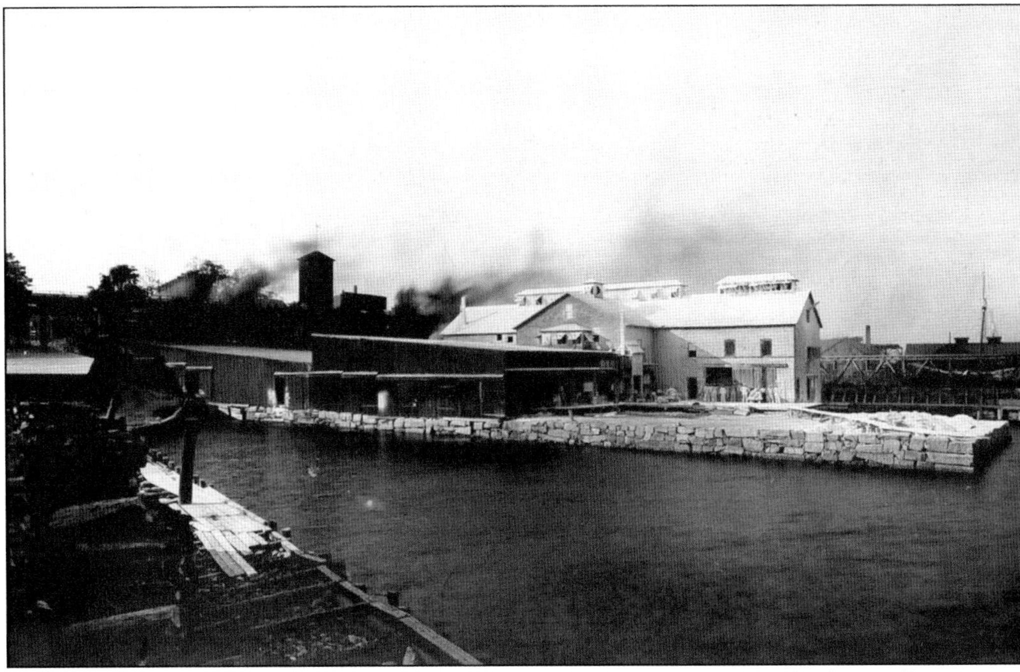

This is an exterior view of the hydrate plant in the 1920s. Hydrated lime had a small amount of water added to it. This was an improvement over the older form of lime because it eliminated a step for masons who were preparing the mortar at the work site. (DH.)

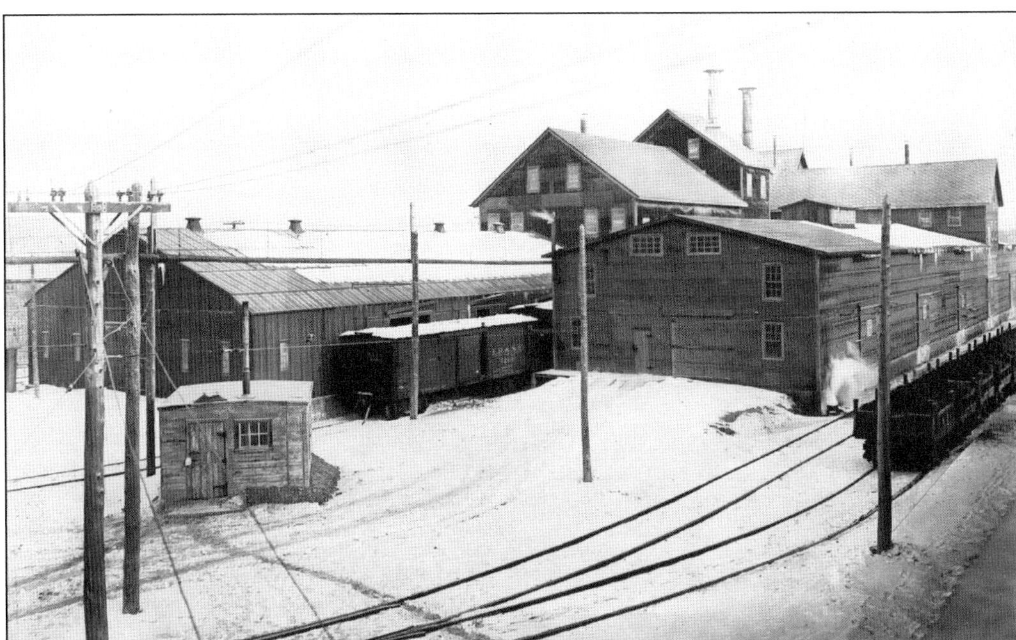

In this winter view of the hydrate plant is a small building on the left that was known to employees as the mystery house. It acquired the strange name because day laborers came here each morning to see if work was available. As they sat waiting to hear whether they were needed, they said, "It's a mystery whether we'll be working today or not," hence the name. (DH.)

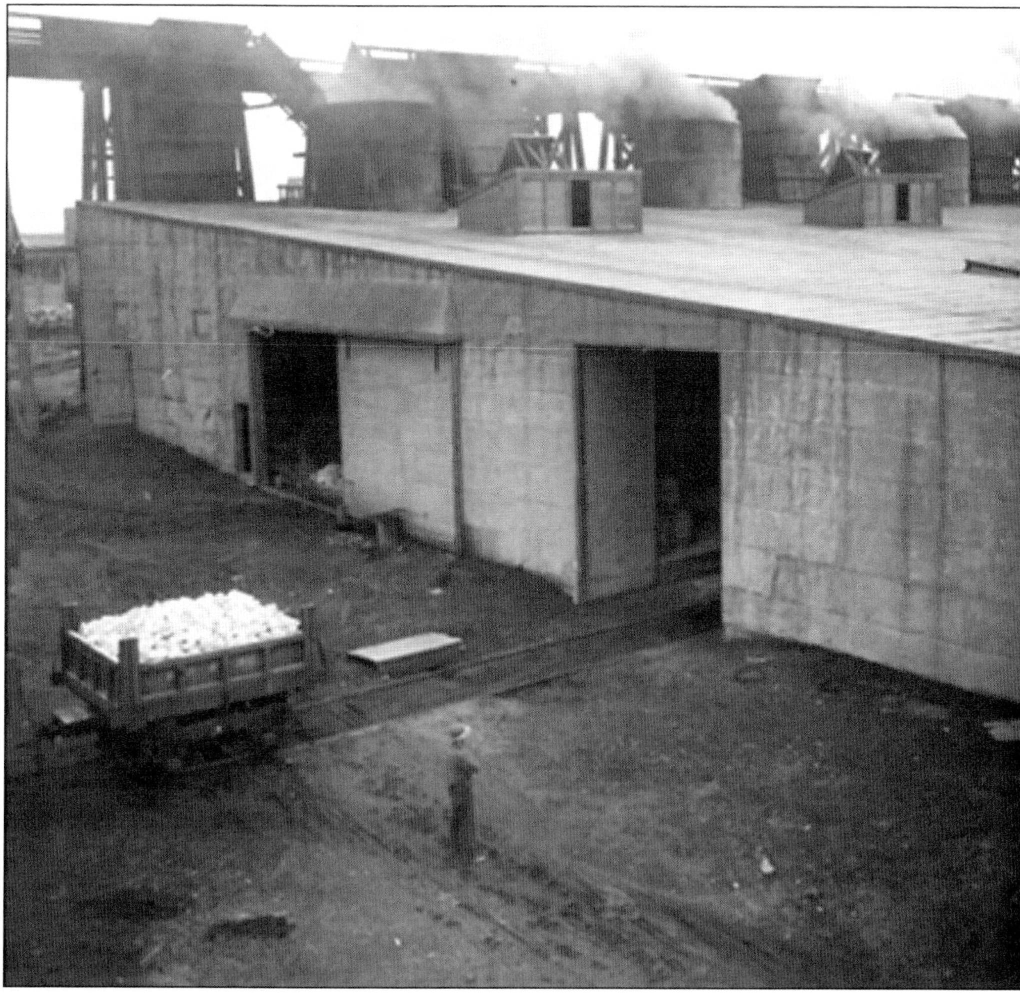

On the tracks coming out of the kiln shed is rock car No. 362, one of a fleet of 500 side-dumping rock cars owned by the Lime Rock Railroad. It contains hot lime from the kiln, which it will carry from this site across the yard to the hydrate plant. (DH.)

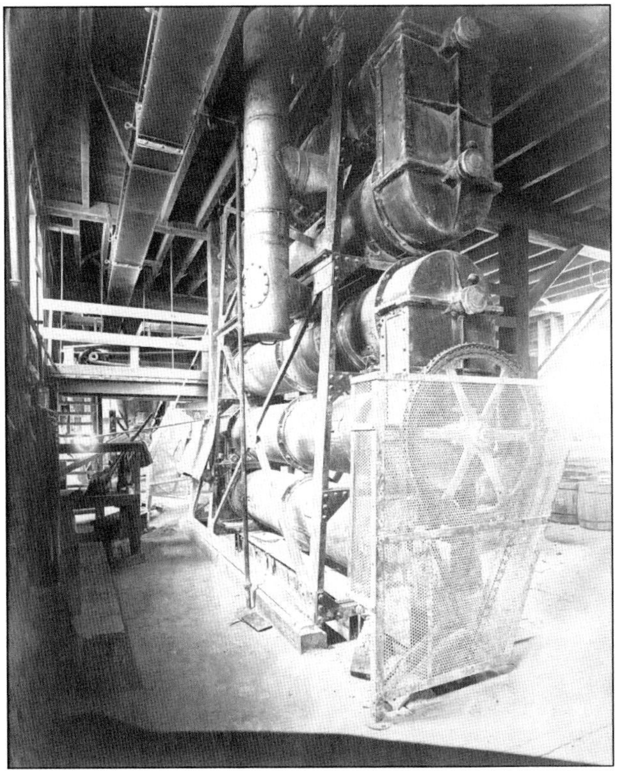

The grinder at the hydrate plant pulverized the hot lime into fine particles, then the hydrators added the proper amount of water to it. After the lime had been hydrated, the product was much safer to ship. Also, much less work was required on the construction site to prepare the product for use. (DH.)

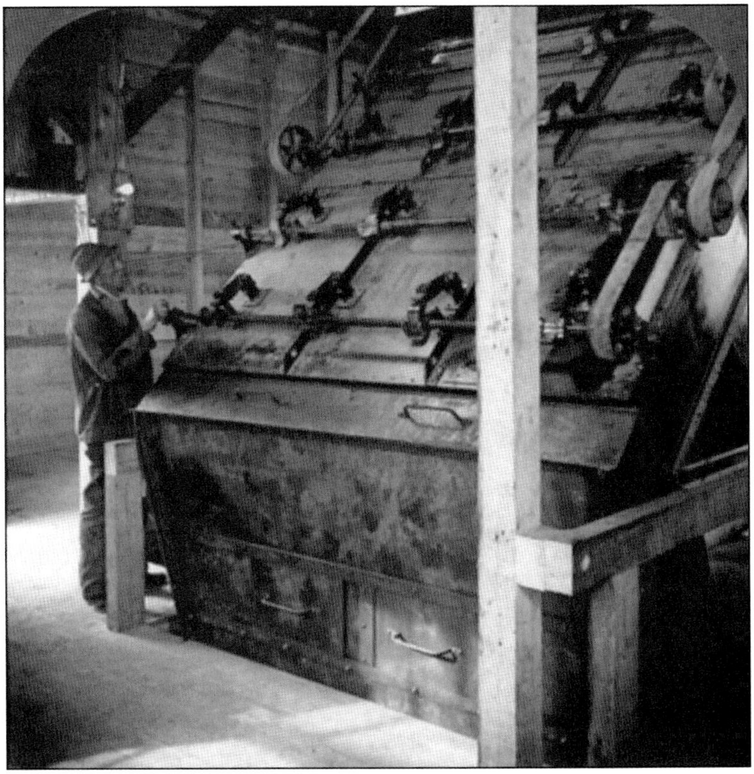

In one of the final steps in the process of refining the hydrated lime, this machine screens the hydrated lime to eliminate the last of the impurities or oversized pieces, getting the product to the standard final specification. (DH.)

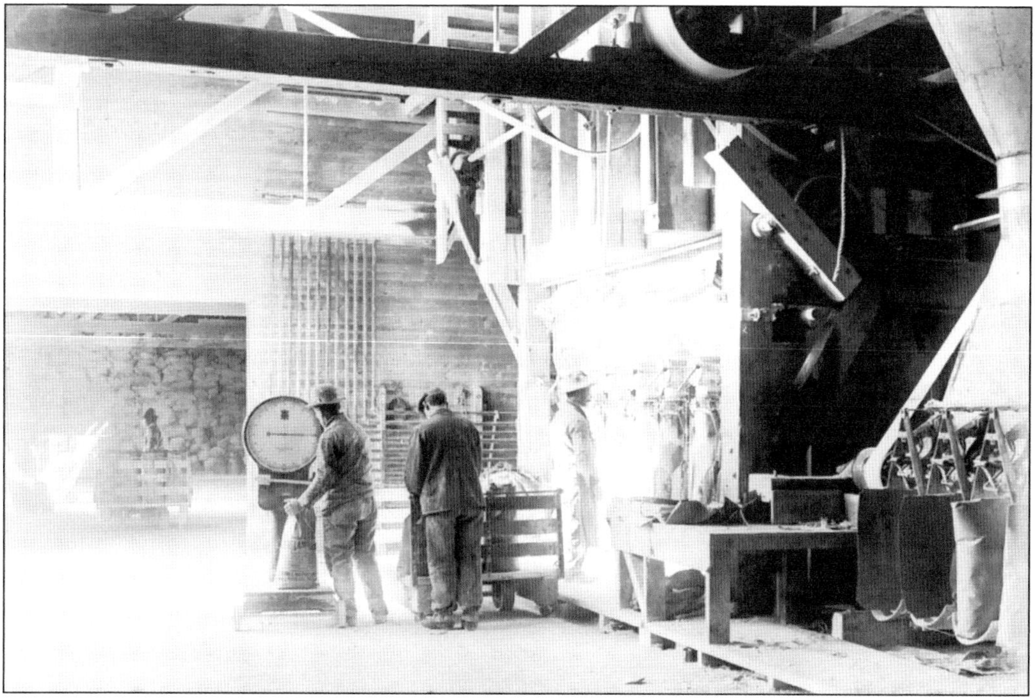

Workers are weighing bagged lime prior to sealing it. Whether paper bags, burlap bags, or barrels, it all had to meet weight requirements before it left the building. (DH.)

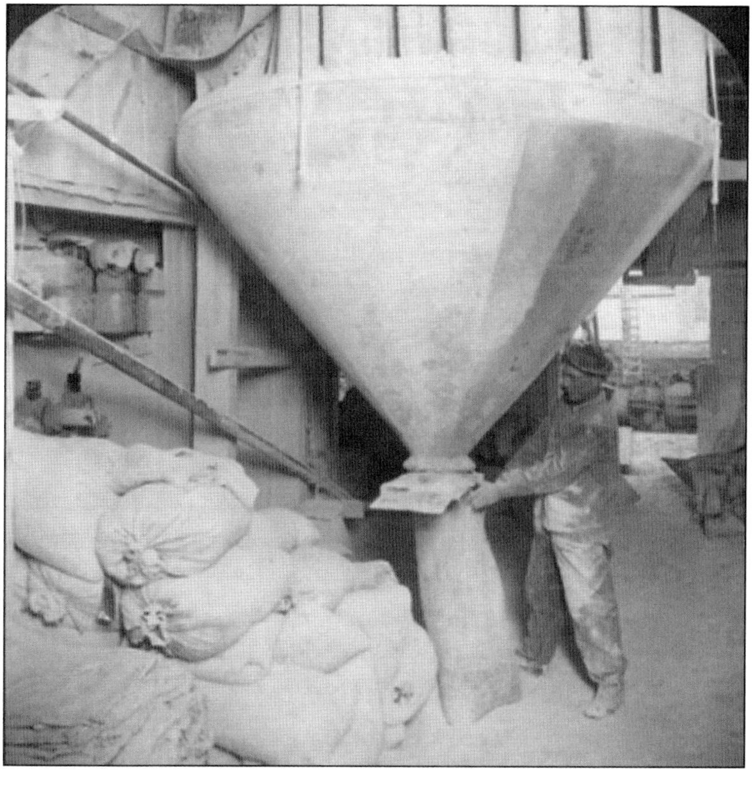

A dust-coated worker bags lime in burlap bags at the hydrate plant. Baggers had to fill and tie each of the floppy burlap bags. Manufacturers later changed to sturdier paper bags, which could be filled automatically. (DH.)

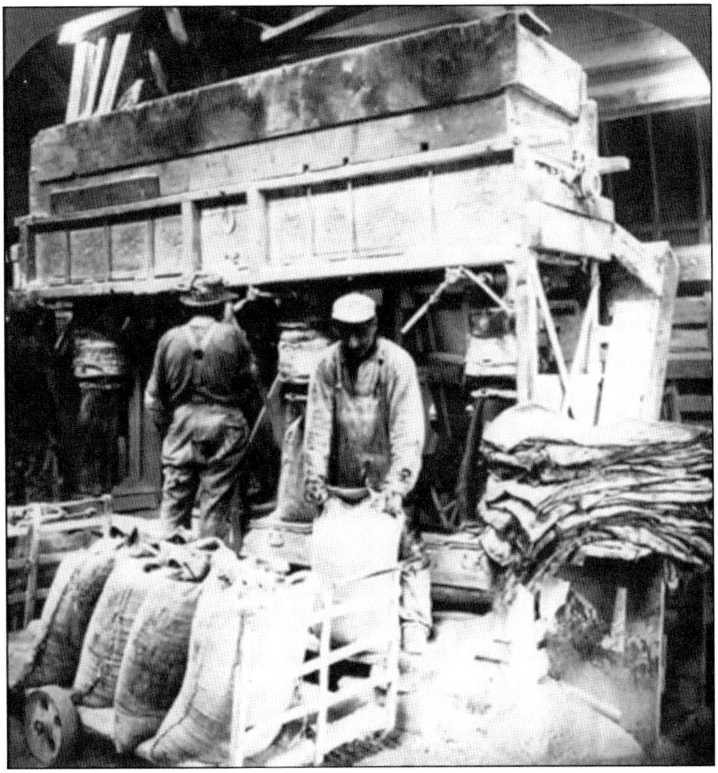

Here men are still bagging in burlap, but this machine is more sophisticated than the one in the previous picture, and the filled bags are propped in carts. Accumulated lime dust gives the workers a ghostlike appearance. (DH)

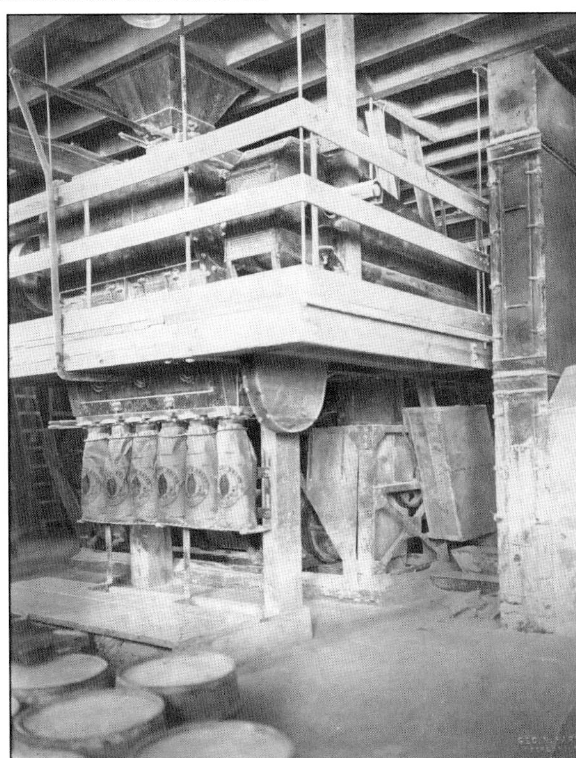

This is the bag machine at the hydrate plant where the finished product is packaged in sturdy paper, several bags at a time. Note the barrels in the foreground. They are intended for shipment on barges; bagged lime was shipped by rail or truck. (DH.)

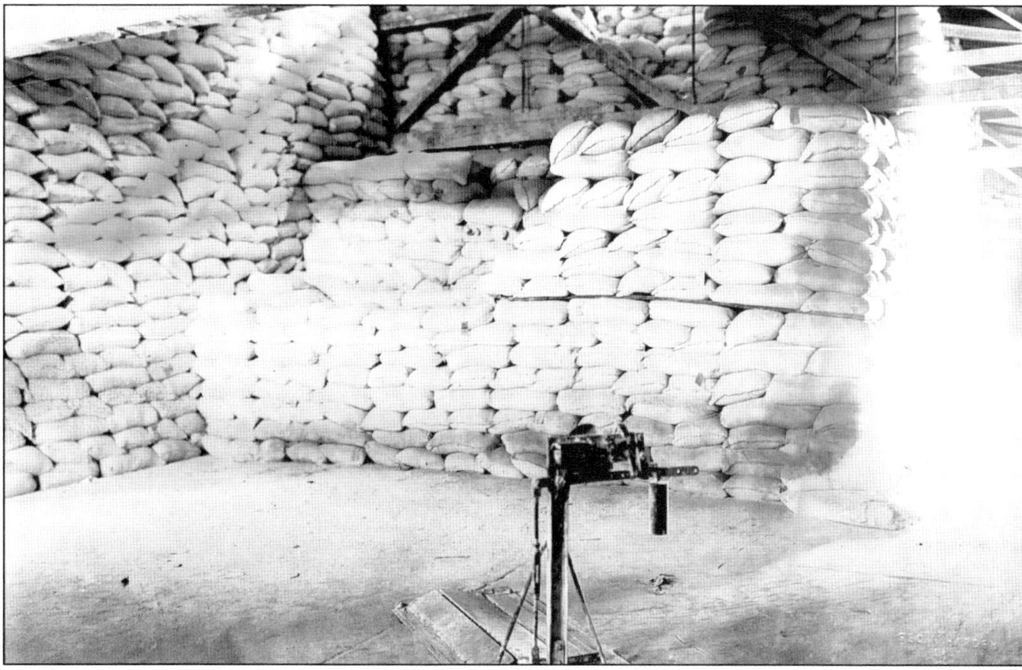

By the 1930s, most barreled lime had given way to bagged lime. Here in the interior of one of the lime sheds are stockpiled bags of lime awaiting shipment. In the foreground are the scales for ensuring that each bag was filled to the required weight. (DH.)

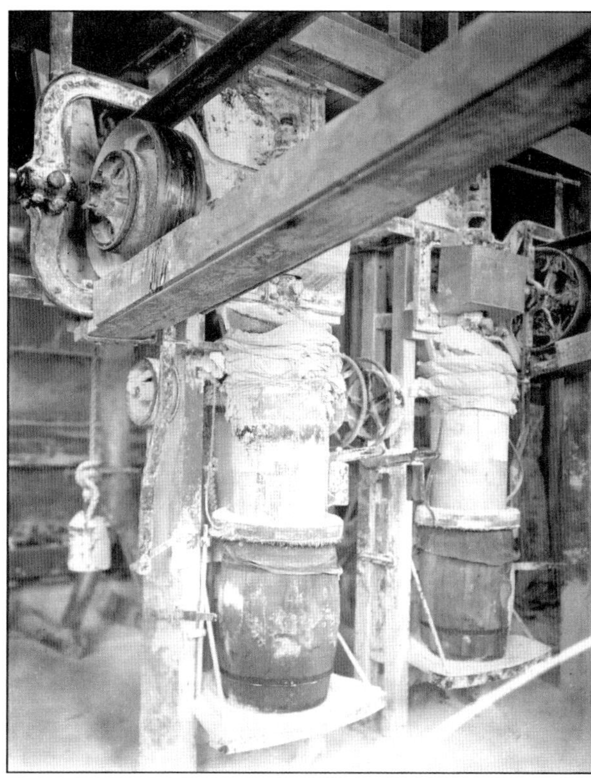

An automatic barrel packer is packing hydrated lime, and now the only human assistance is in overseeing the machine. This machine was used at the Rockland-Rockport Lime Company in the 1920s. A barrel held two bushels and a peck, 185 pounds.

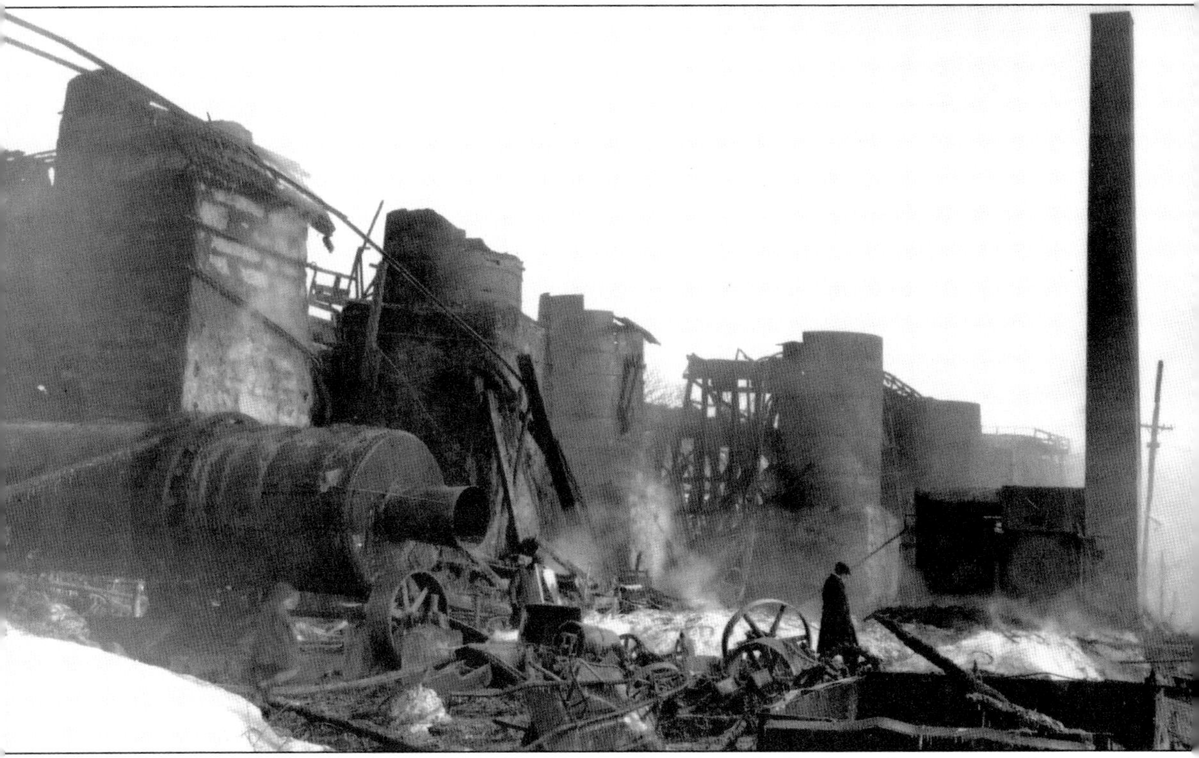

Like so many buildings associated with lime manufacturing, the hydrate plant eventually burned. This fire occurred on July 8, 1932. The country was going through the Depression at the time, and the hydrate plant was not rebuilt. (RHS.)

Four

Fueling the Kilns

Feeding the voracious kilns was a crucial side business that offered work and income to numbers of local men. They cut and delivered the fuel that made lime manufacturing possible. Throughout the 19th century, trees were cut for kiln wood, firewood, shipbuilding, and general construction until the whole coastline, and then all the islands, were virtually denuded of trees. By the 1870s, the demand for kiln wood in "Lime City" was so great that a major side business developed shipping kiln wood from farther down east and from the Saint John, New Brunswick, area. At the height of the trade, about 200 wood boats went back and forth from early spring until freeze-up between the St. Croix River area and Rockland Harbor, with their cargoes of kiln wood to feed the limekilns. This is about the same number of lime schooners that were carrying the finished lime to market. In 1888, serious experiments were conducted using soft coal and oil to fuel the limekilns.

Within the following decade, all the major lime manufacturers switched to less expensive coal as their fuel source. This meant a dramatic change in the fueling of the kilns and spelled the demise of the once-lucrative kiln wood trade, which had enjoyed a 25-year heyday. Lime coasters often brought coal for the kilns as return freight, but after the consolidation of the major Knox County lime companies in 1900, coal started to come in by huge steel barges, each of which could carry thousands of tons of coal. It was off-loaded by a large gantry derrick commonly known as the "coal tower."

A fleet of seven huge barges supplied the demand that numerous individually owned vessels had previously supplied. Although wood and coal were the primary fuel for the kilns, both gas and oil were used as well. In the 1920s, the Rockland-Rockport Lime Company built coal gas kilns at Rockland Harbor, and they ran them for about 10 years. Before that, the firm of McLoon and Stover used oil purchased from the Standard Oil Company to fuel its Warren Lime Company kilns.

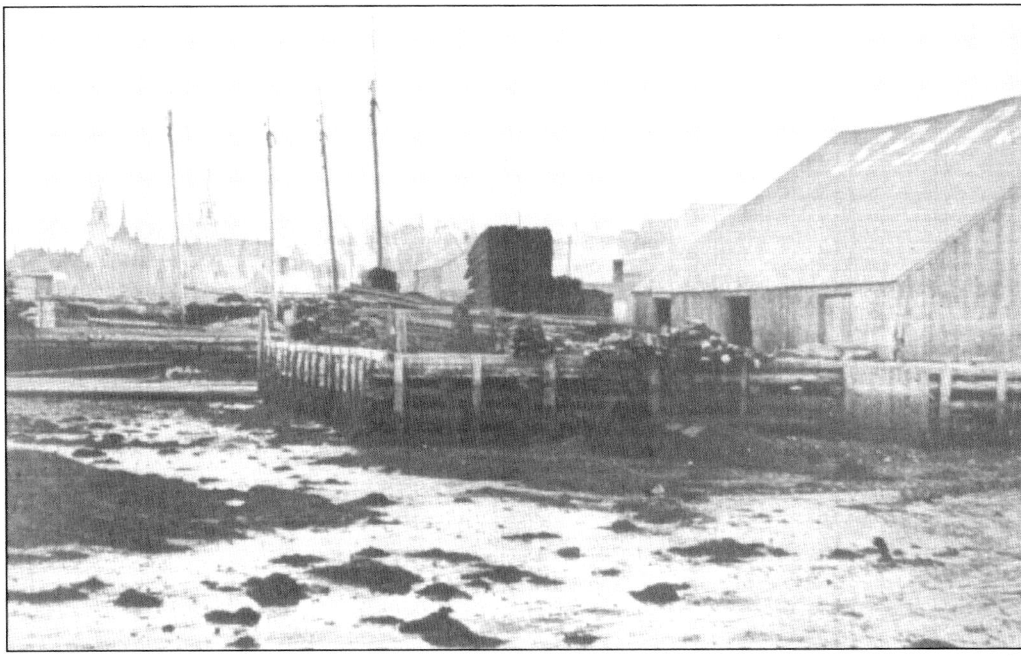

A stereograph image shows a low-tide view of kiln wood stacked on Spear's Wharf near the present-day public landing in Rockland. Thirty cords of wood were required to burn a load of lime in the average kiln. (RHS.)

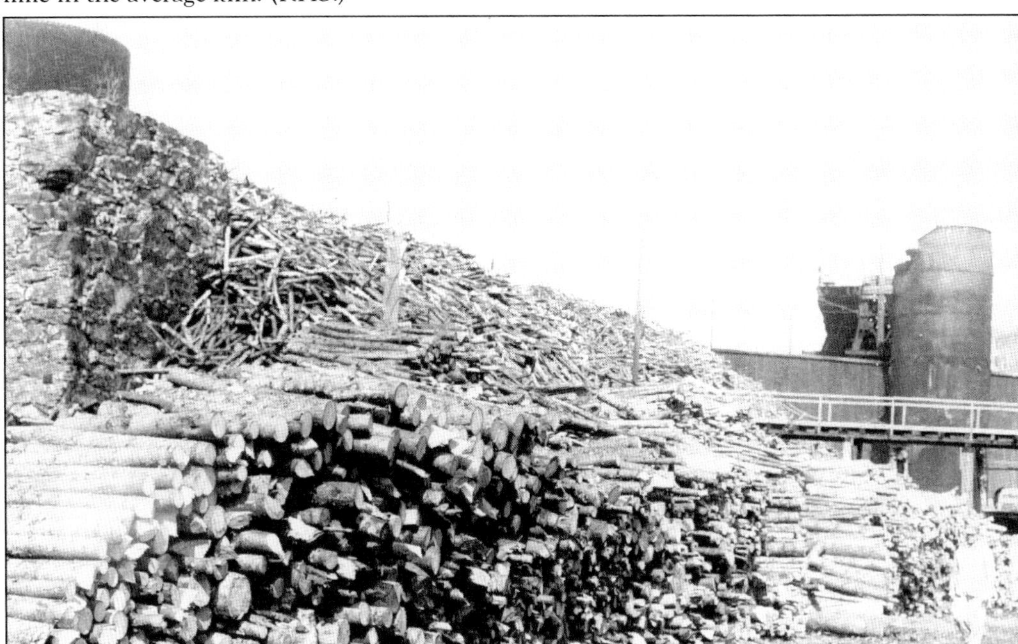

A large stockpile of kiln wood sits near the kilns at the North End of Rockland around 1880. The wood may have come from the Saint John, New Brunswick, area or Nova Scotia. By the 1870s, when local lumber had all been cut, Rockland Harbor swarmed with snub-nosed vessels called "wood coasters" or "Johnny wood boats" delivering wood for the kilns. In 1883, over 11,000 cords were shipped from New Brunswick alone. (RHS.)

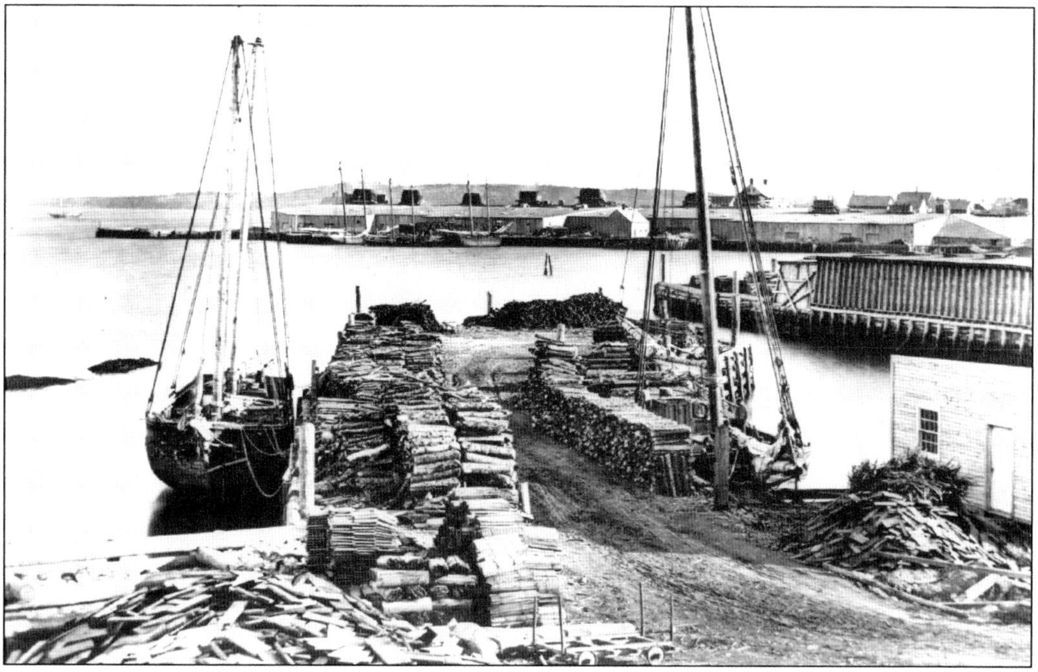

This 1873 stereograph view of Gay's Wharf on the north shore of Rockland Harbor illustrates the vast amount of wood needed to keep the kilns burning. The wharf was built by David Gay. In the 1780s, he was the first person to ship lime to New York from Rockland, called Shore Village at that time. (RHS.)

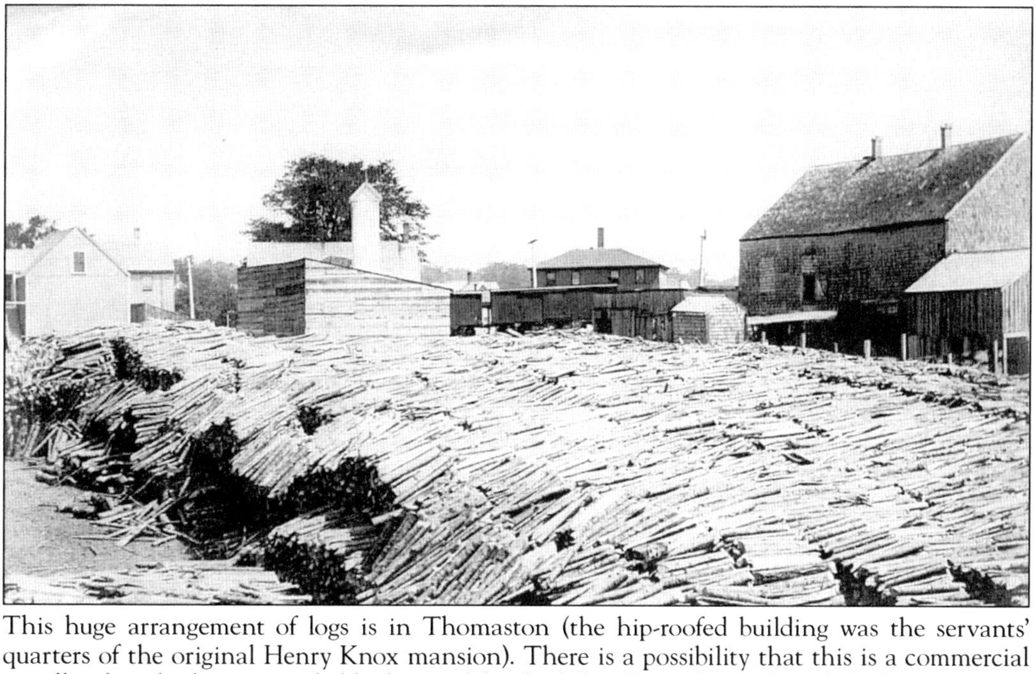

This huge arrangement of logs is in Thomaston (the hip-roofed building was the servants' quarters of the original Henry Knox mansion). There is a possibility that this is a commercial woodlot, but the logs are probably destined for the kilns. Wood burned in the kilns was all cut to four-foot lengths, as this is. (THS.)

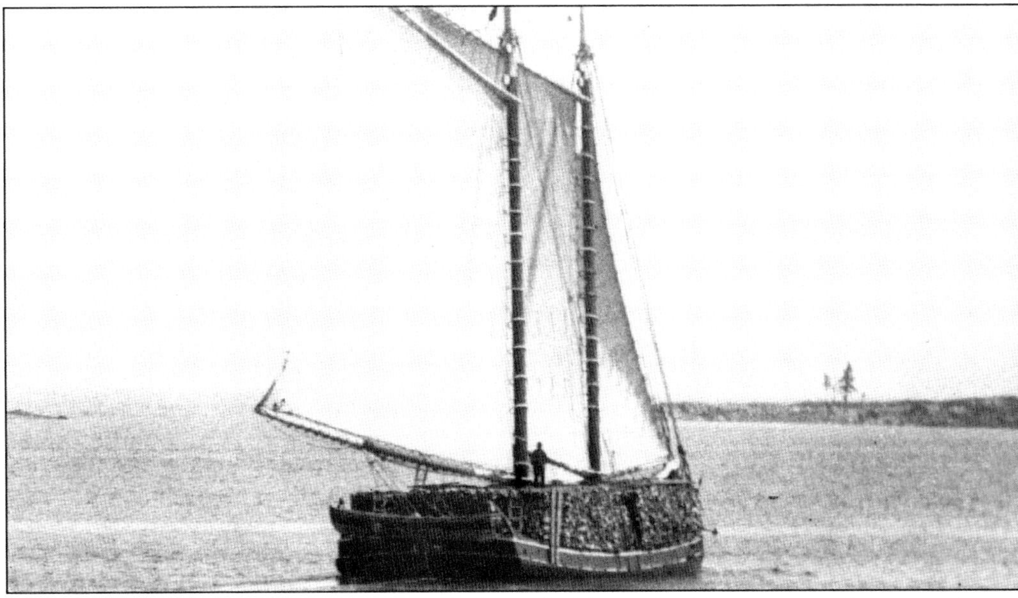

A fully loaded Saint John wood boat is under sail. Along the Maine coast, these vessels were often called Johnny wood boats. Seen here is the square stern with the rudder hung exposed off the stern, thus allowing more space on deck for the lumber. They often came into port loaded to the gunwales, as this one is. They were notorious for being casually built. Stories were told, probably facetiously, about poorly built vessels that brought one load to the kilns and then were broken up and sold for wood, too. (EC.)

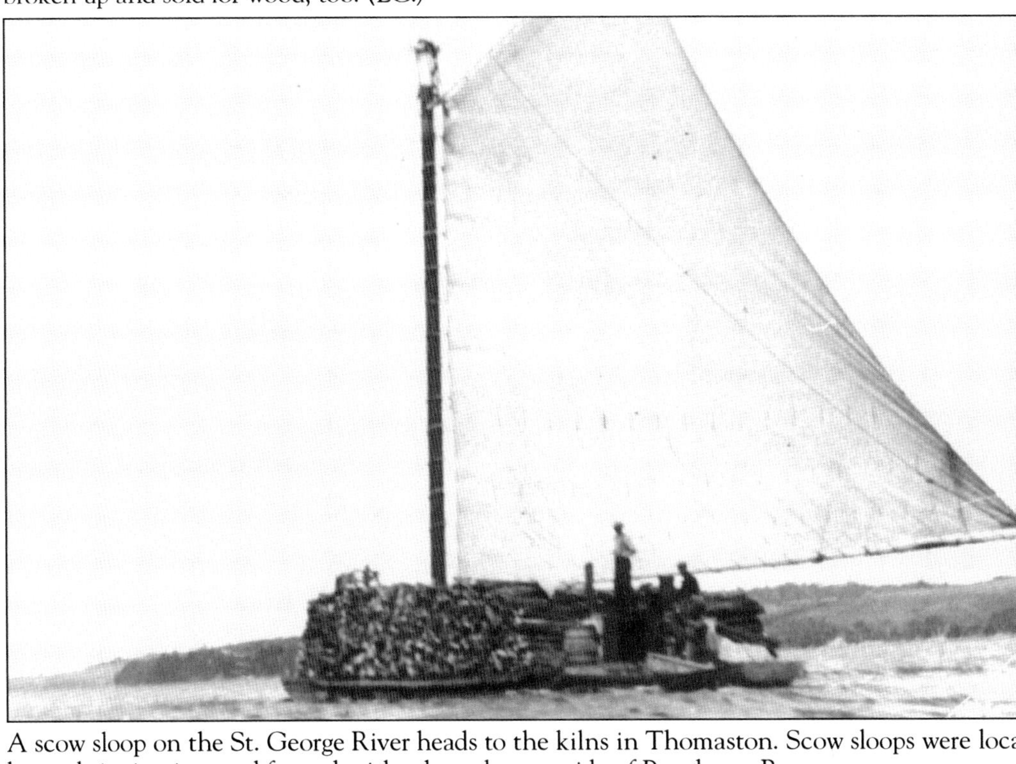

A scow sloop on the St. George River heads to the kilns in Thomaston. Scow sloops were local boats, bringing in wood from the islands or the east side of Penobscot Bay.

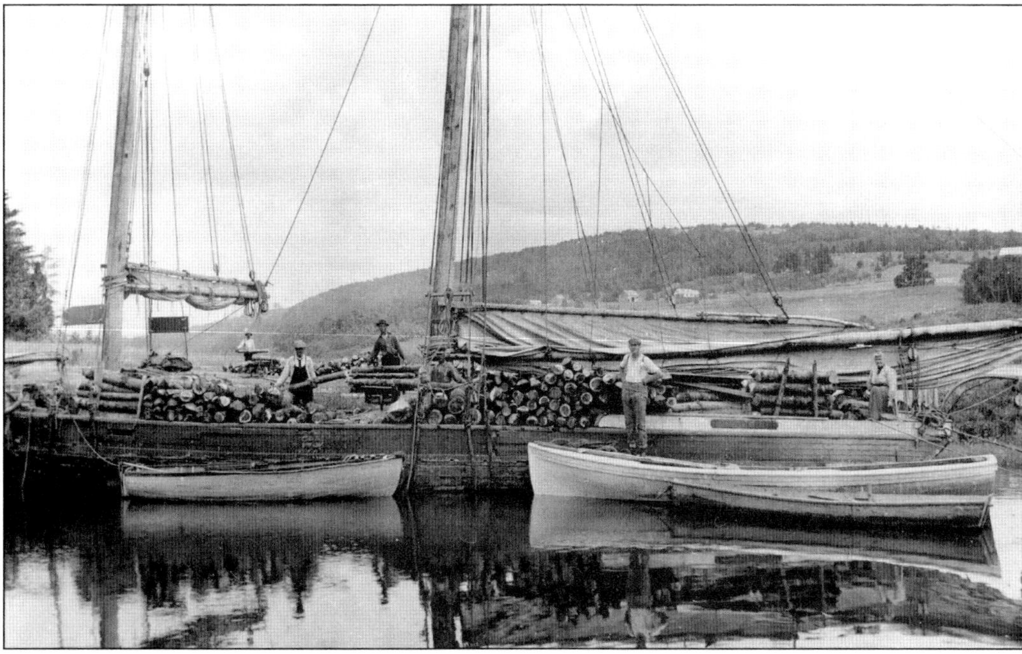

Here are two views of the M. C. *Gray*, built in Sedgwick, Maine, in 1872, loading wood. This vessel is a lumber coaster, not a Saint John wood boat. It has the finer lines of a schooner. Many an older coasting schooner that had had an honorable career but had become too expensive to repair ended up in the lumber trade. (EC.)

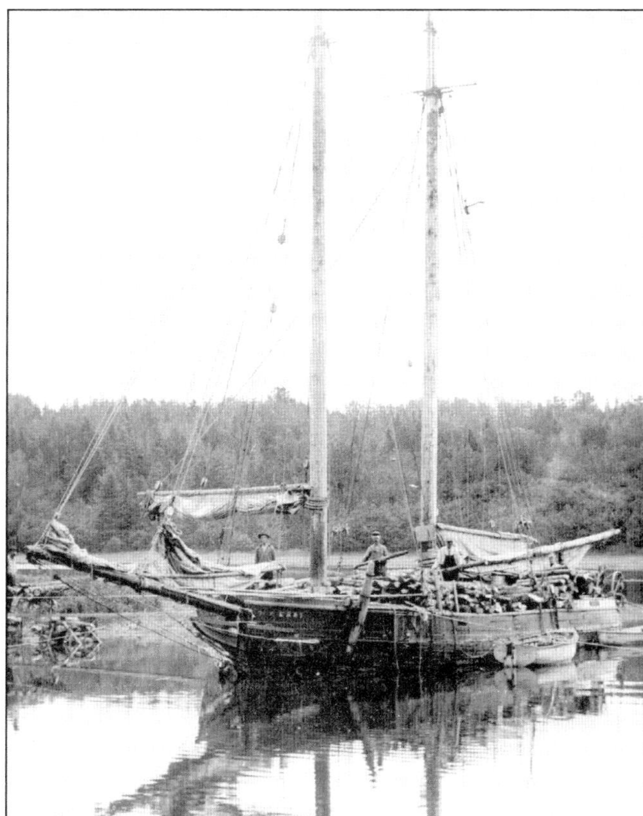

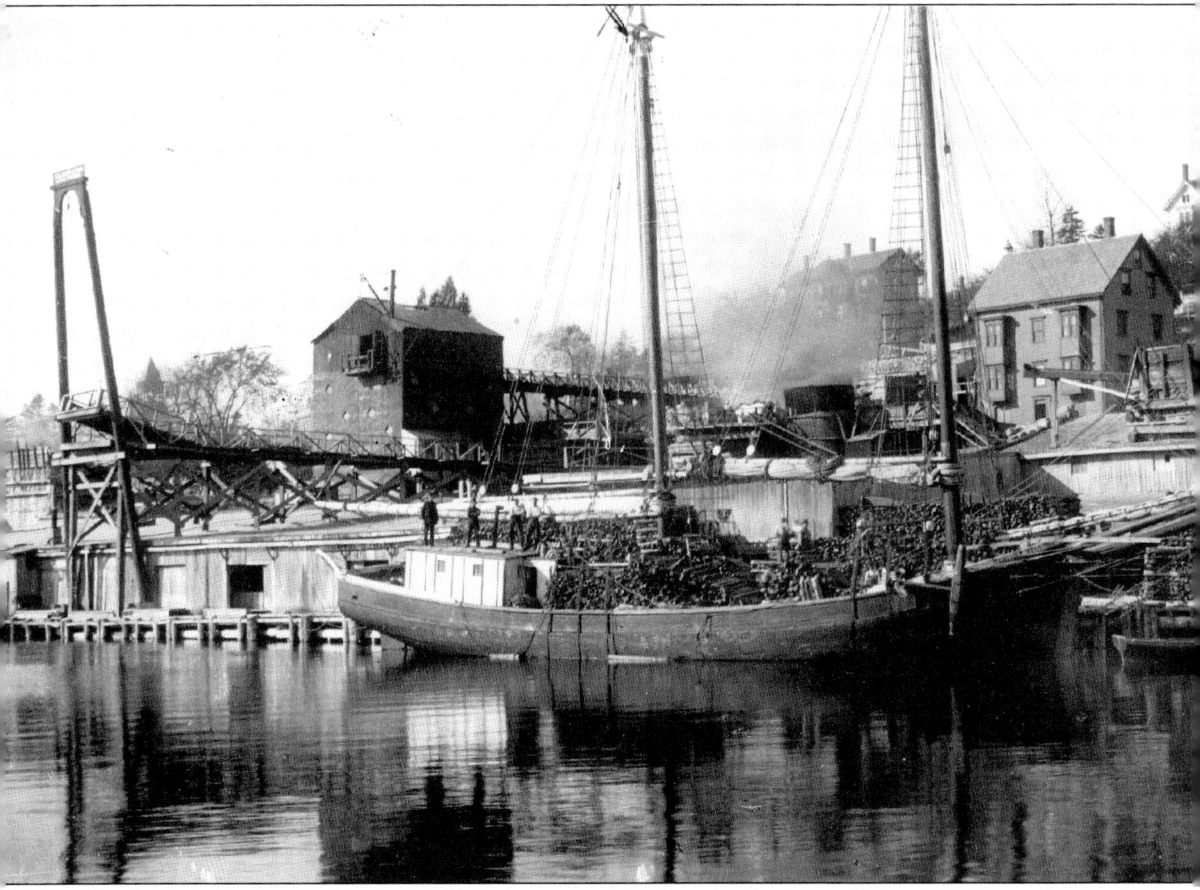

The wood boat *Heather Dell* or *Belle* brings in wood to the Rockport kilns from Nova Scotia. It was not unusual to find a wood boat built, sailed, and owned by the same man, many of whom were farmers or lumber merchants. The foremast was often placed up in the bow and the single deckhouse far in the stern to allow maximum space for cargo on deck. (EC.)

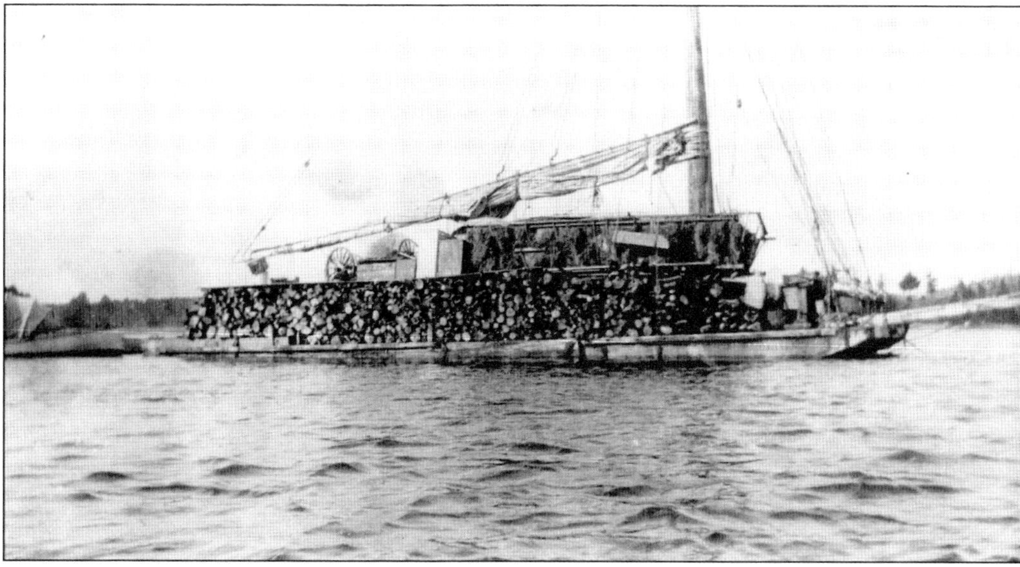

A heavily loaded scow sloop has arrived in the harbor. When under way, the captain often had one of his crew stand on top of the cargo to give him directions since he could not see over the wood. (EC.)

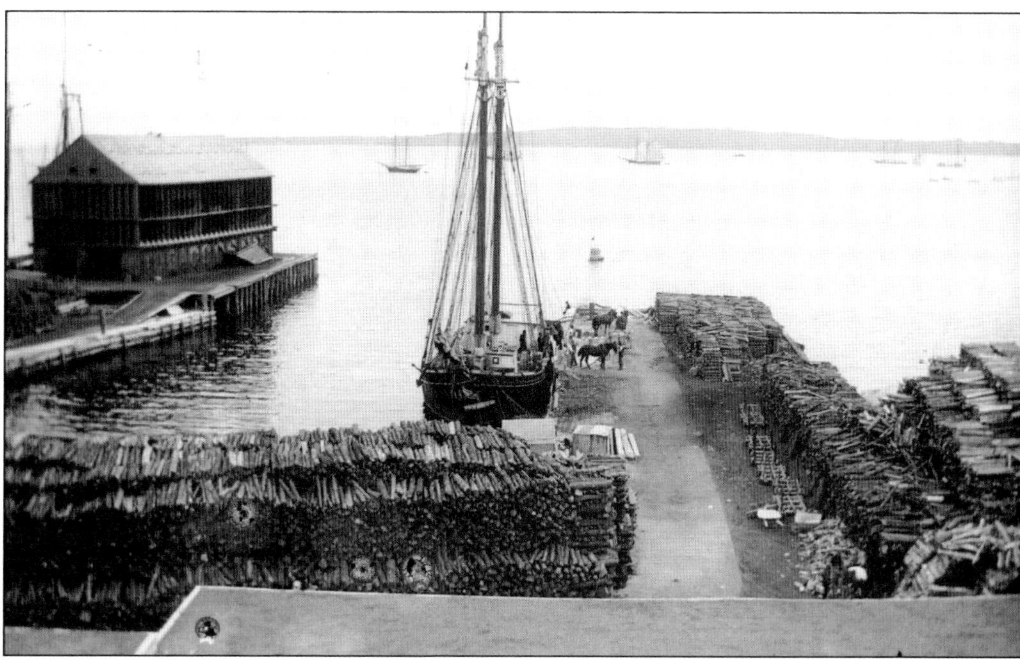

Neatly stacked and piled high, kiln wood seems to occupy every available place along the dock except the space where the schooner is tied. Notice that there is no breakwater in the harbor yet to protect shipping from dreaded easterly storms. Construction began on the breakwater in 1881. (DH.)

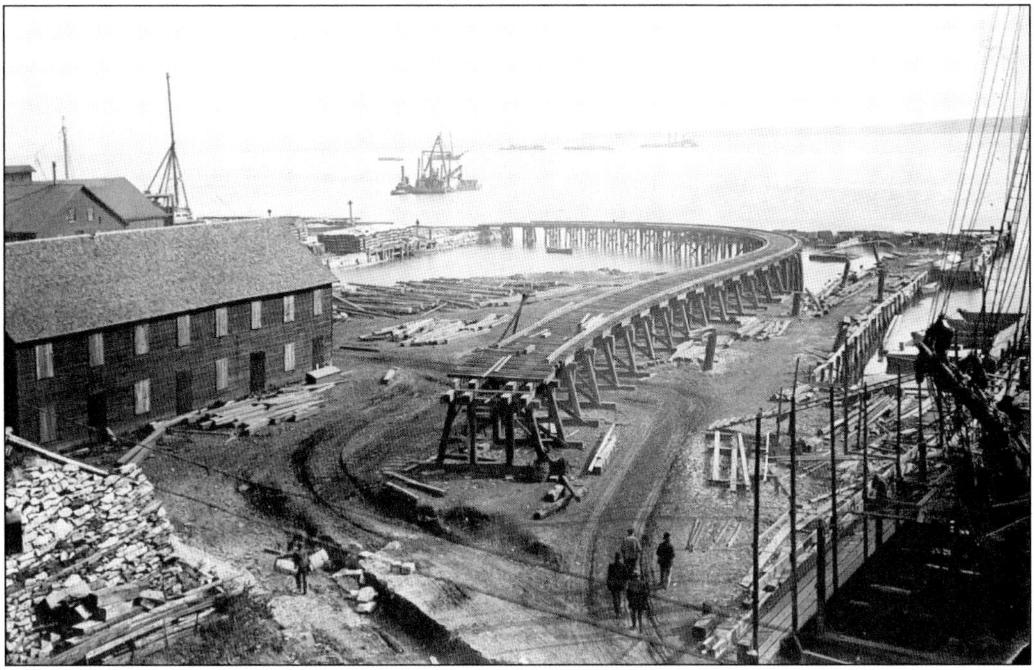

The Lime Rock Railroad trestle track is under construction at Rockland Harbor in October 1912. In the background, they are dredging a new channel in preparation for building the derrick and coal tower. This construction project marked the transition from wood to coal as the main fuel source for the industry. (DH.)

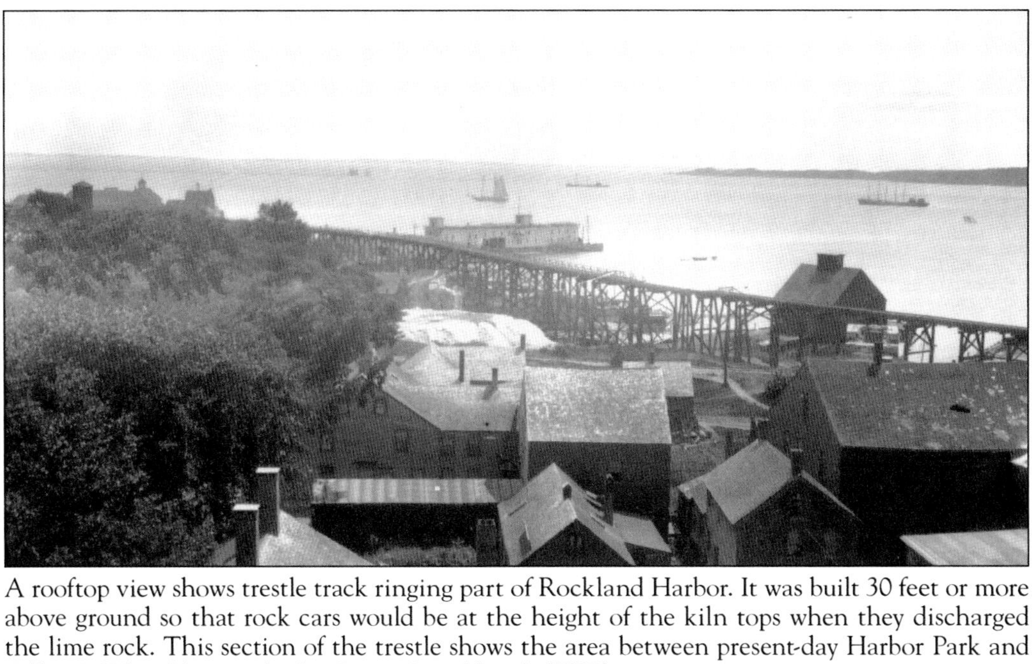

A rooftop view shows trestle track ringing part of Rockland Harbor. It was built 30 feet or more above ground so that rock cars would be at the height of the kiln tops when they discharged the lime rock. This section of the trestle shows the area between present-day Harbor Park and Tillson's Wharf (currently the Coast Guard base). (WT.)

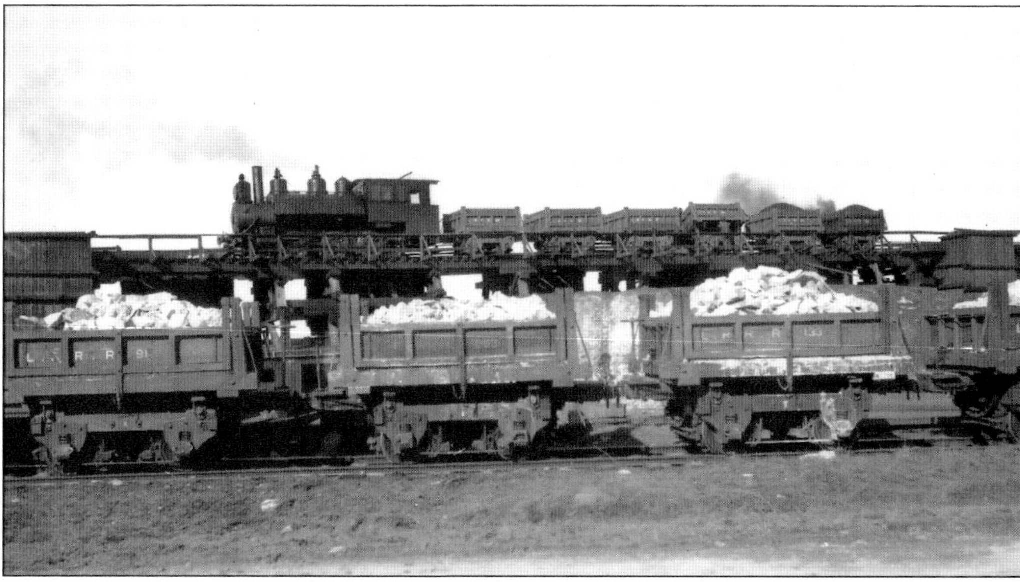

The Lime Rock Railroad had a dual role, and this image illustrates it perfectly. Not only did the rock cars below carry the lime rock from the quarry to be burned in the kilns, but the coal cars provided the kilns with the fuel they needed to burn the lime rock. (WT.)

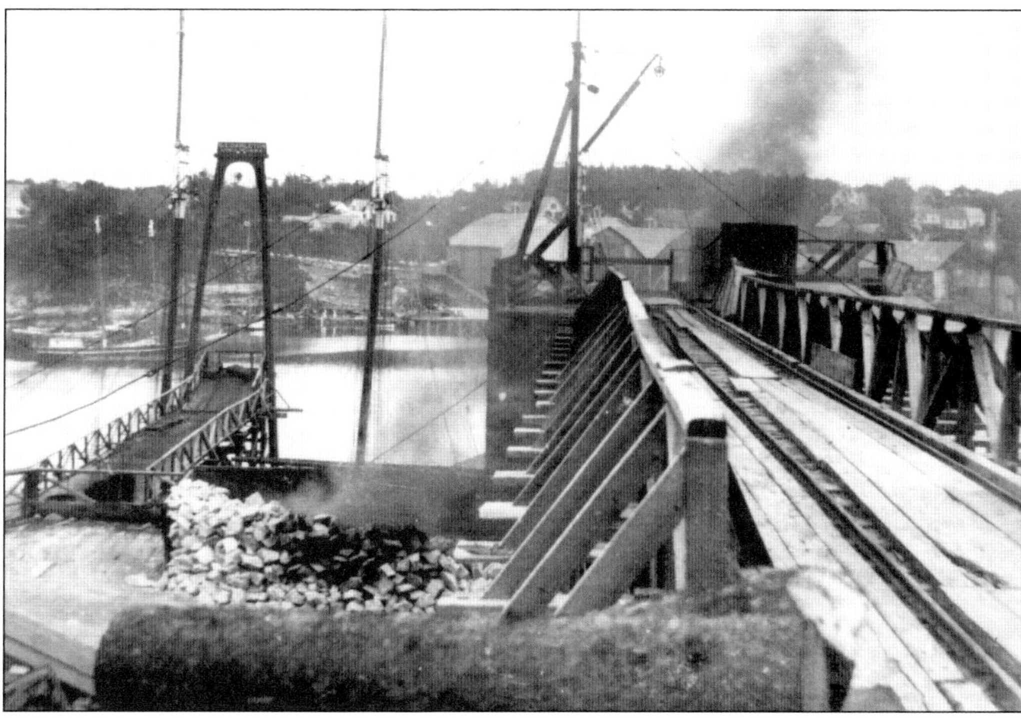

This photograph was taken from the trestle track that goes out to the kiln top of one of the Rockport kilns. To the left is a hoisting conveyance for unloading the sailing vessels. Notice the two masts of a schooner, which is docked beneath it. To the right one can see the smoke and steam from an operating kiln. (CRHS.)

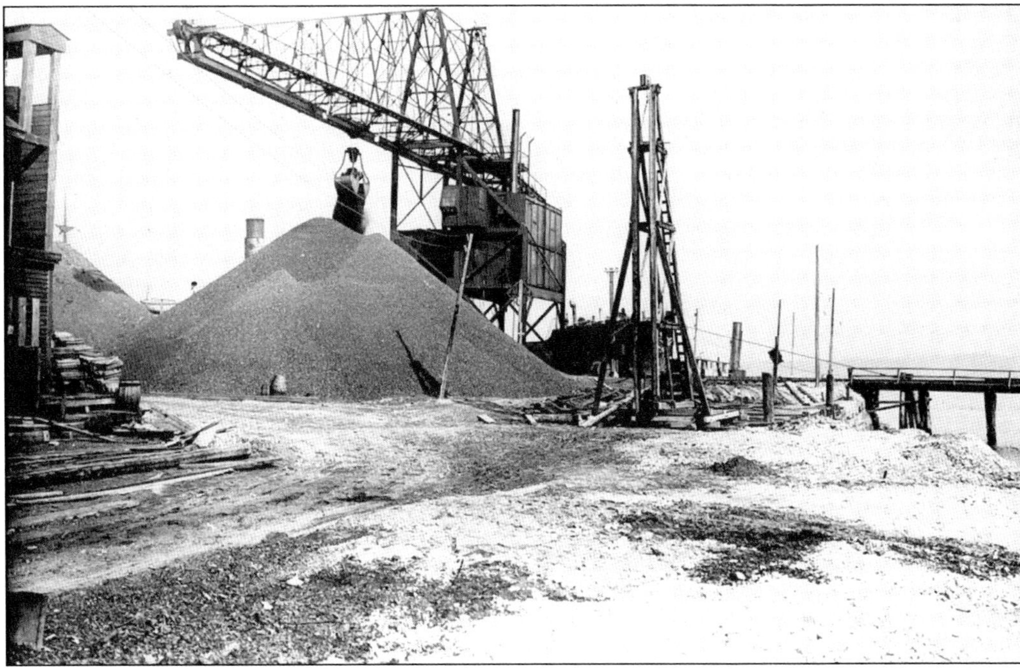

Rockland-Rockport Lime Company's gantry derrick (popularly known as the "coal tower") at its North End facility dominated the harbor. Here coal for the kilns was delivered from the barges. Later it was also used to discharge gypsum for the Dragon Cement Company. Two steam engines were used, one to move the bucket and the other to move the gantry. (DH.)

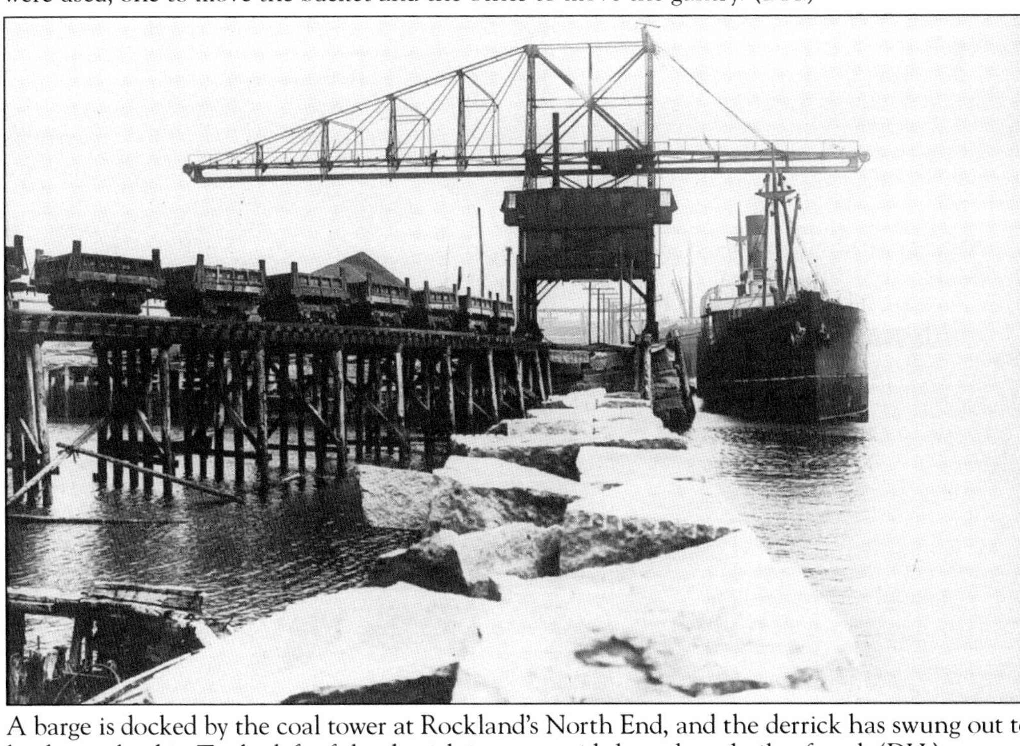

A barge is docked by the coal tower at Rockland's North End, and the derrick has swung out to load or unload it. To the left of the derrick is a pyramid-shaped stockpile of coal. (DH.)

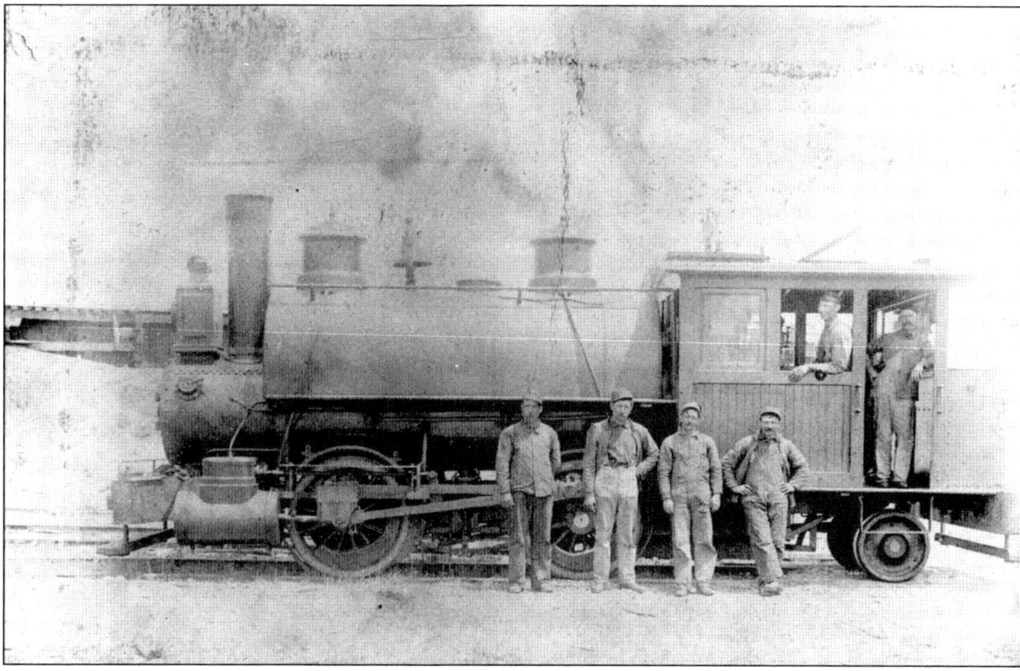

The 12.5-mile Lime Rock Railroad, which carried coal and lime rock to the kilns, was a standard-gauge railroad that connected to the Maine Central tracks. This is engine No. 2, near the Five Kilns in Rockland's South End in the early 1900s. In the cab are engineer Irving Gray or Cray and fireman Howard Walsh. The men standing next to the locomotive are unidentified. (DH.)

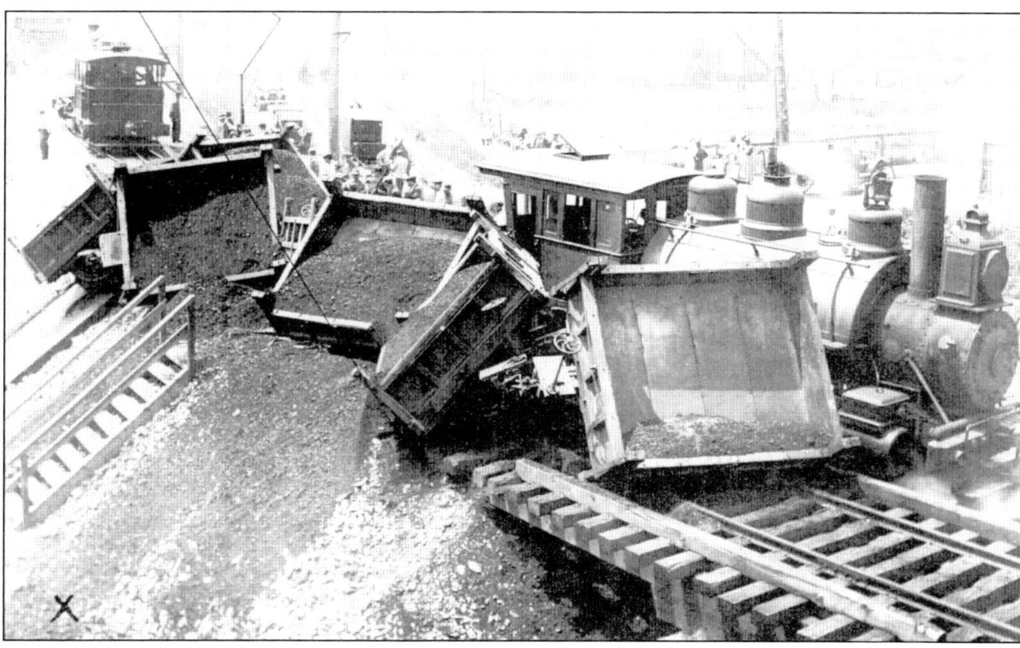

Two trains have collided, and the rock cars hauling coal to the North End kilns have "left the irons." The accident has collected a crowd—judging by their clothing and the cars, this accident happened in the early 1920s. (DH.)

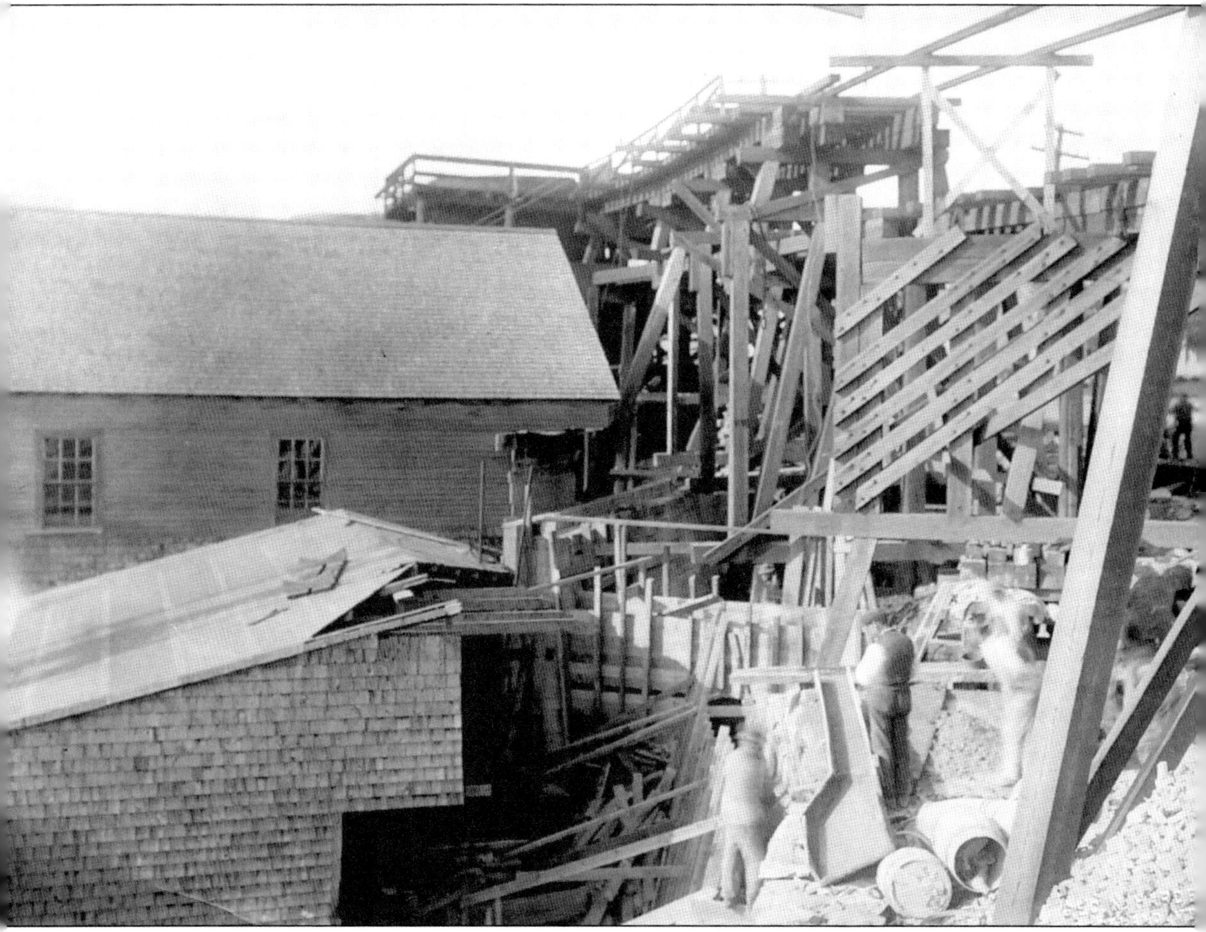

Lime rock and coal were both heavy to transport, and the train trestle that ringed the harbor needed constant upkeep. Here some repair work is under way on the trestle supports. (DH.)

Five

Cask Building

Cask (or barrel) building was an important side business that provided dependable employment to many local farmers and fishermen in their off-seasons. Many up-country farms within a 25-mile radius of the Rockland area had their own cooper shop. Men often built lime casks during the winter or in poor weather in other seasons. Building material was usually oak or ash but could also be spruce, from the farmer's own woodlot. The making of lime barrels required moderate coopering skills on the part of the builder. These builders were called dry coopers because they built their barrels for dry goods (such as lime). The barrels needed to be tight enough to protect the contents from getting wet if they were left out in the rain. Highly skilled wet coopers, in contrast, built barrels that were tight enough to hold liquid without any leakage. Lime barrels were built to specific standards set by the state. The law required that they be built of well-seasoned wood with strong one-inch-wide hoops on each cask and built to standard dimensions. Later, when cask building was mechanized, some lime casks were built with tongue-and-groove staves to keep the lime dry. Each barrel was branded with the name of the manufacturer.

Every town that produced lime had its own lime inspector whose duty was to inspect the quality of lime at the kilns and also the casks. The inspector stamped the name of the town and his own name on each filled cask that passed inspection. However, even though regulations such as these were in place, when the demand became great, casks were put together hastily, and laws were overlooked by both builders and purchasers. As the industry continued to grow, barrel making became mechanized and year-round lime barrel factories were established to fill the demand. From 1900 on, the Rockland-Rockport Lime Company had its own large mechanized cooper shop next to its kilns. Many small lime-barrel makers were unable to compete. But barrel making, not only for the packaging of lime but also for packing salt fish and other local products, remained a crucial part of the regional economy for some time after this.

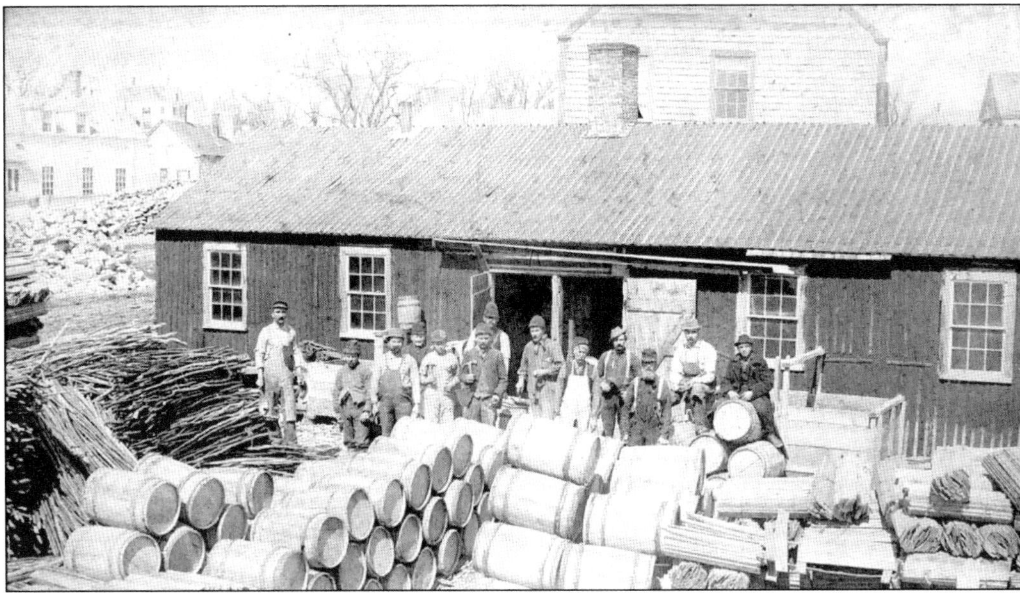

The crew in this cooper's shop is involved in making lime casks. The man on the left is splitting saplings, often alder or birch, for barrel hoops. The bundles of wood on the right are machine-cut staves, probably cut in a stave mill using a barrel saw or a cylinder saw. The men in this building are assembling the barrels by bending the staves, preparing the ends to receive the heads, putting the heads on the barrels, and hooping the barrels. (CM.)

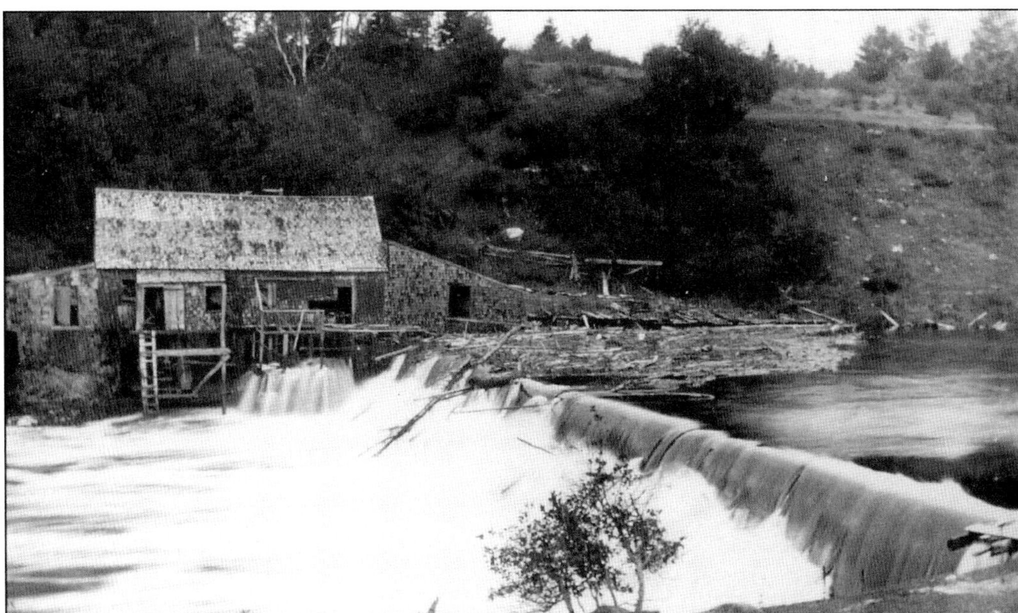

The mill dam at Ducktrap is just upriver from the Ducktrap bridge in Lincolnville. The sawmill used waterpower from the dam to cut barrel staves for lime barrels, among other things. Towns like Union, Waldoboro, Warren, and Jefferson all had mills similar to this one. Such mills could not run in dry spells in the summer when the water level was too low or in cold snaps in the winter when the river was frozen. (LHS.)

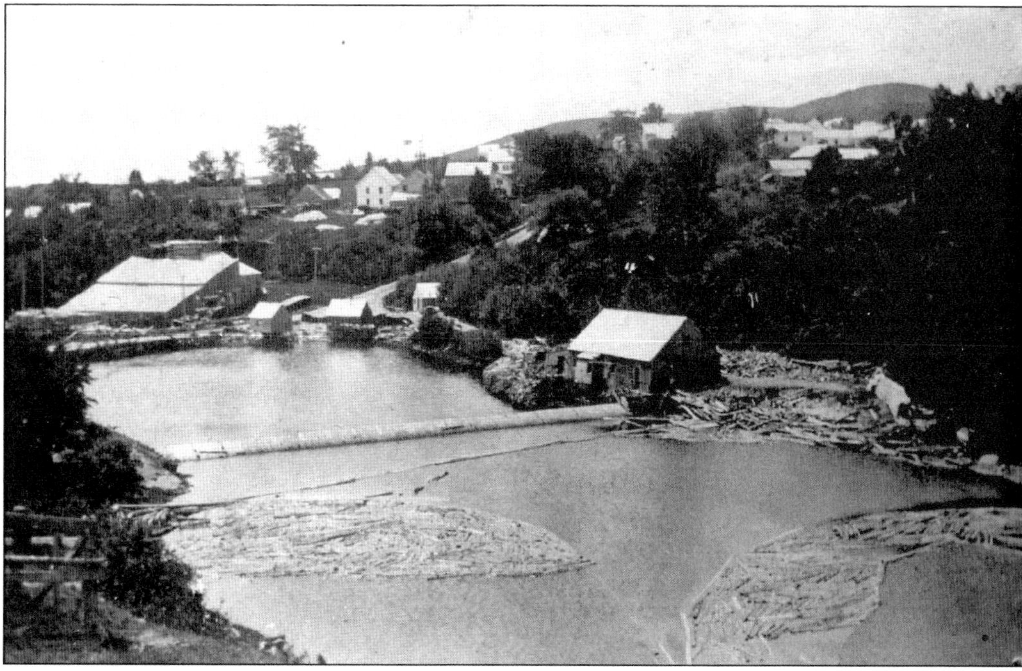

This is a broader view of the mill dam, the mill, and the lime kiln and shed on the Ducktrap River in Lincolnville, looking southeast. Staves are floating in the containment area, staying flexible in the water, awaiting assembly into barrels. (LHS.)

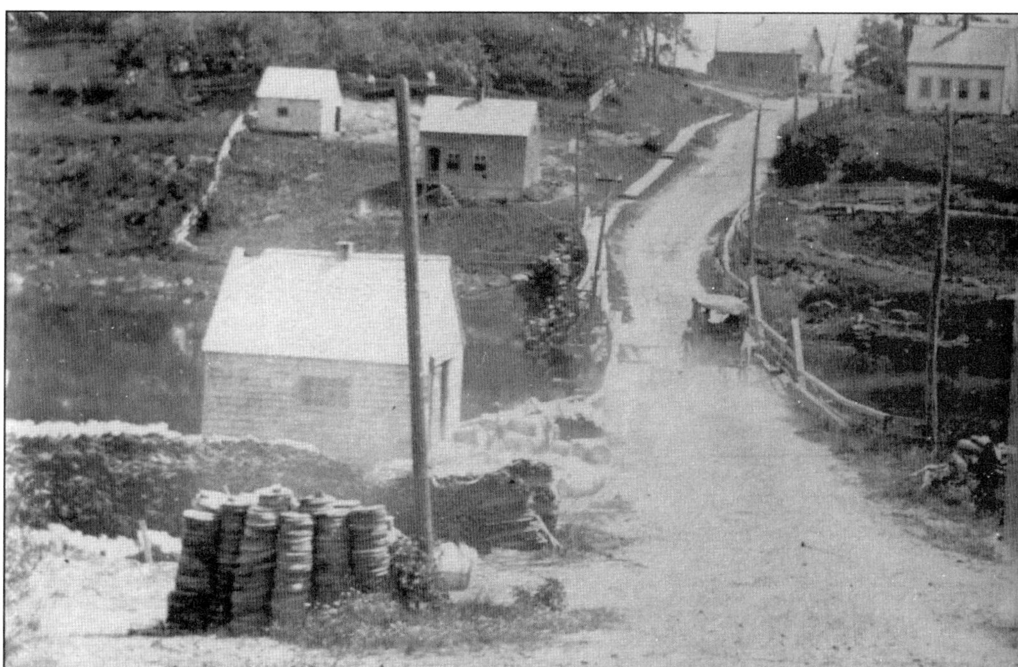

In this eastern view, barrelheads are stacked at the roadside near the mill at Ducktrap in Lincolnville. Wooden sidewalks line the road on the other side of the bridge, and an early automobile kicks up dust as it heads north. (LHS.)

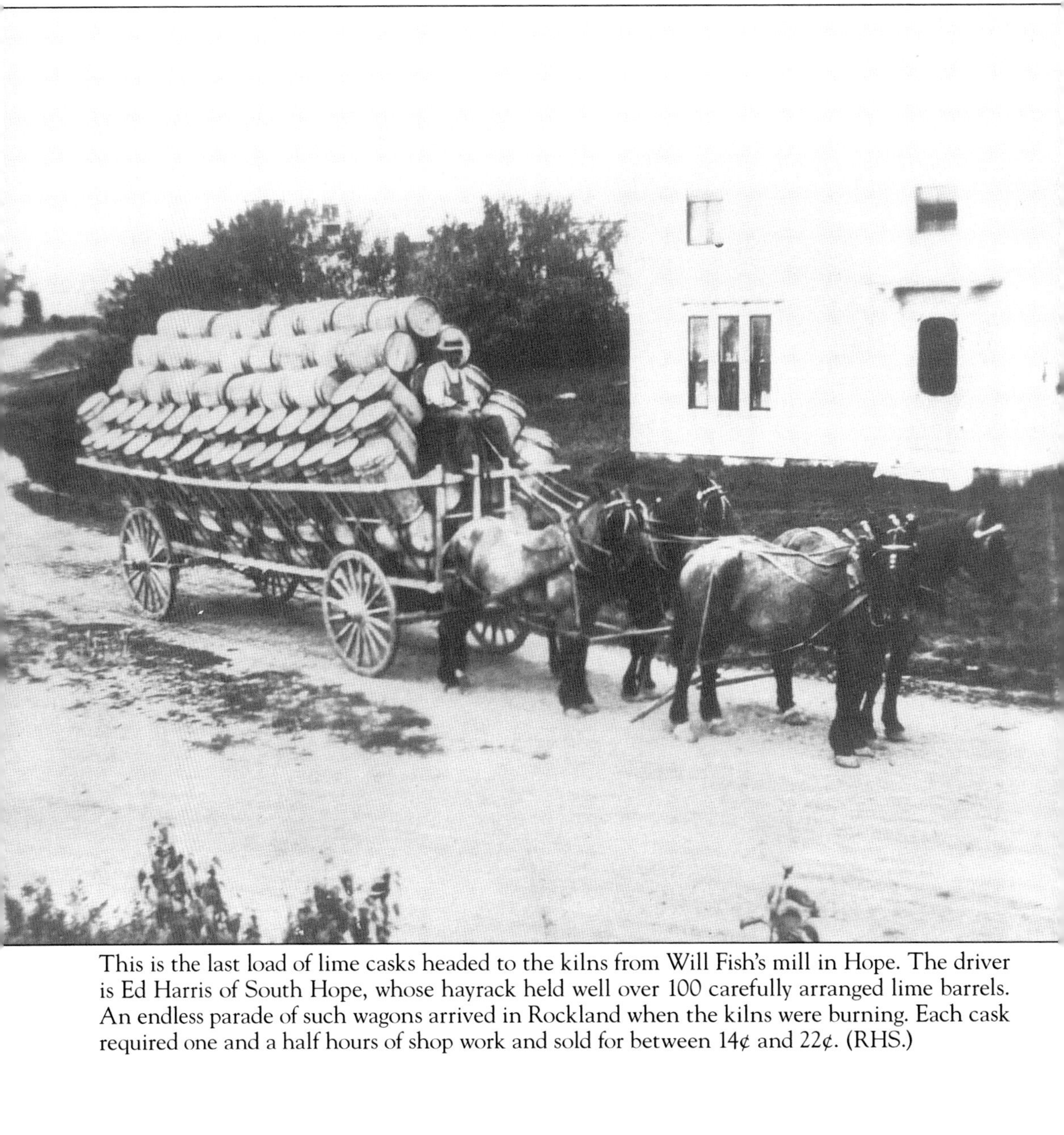

This is the last load of lime casks headed to the kilns from Will Fish's mill in Hope. The driver is Ed Harris of South Hope, whose hayrack held well over 100 carefully arranged lime barrels. An endless parade of such wagons arrived in Rockland when the kilns were burning. Each cask required one and a half hours of shop work and sold for between 14¢ and 22¢. (RHS.)

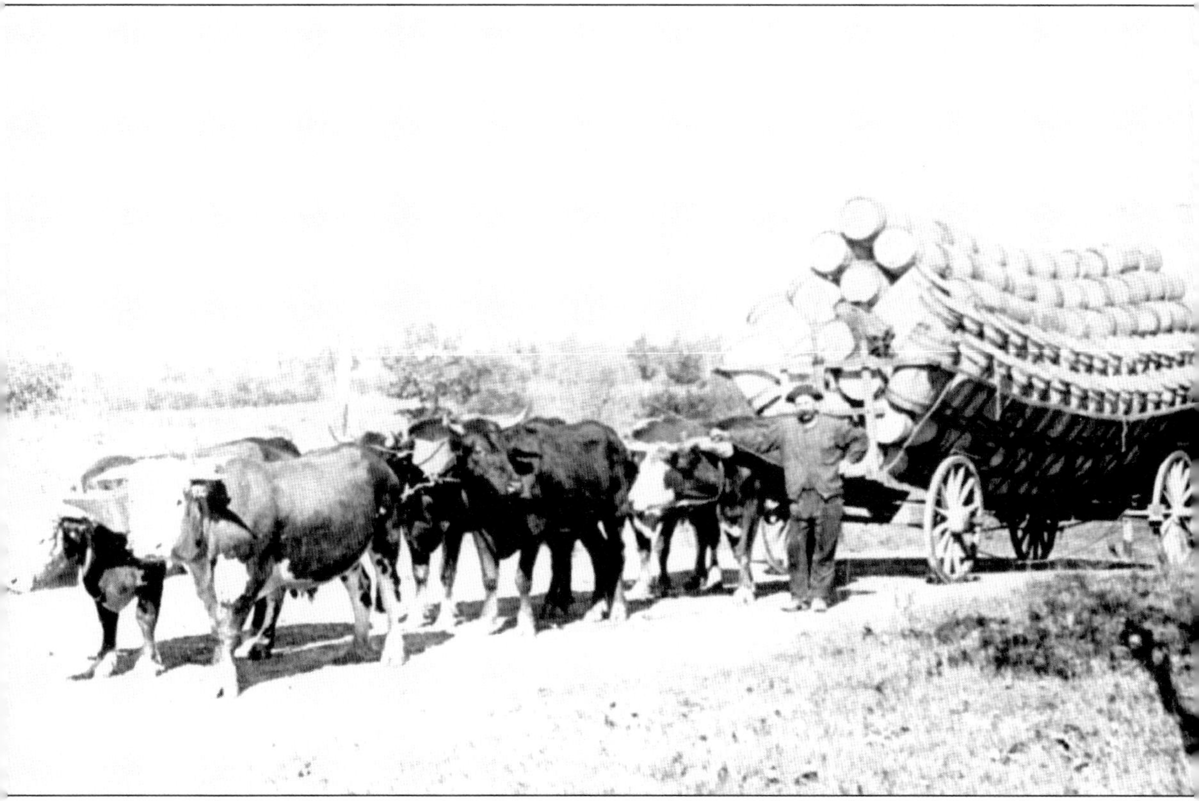

Farmers from outlying towns often left their homes in the evening and walked all night in order to reach Rockland in the morning. It took several hours to walk from towns like Union, Appleton, and Searsmont. If a farmer had a team of oxen, he had to walk the whole way beside them with a goad, but if he had a team of horses pulling his wagon, he could ride at least part of the way. (WHS.)

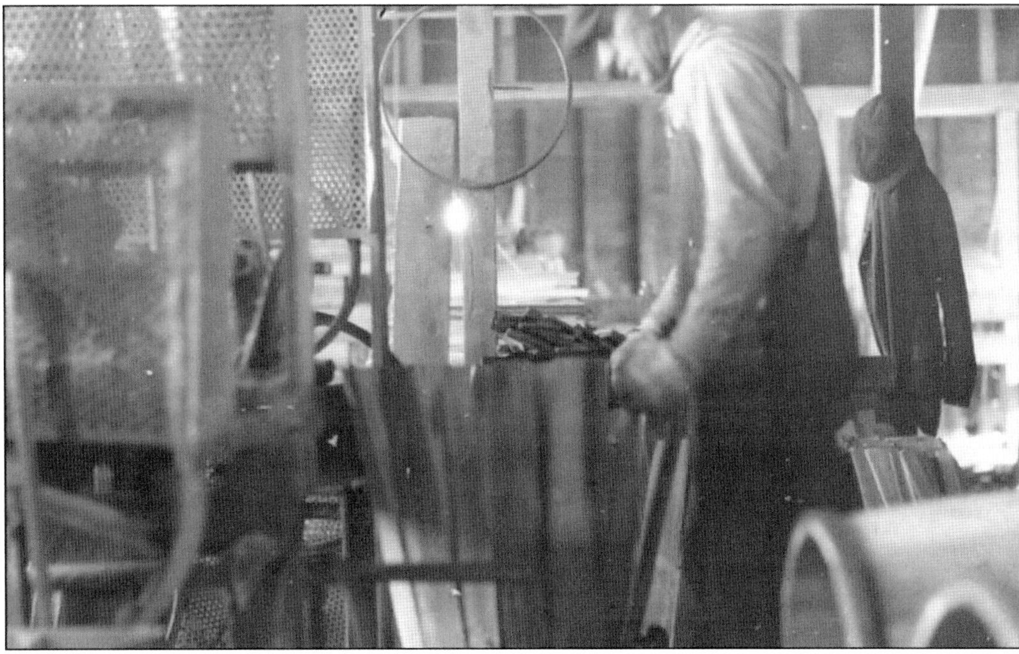

Barrel making required several steps. After staves are cut, tapered, and beveled, the cooper arranges the staves in an upright position inside a metal hoop that serves as an assembly jig. They are held in place with metal hoops that have been forced into place. This is called raising the barrel. Sometimes a barrel at this stage of construction is called the rose. (DH.)

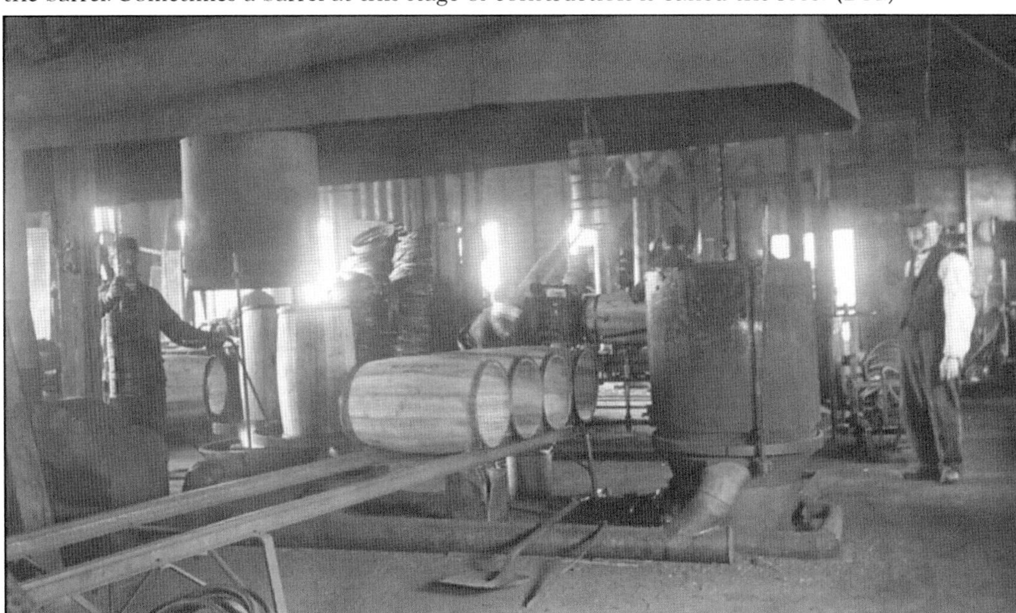

This and the following photographs are of the Rockland-Rockport Lime Company's cooperage shop at the company's North End facility. Here all aspects of barrel construction were mechanized. In this image is an assembly line of partially finished barrels without hoops, except for the hoops at the top and bottom of the barrel, called the chime hoops, which hold the staves in place. (DH.)

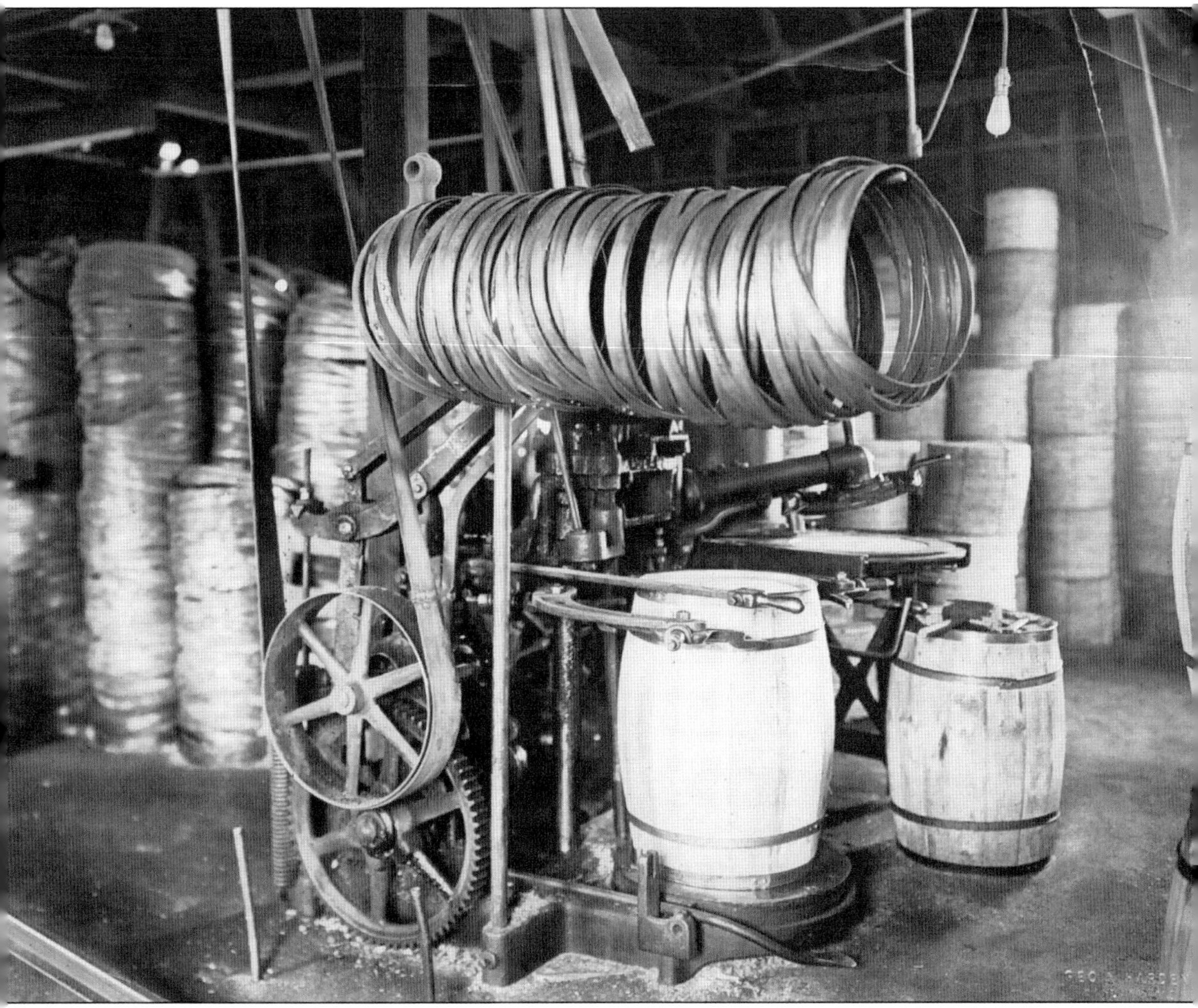

This image shows the hoop machine in the cooper shop at the Rockland-Rockport Lime Company. One can see the mechanism by which the metal hoops are cinched tight to draw in the staves. In the left background, stacks of hoops are piled high, and in the right background, the unhooped barrels await their turn. (DH.)

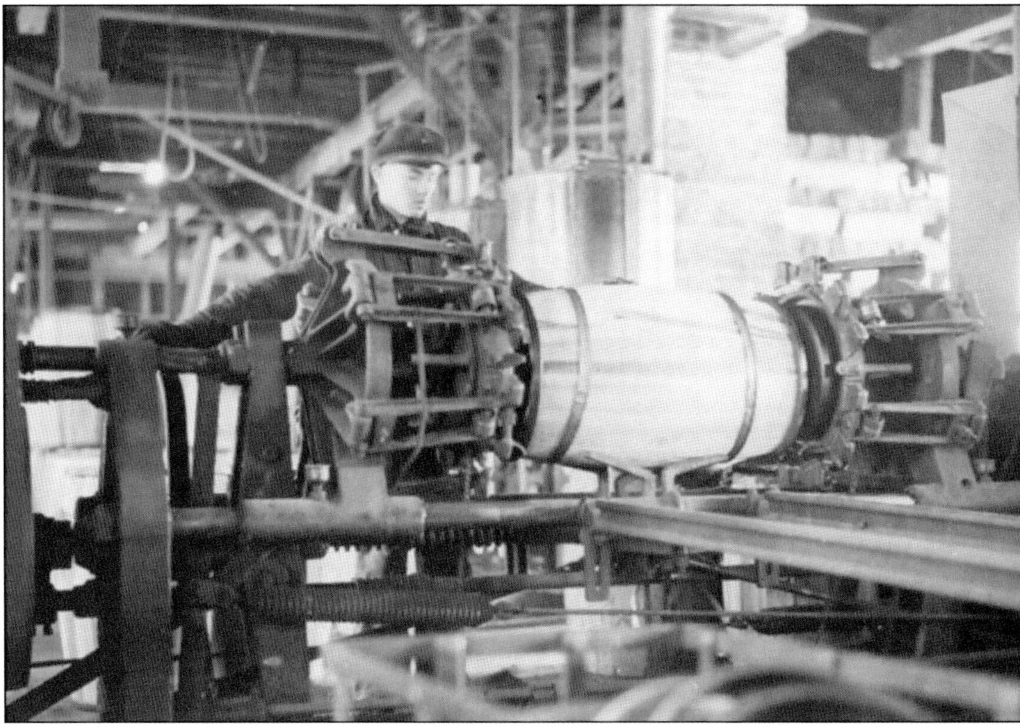

This machine adds hoops to the section of the barrel called the booge, which is between the center of the barrel and the two ends. Lime barrels were required to have inch-wide hoops for strength. Barrels have maintained popularity over the ages because they are structurally very strong, and they can be rolled instead of carried. (DH.)

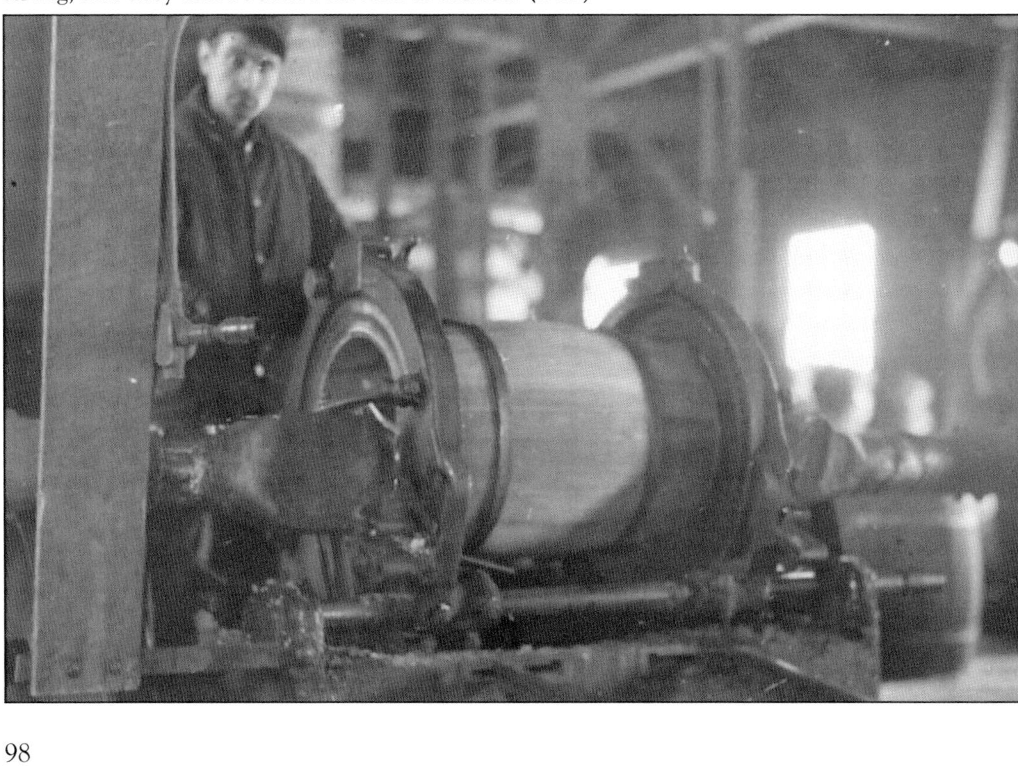

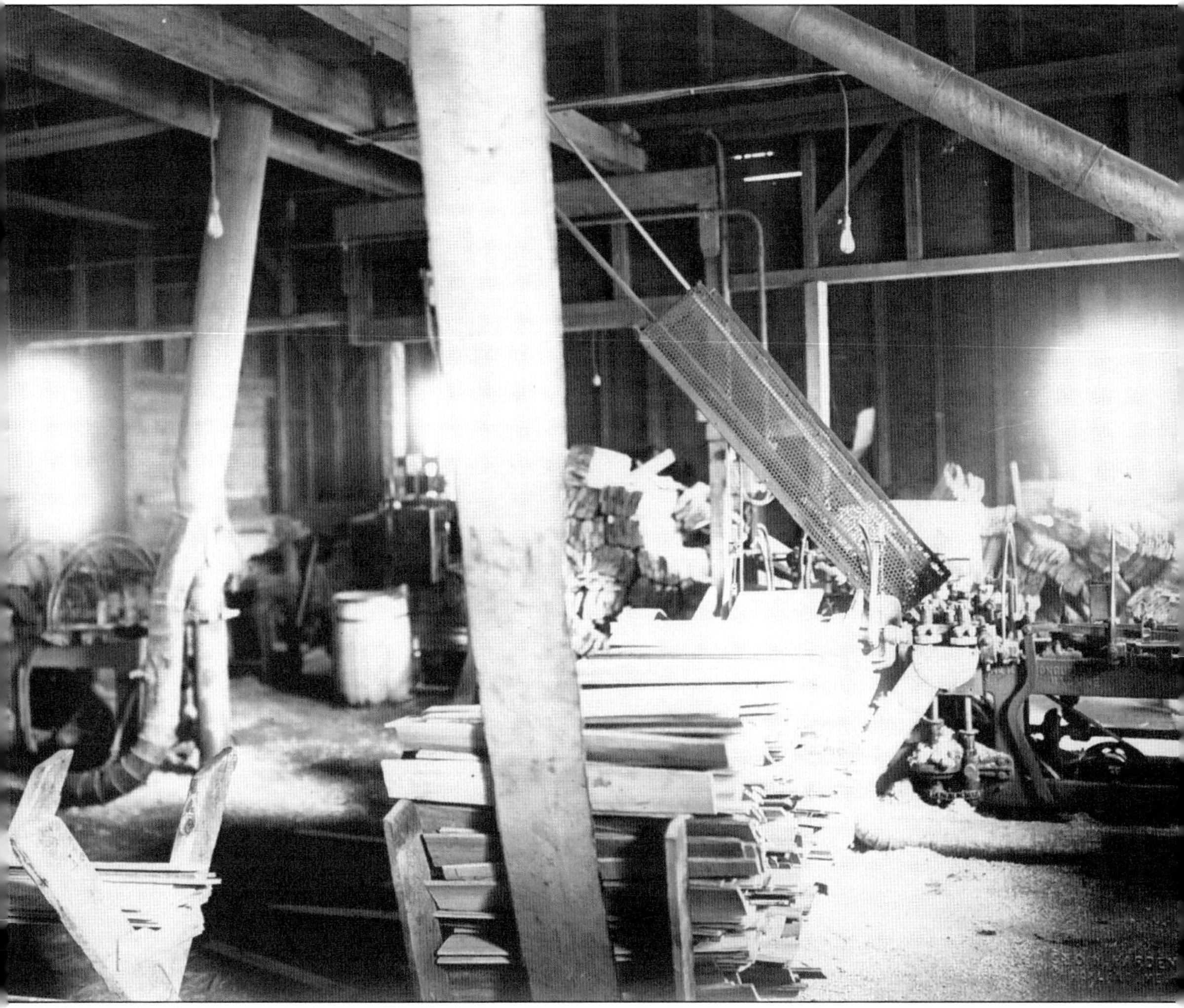

This is a tongue-and-groove machine in a large cooper shop. Tongue-and-groove construction made lime barrels much safer because they were watertight. Barrel staves are stacked in the foreground, and one can see grooves in some of them. (DH.)

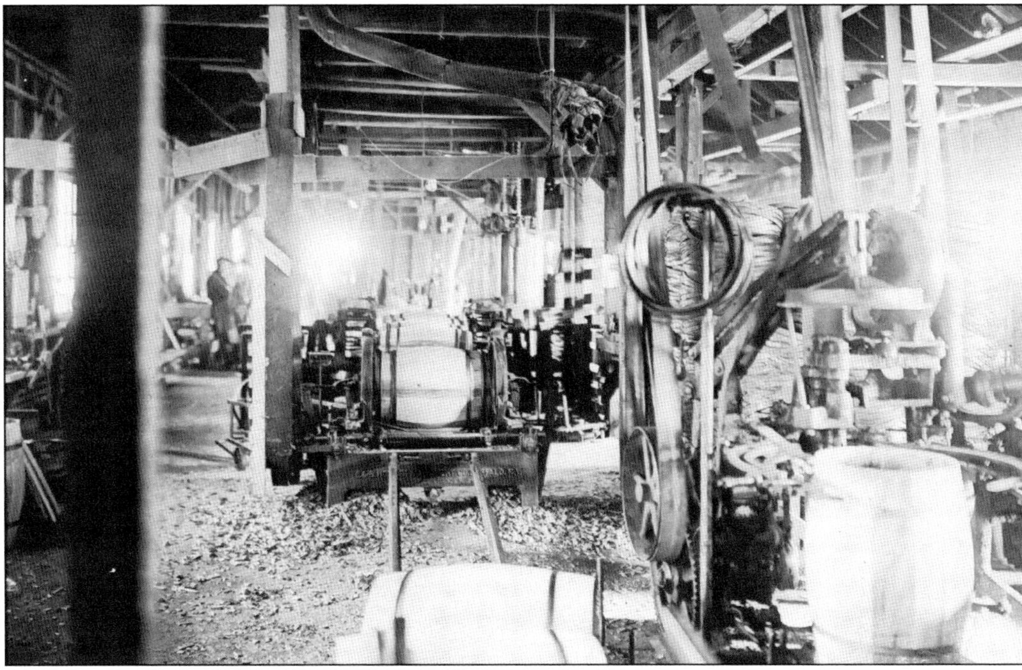

A stave working-off machine trims off the ends of the staves so that the heads can be applied. This is a precise machining step that not only trims the stave ends but also cuts the "croze," the grooves in the staves that receive the barrelhead. On the left, a worker is keeping an eye on the machine. (DH.)

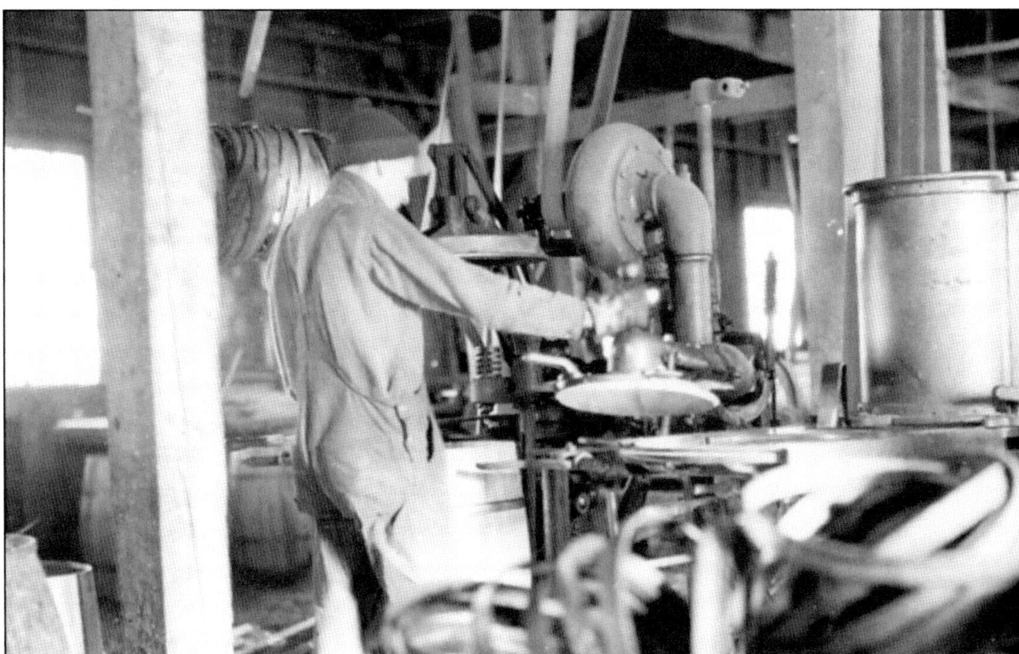

Here a worker is running a machine that attaches the ends of the barrels. The barrelhead is custom cut to fit the croze. The parts of the barrelhead are assembled with dowels so that the whole end is very tight. The barrel will be "headed" when it is full. (DH.)

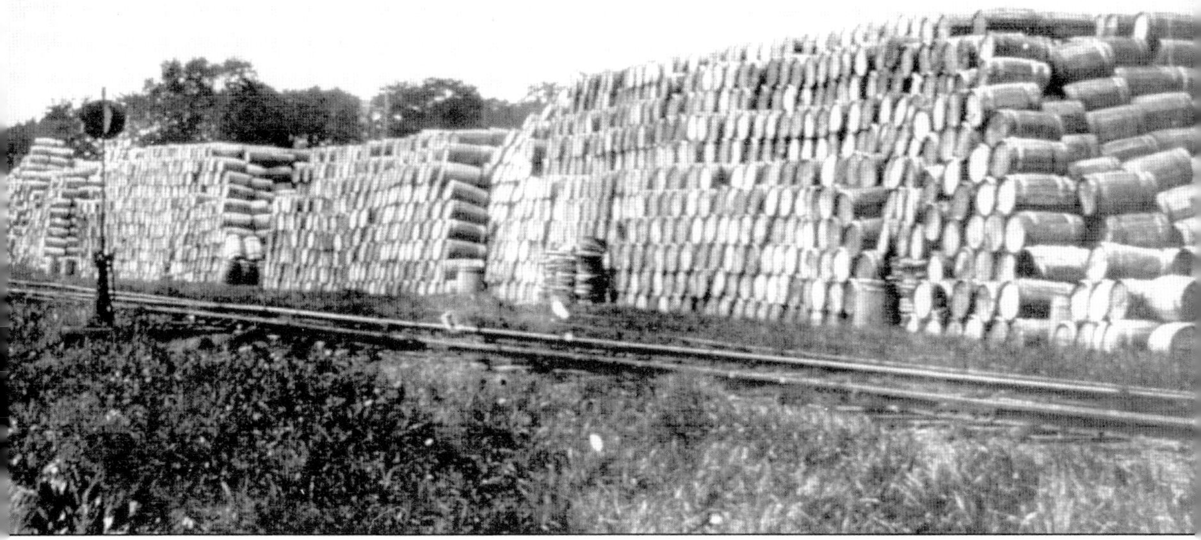

An immense stack of barrels sits by the tracks of the Georges Valley Railroad, nicknamed the Doodlebug Railroad, which ran between Warren and Union. Some of these barrels are destined for the Stover and McLoon kilns in North Warren; others most likely will go to the Rockland kilns. (WHS.)

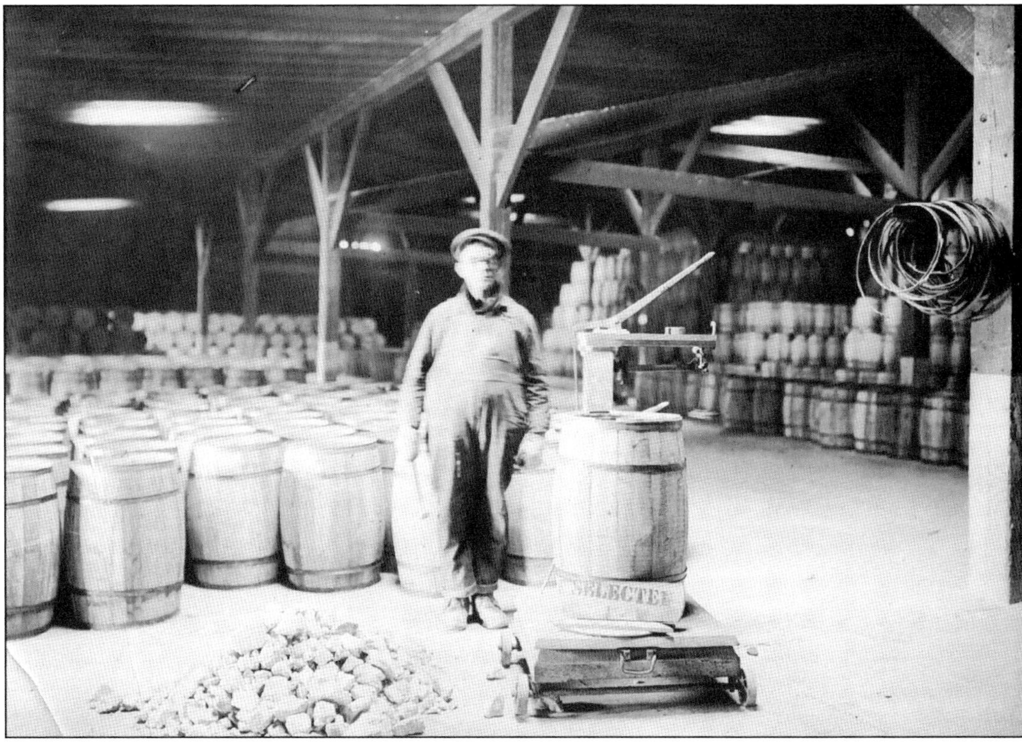

Lime trimmer Albert McLellan fills barrels of lime at the kiln shed at the Rockland-Rockport Lime Company. There is a barrel of lump lime on the scale. (DH.)

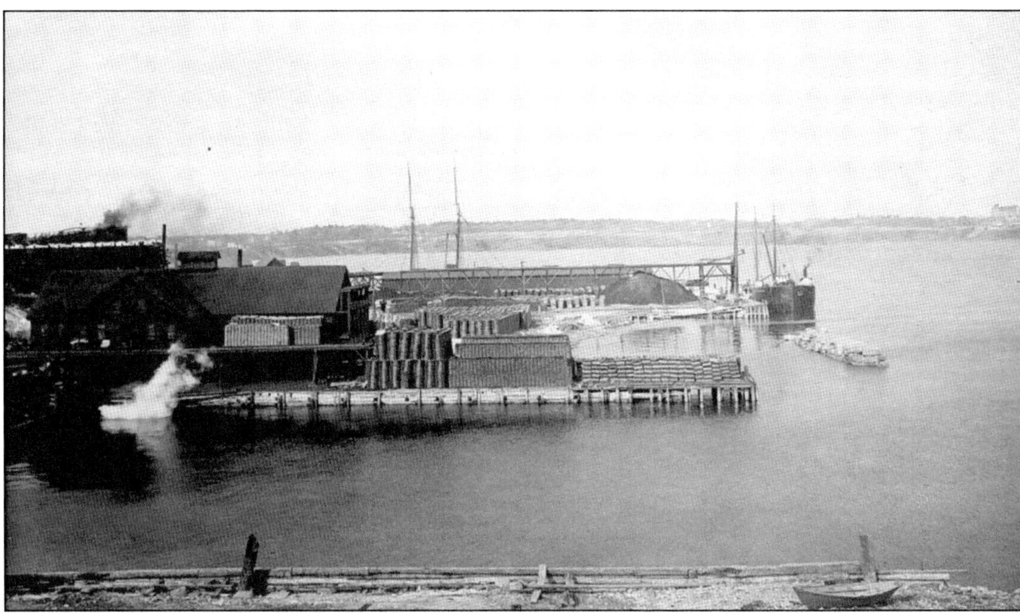

As the industry grew more mechanized, it became cheaper to import premade barrel parts and assemble them at the shop rather than actually manufacture barrel parts there. Stockpiled on this wharf are parts of barrels—heads, staves, and hoops—awaiting assembly. A barge is docked on the right by the coal dock, and behind that, farther to the right, is the Samoset Hotel. (DH.)

Six

Shipbuilding and Shipping Lime

Shipping barreled lime to market was the final step in lime production. Until the beginning of the 20th century, lime was carried to market in two- or three-masted schooners. Many or most of the lime schooners were built locally. The need for these vessels spurred the shipbuilding industry in this area. Indeed, it can be said that shipbuilding and lime production went hand in hand.

Like all vessels, lime coasters were subject to the hazards of storms, fog, stranding, and collisions. But the foremost danger to a limer was fire, caused when leaking water came in contact with the quicklime. Water causes lime to expand and generate intense heat, resulting in casks or the wooden timbers of the vessels splitting and catching fire. The only way to extinguish burning lime is to smother it since dousing burning lime with water results in increased heat and expansion. Most lime schooners carried a few casks of lime above deck, and when the crew detected a fire below, they opened a cask, mixed up plaster, and tried to smother the fire by plugging every hatch and hole that might allow air into the vessel. After coming in to port and finding a mooring away from other vessels, the captain would often dismiss his crew, and he would stay with the ship. Periodically he would open a hatch and check for wisps of smoke or the telltale smell of slaked lime. In time, either the fire would die out, at which time the captain would recall his crew and they would continue the voyage, or it would continue to smolder. Then the captain had to decide whether to open the hatches and try to off-load the offending lime or to scuttle the burning limer. Scuttling was rare since the shipmaster was quite prepared to use patience in letting the fire burn itself out.

By the end of the 19th century, the lime fleet from Rockland, Thomaston, and Camden-Rockport included up to 200 vessels. Ten years later, however, when the Rockland-Rockport Lime Company began buying up the smaller companies and shipping lime to market in huge barges towed by steam tugs, the number of lime schooners dropped significantly. By 1930, there were only 30 to 50 lime schooners remaining, all of which had left the scene by the beginning of World War II. The larger and more efficient barges had completely taken over.

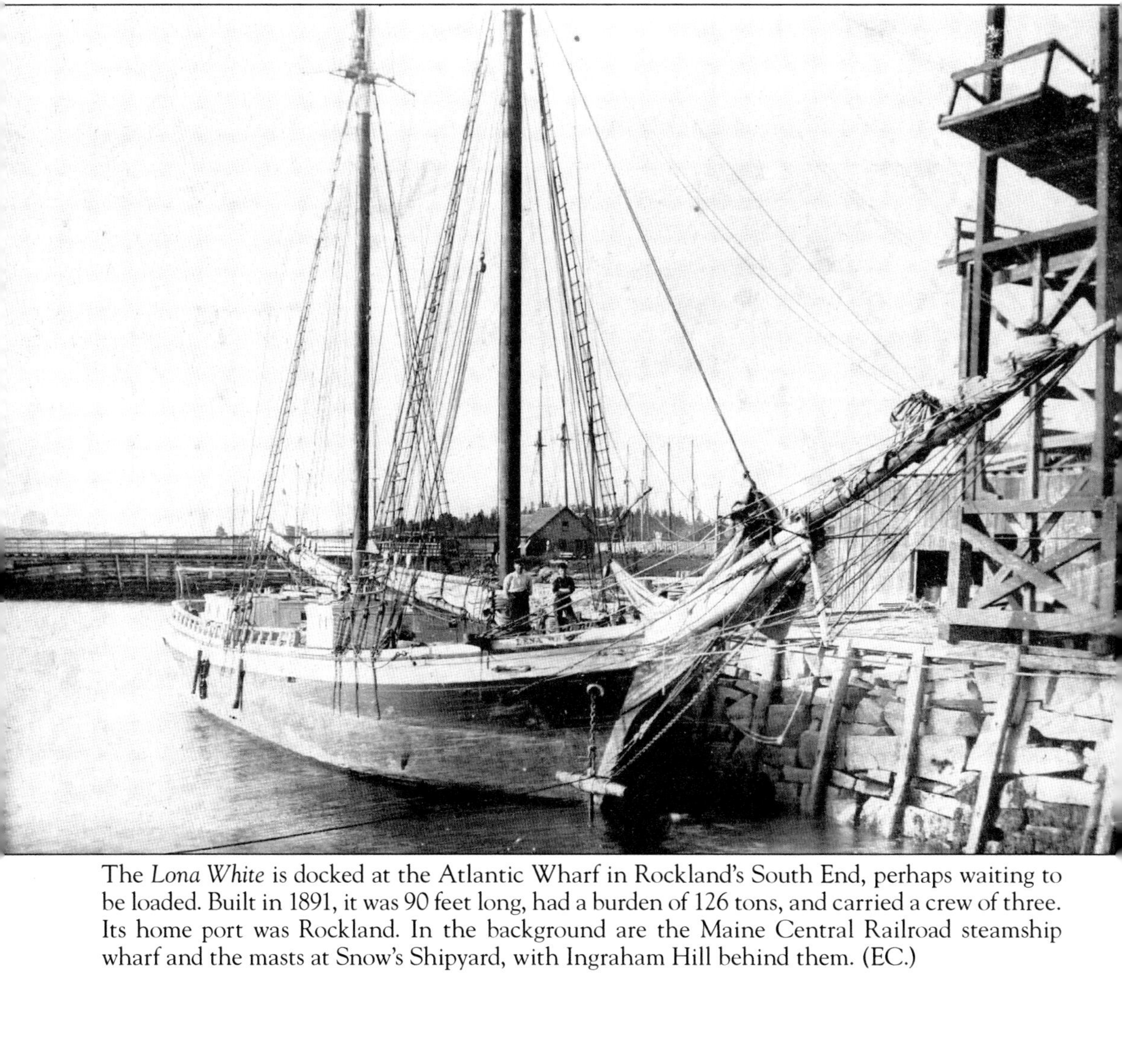

The *Lona White* is docked at the Atlantic Wharf in Rockland's South End, perhaps waiting to be loaded. Built in 1891, it was 90 feet long, had a burden of 126 tons, and carried a crew of three. Its home port was Rockland. In the background are the Maine Central Railroad steamship wharf and the masts at Snow's Shipyard, with Ingraham Hill behind them. (EC.)

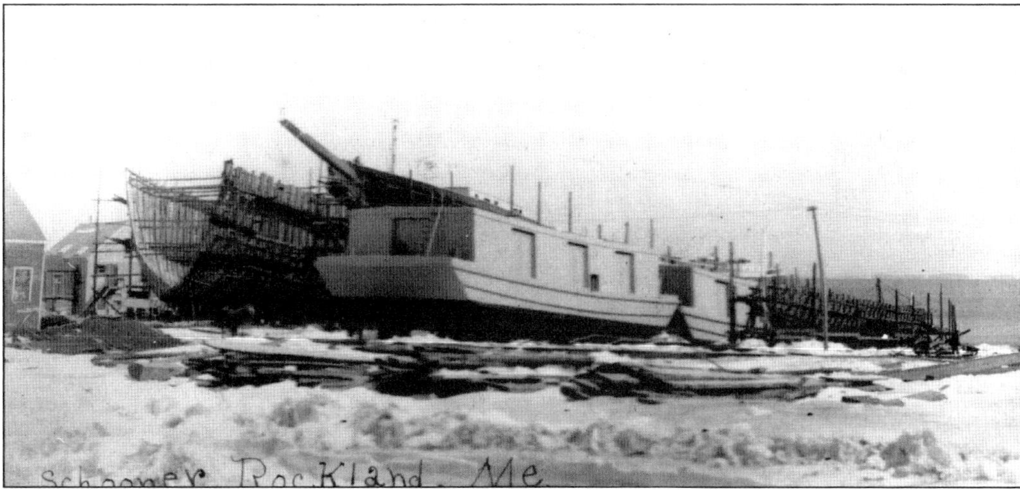

Two types of vessels are being constructed in a Rockland shipyard. On the left are the ribs and framing of new schooners. In front of them are two barges, to be used as lime storage barges in New York Harbor, thus saving wharf and dockage fees. (EC.)

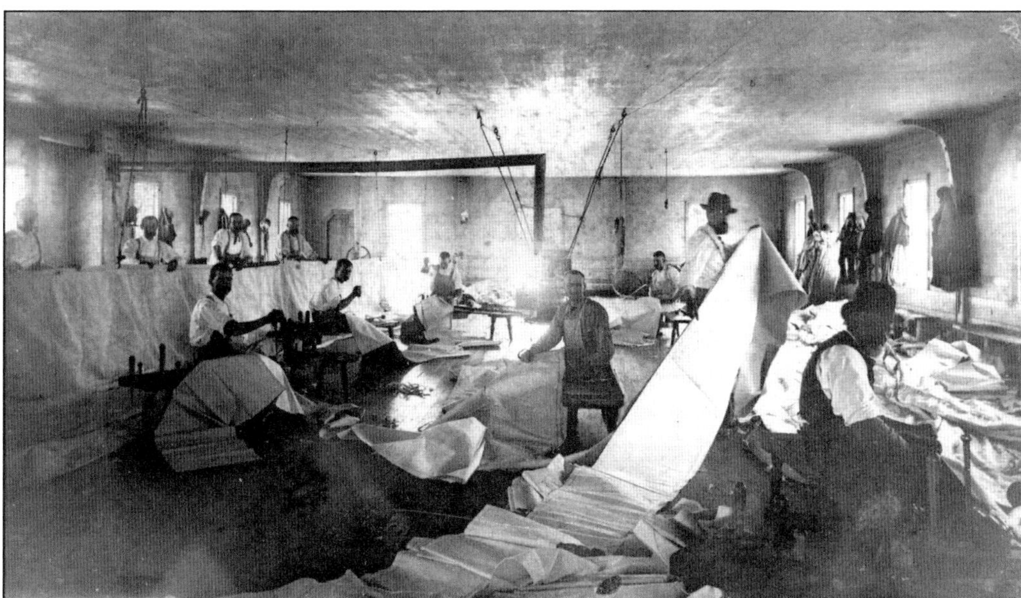

Sailmakers are at work in the Dunn and Elliot sail loft in Thomaston in 1875. Sail lofts were often on the second floor with numerous windows to take advantage of the natural light. This picture shows the stove hung from the ceiling so the floor space would remain unobstructed when sails were spread out. Sailmakers seen here, from left to right, are George Hanley, Orren Perry, Henry Mathews, Arn Morse, Pat Soucey, R. E. Dunn, Irving Harrington, William Hodgkins, Levi Bucklin, George Elliot, and T. W. Dunn. (THS.)

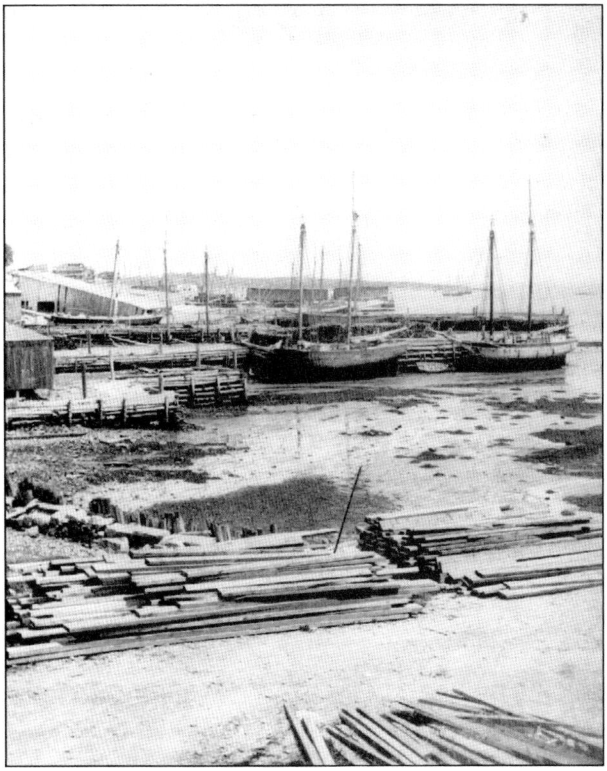

This is a typical scene of Rockland's waterfront at low tide, taken in 1875. The view is looking northeast from "the brook," which empties into Lermond's Cove. On the left are kilns and kiln sheds. Kiln wood is piled high on the wharf behind the grounded-out schooners. (RHS.)

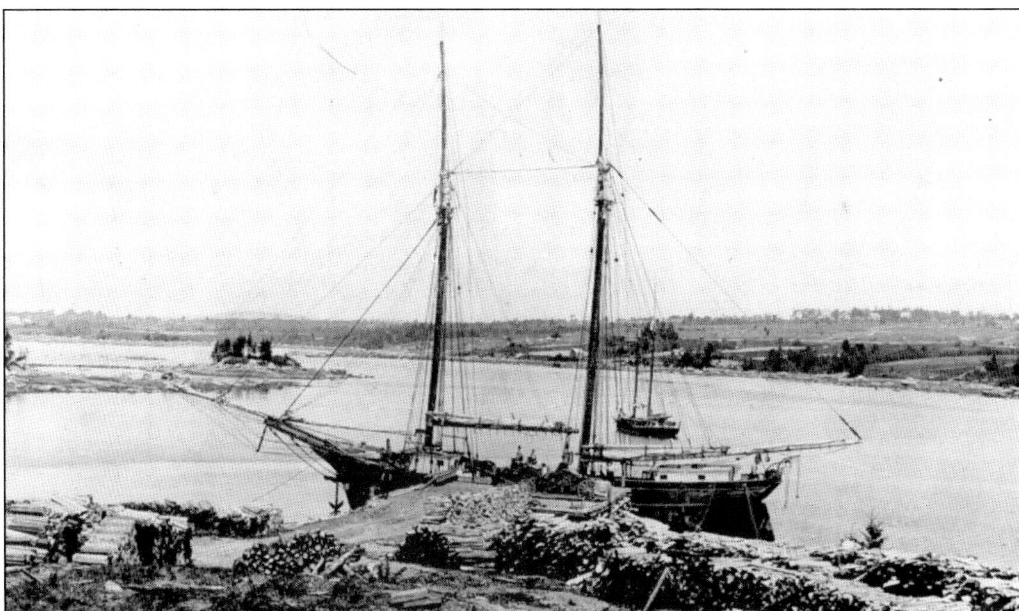

A coasting schooner lies at the dock by the kilns in Thomaston. Lime coasters were mostly two-masted schooners, about 60 to 80 feet long. They were well caulked and frequently pumped. As a vessel aged, its seams loosened, and a vessel that became too loose to carry lime was often reassigned to carrying lumber. Lumber coasters were often older vessels and less well cared for because owners knew that with a cargo of wood they could not sink. (DH.)

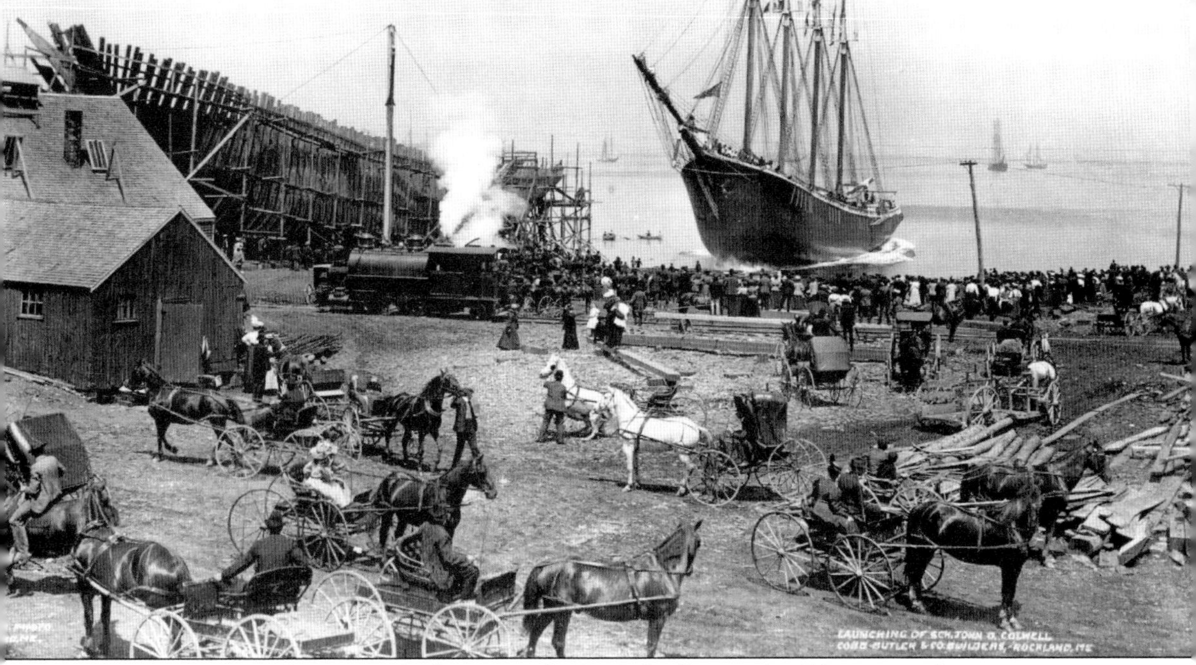

The launching of a four-masted schooner, *John D. Colwell*, as with all large vessels, was a major occasion in town. This ship probably was too large to be used as a lime coaster. Its picture is included here to show how many people attended a launching, including even the train crew, who are blowing the whistle to add to the general din and excitement. The vessel was launched on June 9, 1906, at the Cobb-Butler shipyard in Rockland. (WT.)

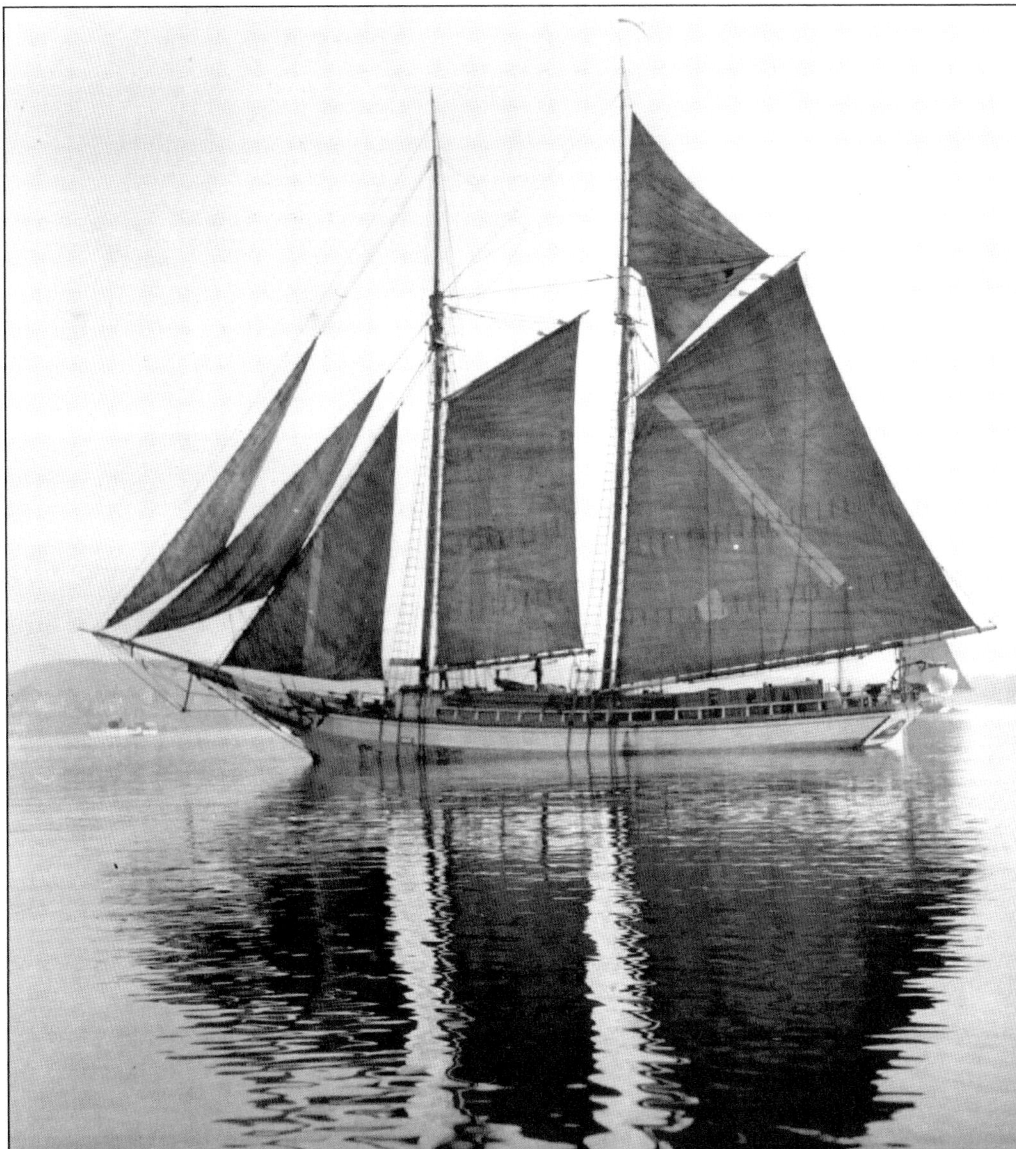

The 99-ton *Mary Langdon* is under way in Penobscot Bay. The 73-foot coasting schooner was built in Thomaston in 1845. It sailed for the next 80 years, in an era when the life of an average vessel was 12 years. During that time, it not only carried lime to eastern seaboard cities but also served as a rumrunner and a lumber drogher. Here it is seen loaded with cargo in its hold, and it also carries a deck load of lumber. (EC.)

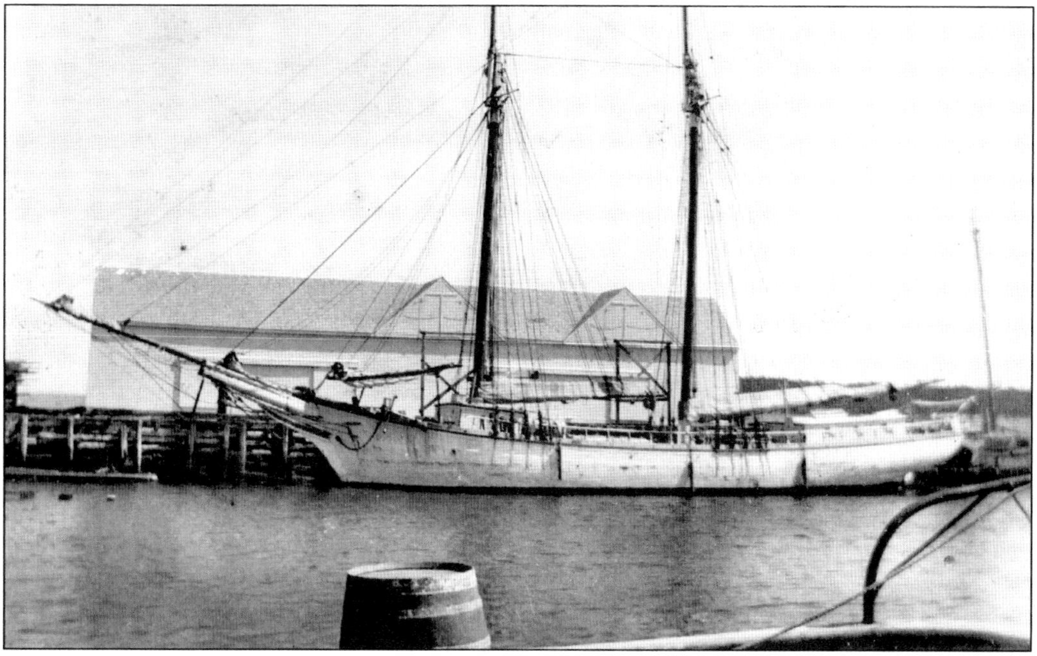

The *Lulu Everett* awaits repairs in the Snow Farwell Shipyard in Rockland in 1891. It is being converted from carrying general merchandise to carrying lime. When a vessel was rebuilt for the lime trade, its original main deck and beams were removed, the poop deck was extended all the way forward to the fore rigging, and an open fly rail was installed all around. This made room for an extra layer of lime casks below deck. (EC.)

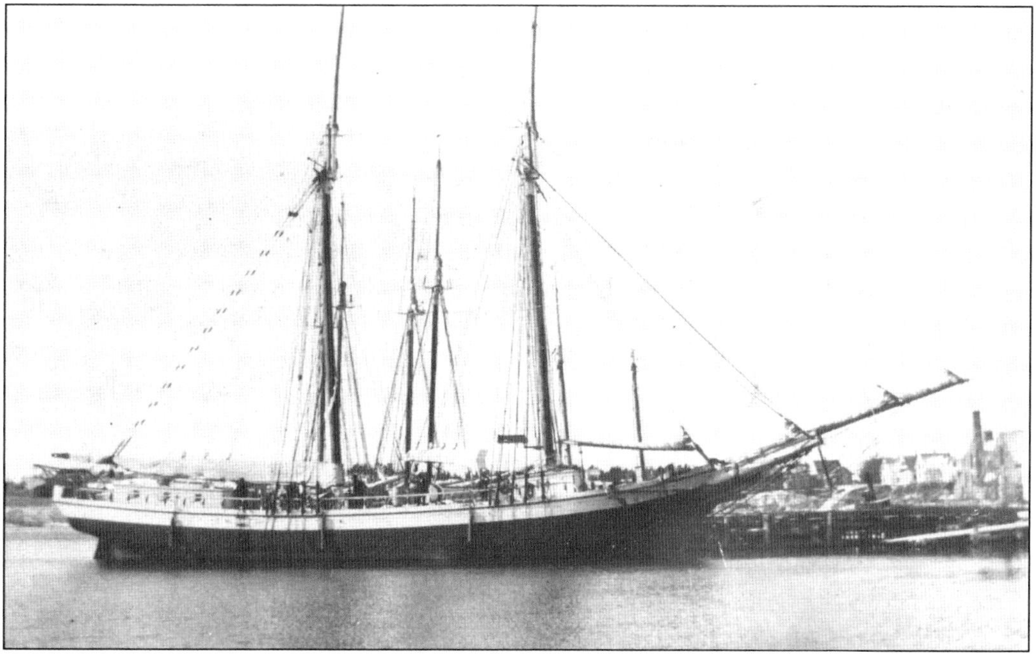

Here is the newly painted *Lulu Everett* in 1892, after the work is completed on its conversion. The Snow Farwell Shipyard, where the work was done, was well known for specializing in ship repairs and modifications. It also built new vessels.

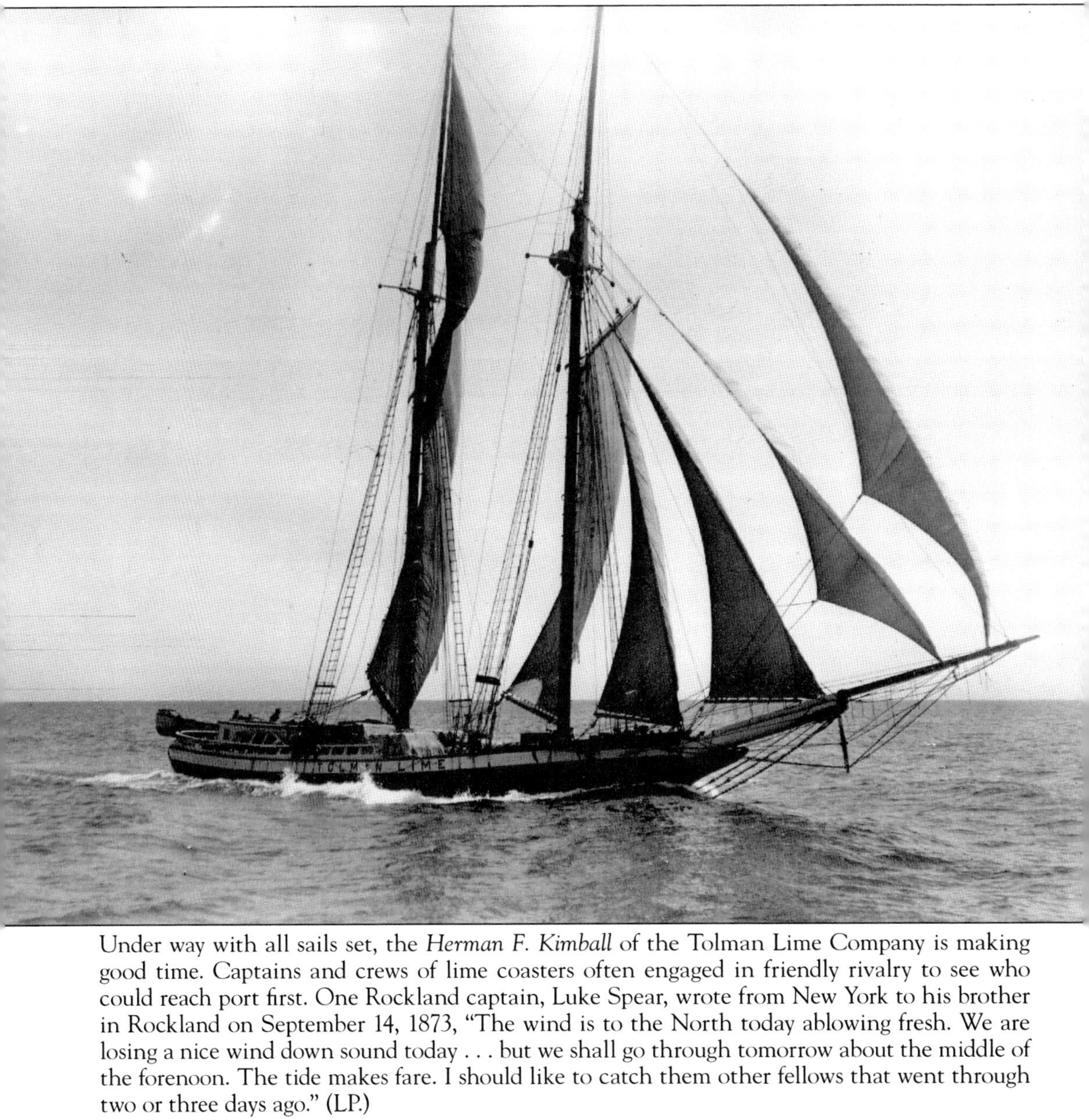

Under way with all sails set, the *Herman F. Kimball* of the Tolman Lime Company is making good time. Captains and crews of lime coasters often engaged in friendly rivalry to see who could reach port first. One Rockland captain, Luke Spear, wrote from New York to his brother in Rockland on September 14, 1873, "The wind is to the North today ablowing fresh. We are losing a nice wind down sound today . . . but we shall go through tomorrow about the middle of the forenoon. The tide makes fare. I should like to catch them other fellows that went through two or three days ago." (LP.)

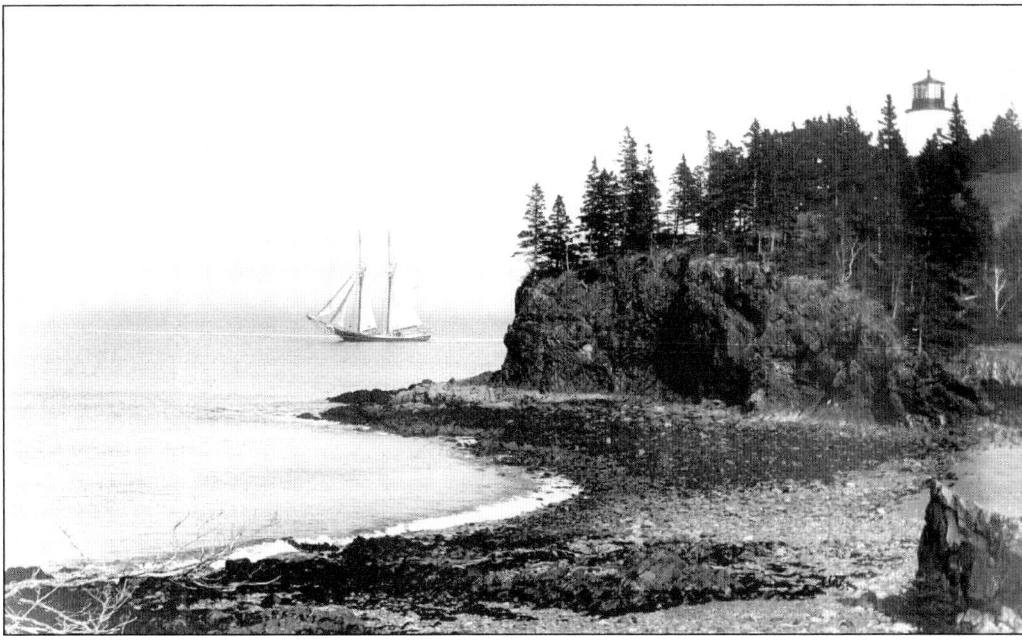

Rounding Owl's Head Light, a schooner passes Rockland Harbor's southern point of entry on May 26, 1892. Lime coasters returning from the New York market carried a variety of cargoes to various ports between Boston and Bangor. Schooners often carried coal from Hoboken, New Jersey, or Rondout, New York, 90 miles up the Hudson River. They also carried flour, mixed cargoes for local merchants, gravel, and firebrick for the kilns. (RHS.)

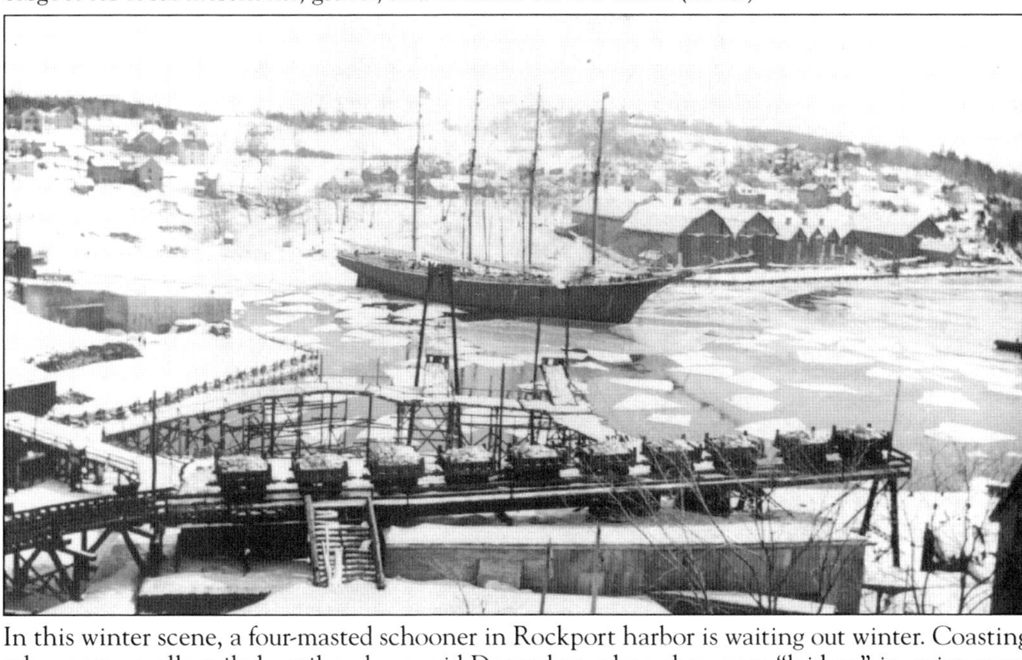

In this winter scene, a four-masted schooner in Rockport harbor is waiting out winter. Coasting schooners usually sailed until early or mid-December, when they were "laid up" in quiet coves to wait for the ice to break up in March. Notice the rock cars in the foreground. Quarrying was not done in winter, but they did transport rock that had been dug earlier in the season and stockpiled at the quarry rim. (DH.)

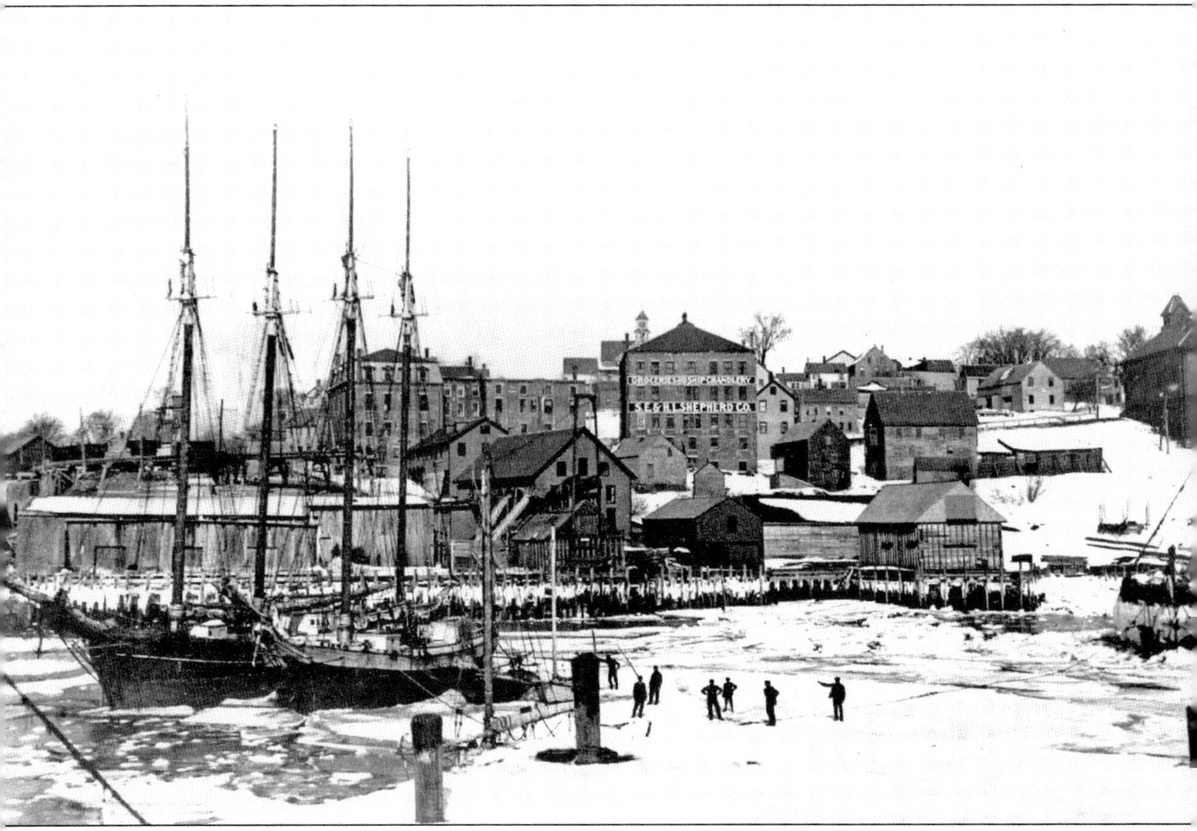

Several vessels are caught in the ice in Rockport harbor. In the foreground, one can see just the mast of a sloop that has sunk. Men standing on the snow-covered ice appear to be considering the situation. To the right, a small schooner has been grounded out for the winter. There is a line coming from it to the sunken sloop and another line to the sloop from the large schooners on the left of the picture. They indicate that the men may be trying to pull the sunken sloop away from the grip of the ice that formed between the vessel and the wharf. The grinding ice tended to pull out or loosen the oakum caulking between the planks of the vessels. (CRHS.)

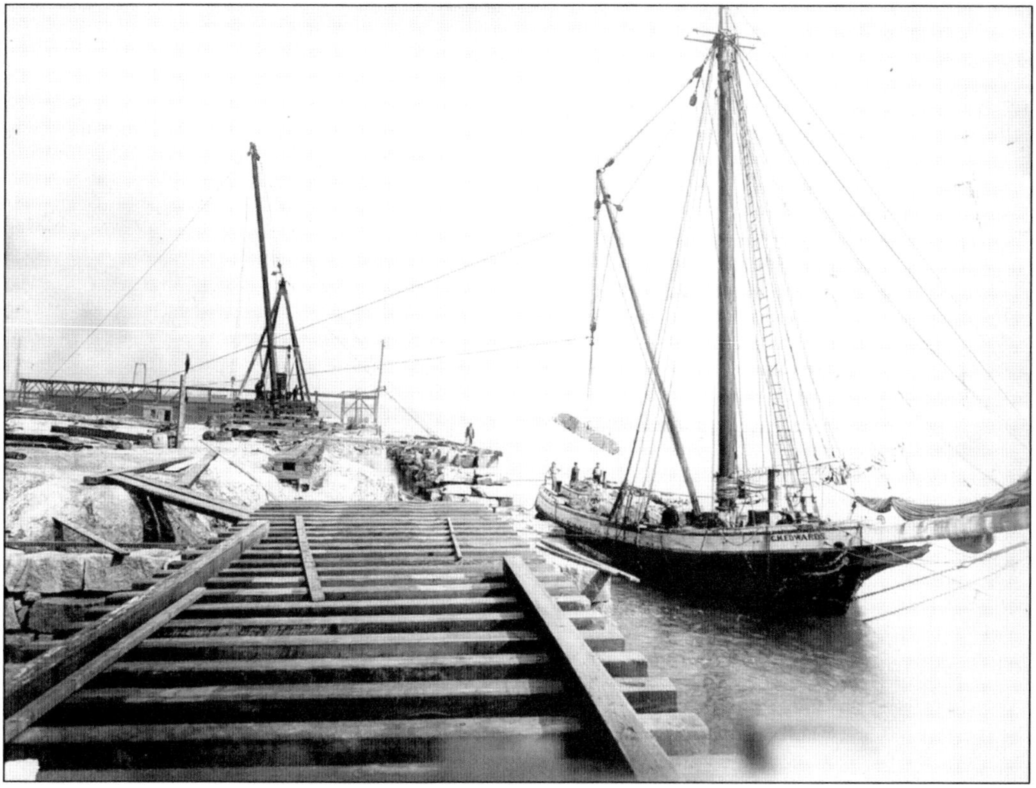

The lime industry employed many vessels to transport its product to market, and it also employed work boats around the harbor to support the industry. Here is a granite sloop working on the partially constructed sea wall for the coal wharf in Rockland's North End. Granite is being laid as the foundation for the railroad, which will run along the edge of the harbor. Notice the crane and pulley arrangement as the *C. H. Edwards* lifts a large slab of granite to be set as part of the foundation. Vessels like this were also used in the construction of the Rockland breakwater, built between 1881 and 1899. This image was taken on October 15, 1912. (RHS.)

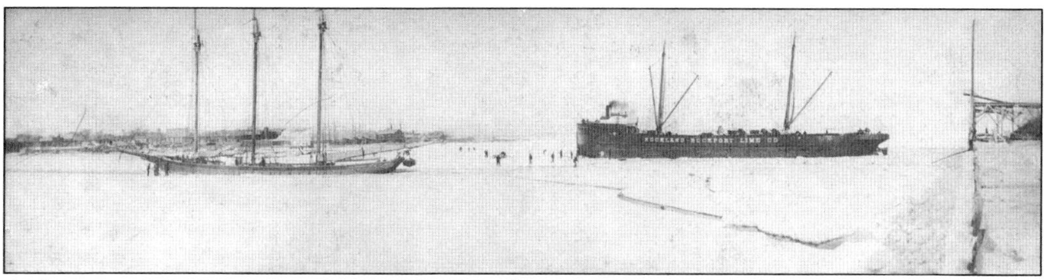

A three-masted schooner and a Rockland-Rockport Lime Company barge are frozen in the ice in Rockland Harbor in February 1904. Men are out on the ice near both vessels. The harbor ice was over 14 inches thick that winter, a depth that had not been reached for years. (CRHS.)

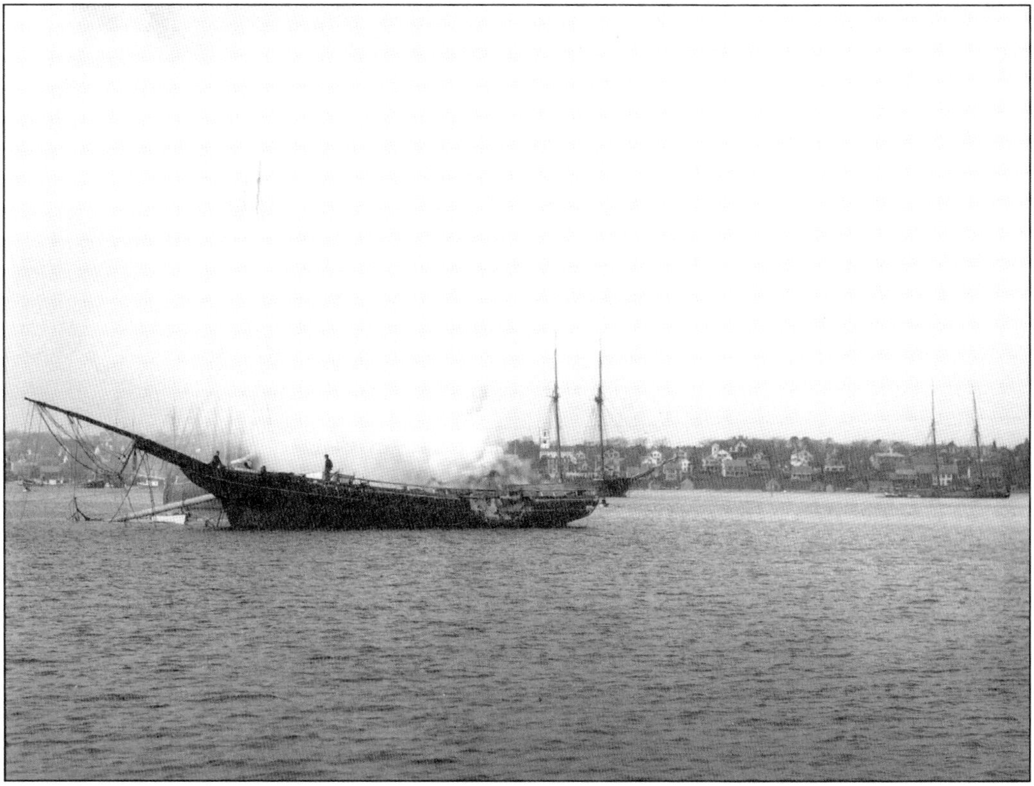

The schooner *Bertha E. Glover* has a burning cargo of lime in Edgartown, Martha's Vineyard, in January 1898. Capt. Frank Chandler Farr had decided to put in to Edgartown before the big gale of January 1898, but the *Glover* was severely damaged when water got into the cargo. The masts and rigging have been cut away, to be salvaged. This image shows Captain Farr and his crew standing on board, possibly deciding if anything else can be salvaged. The vessel was declared a total loss. (PMM.)

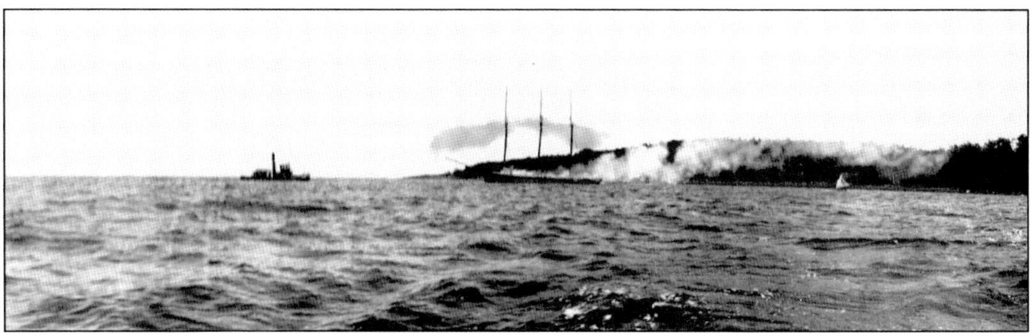

An undated photograph shows the three-masted lime coaster *James R. Talbot* on fire at Rockland Harbor, near the Owl's Head shore. If possible, captains of burning limers tried to segregate their vessels from other shipping in the harbor. (DLL.)

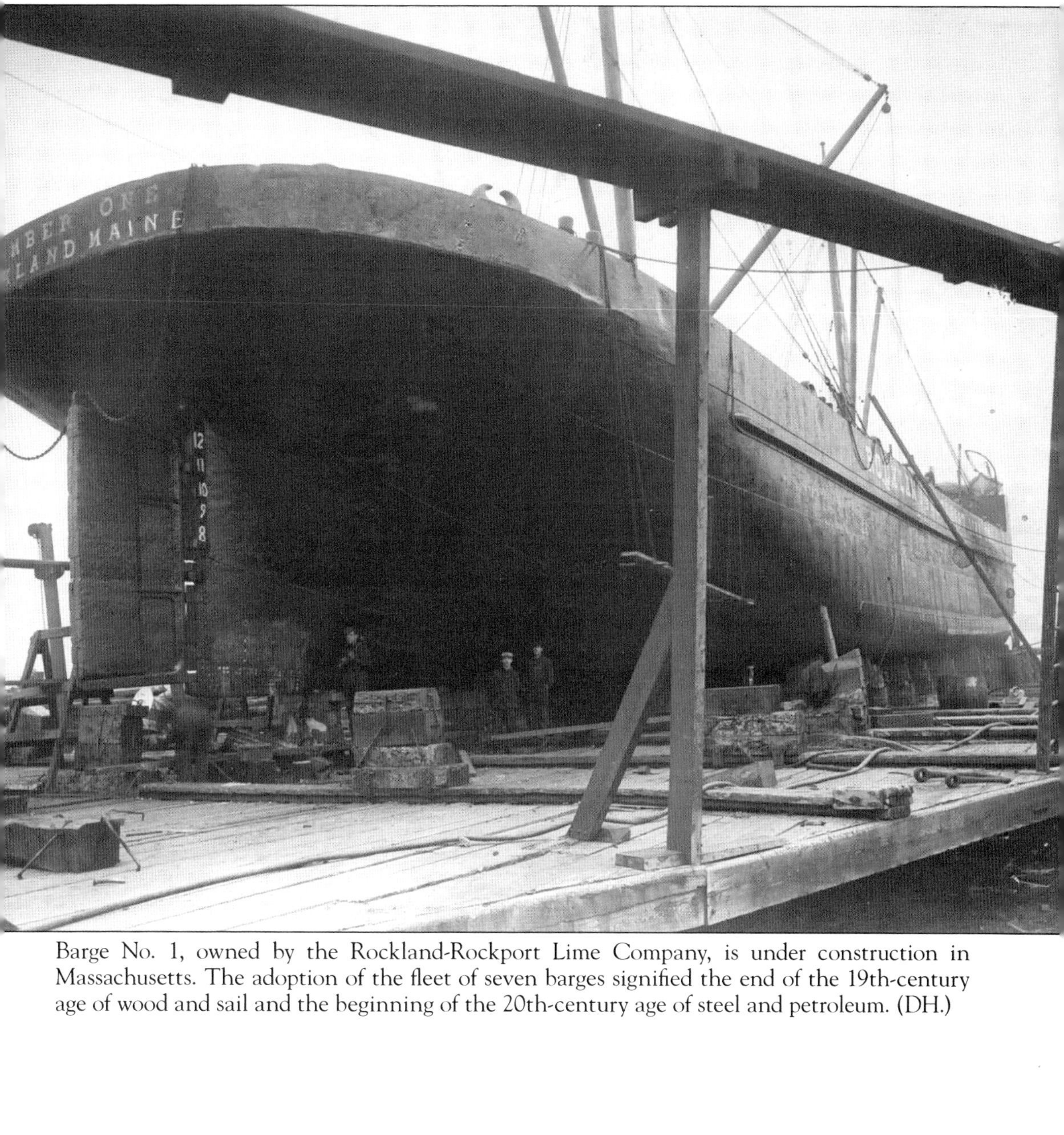

Barge No. 1, owned by the Rockland-Rockport Lime Company, is under construction in Massachusetts. The adoption of the fleet of seven barges signified the end of the 19th-century age of wood and sail and the beginning of the 20th-century age of steel and petroleum. (DH.)

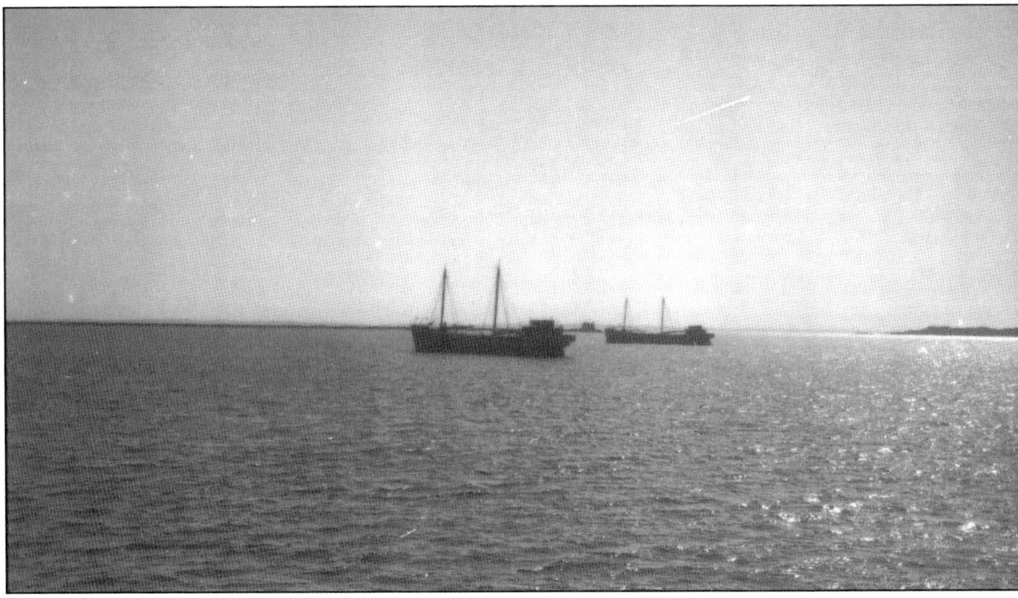

These two barges in the harbor are part of the second barge fleet bought by the Rockland-Rockport Lime Company. After selling the first fleet to the federal government during World War I, the company bought a second fleet. They kept this second fleet of seven barges until the outbreak of World War II and sold them to the federal government. They are easily identifiable because the first barges had cabins in the bow, and the second barges had cabins in the stern. (DH.)

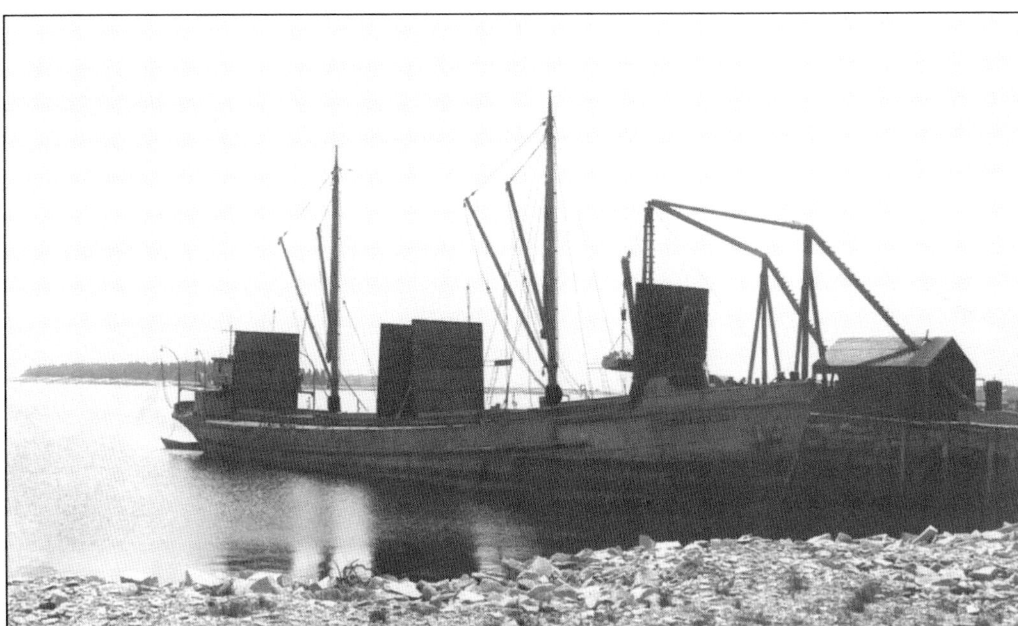

One of the Rockland-Rockport Lime Company's barges sits at a loading dock with its hatches open, waiting for loading. (DH.)

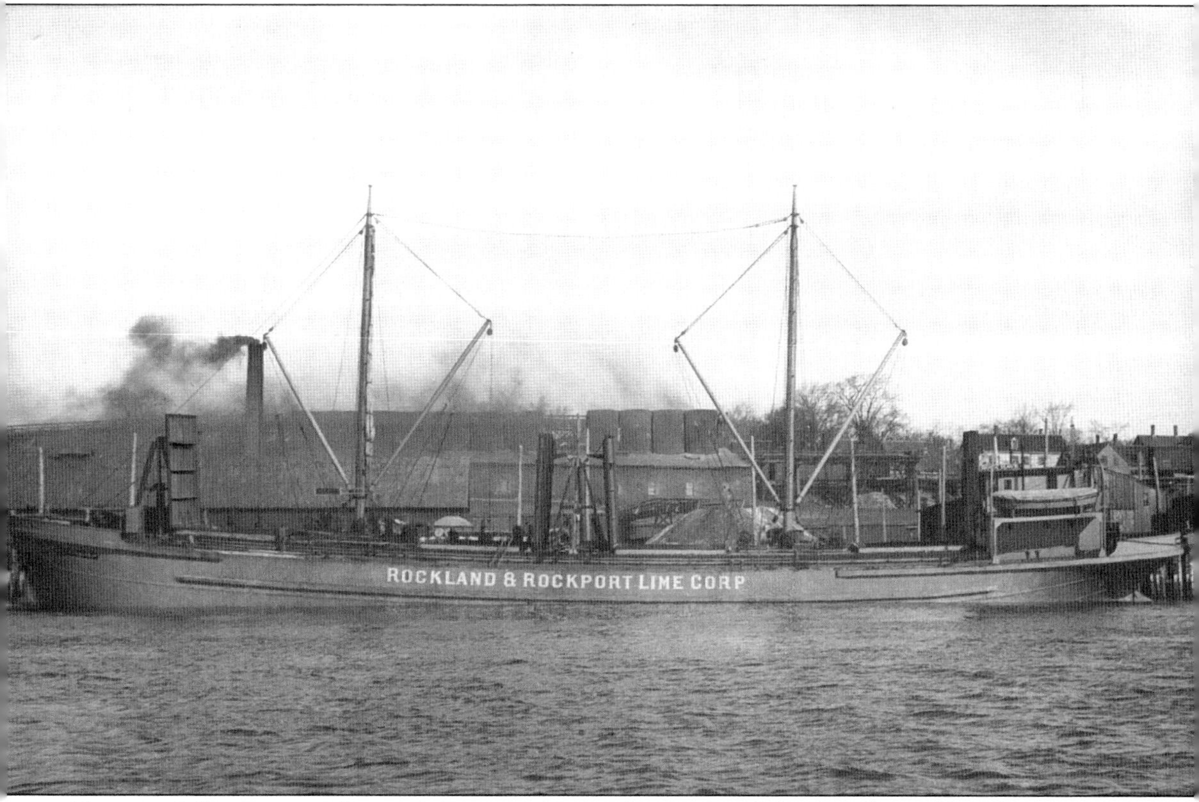

Here is a full side view of one of the seven barges that replaced the first fleet of lime barges in 1920. In the background, lime is being burned in the kilns. When the kilns were wood-fired, the smoke was white and wispy, but when the lime manufacturers shifted to coal-fired kilns, the smoke came out in black billows. This photograph was taken by A. L. Babbidge. (DH.)

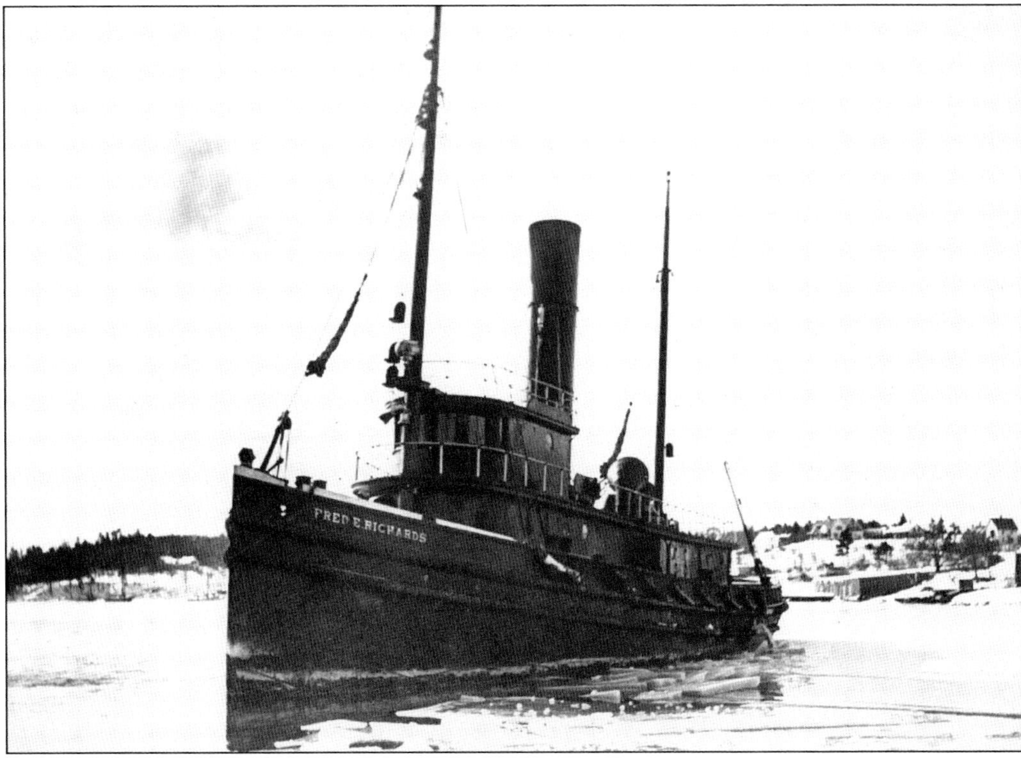

The tug *Fred E. Richards* was named after the president of the Rockland-Rockport Lime Company when the vessel was built. The main job of the *Fred E. Richards* was to tow the barges to and from New York and to guide them into the loading docks. It was built in 1901–1902 at the same time as the initial fleet of seven barges. (DH.)

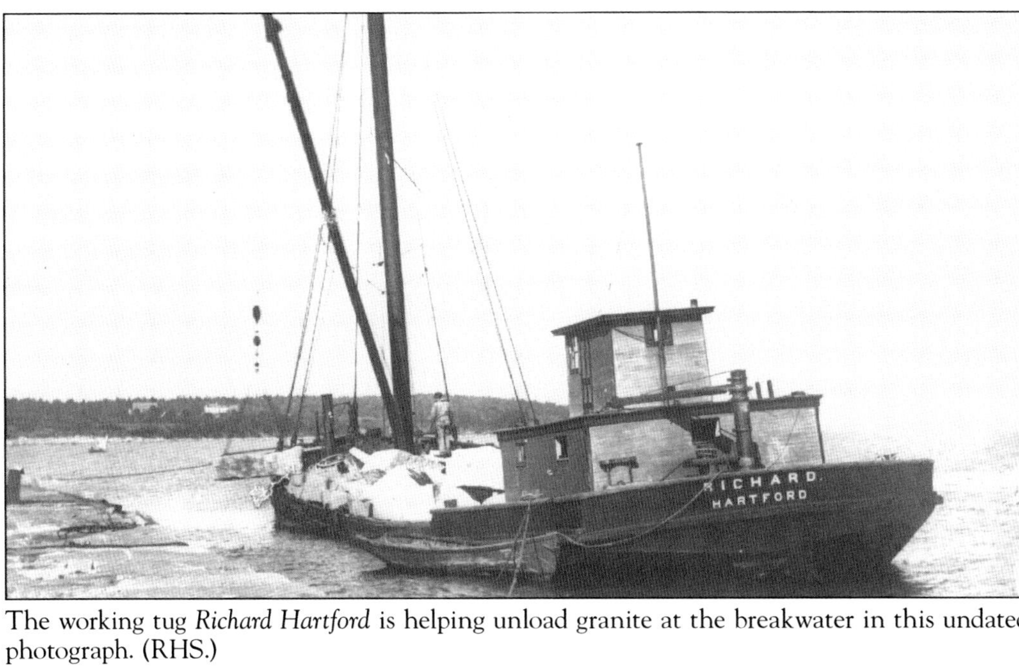

The working tug *Richard Hartford* is helping unload granite at the breakwater in this undated photograph. (RHS.)

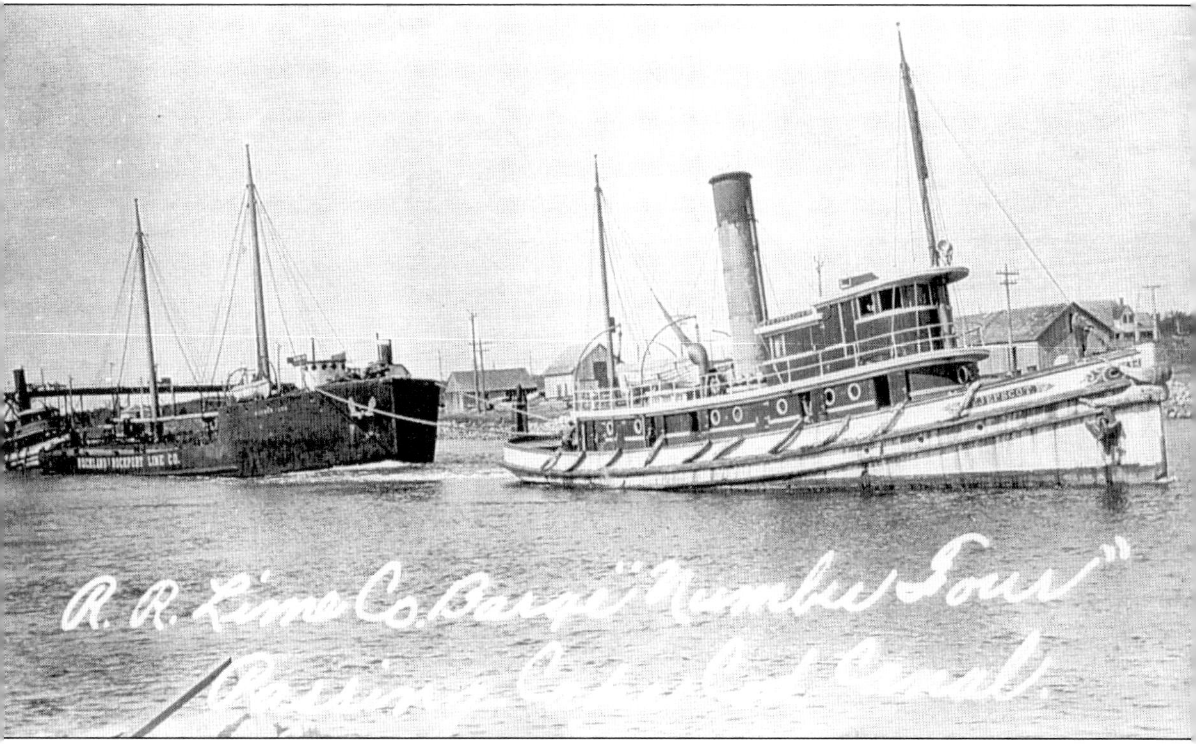

Rockland-Rockport barge No. 4 is passing through the Cape Cod Canal. To help it through the narrow waters, it has the tug *Pejebscot* pulling it and another tug behind to push and guide. (RHS.)

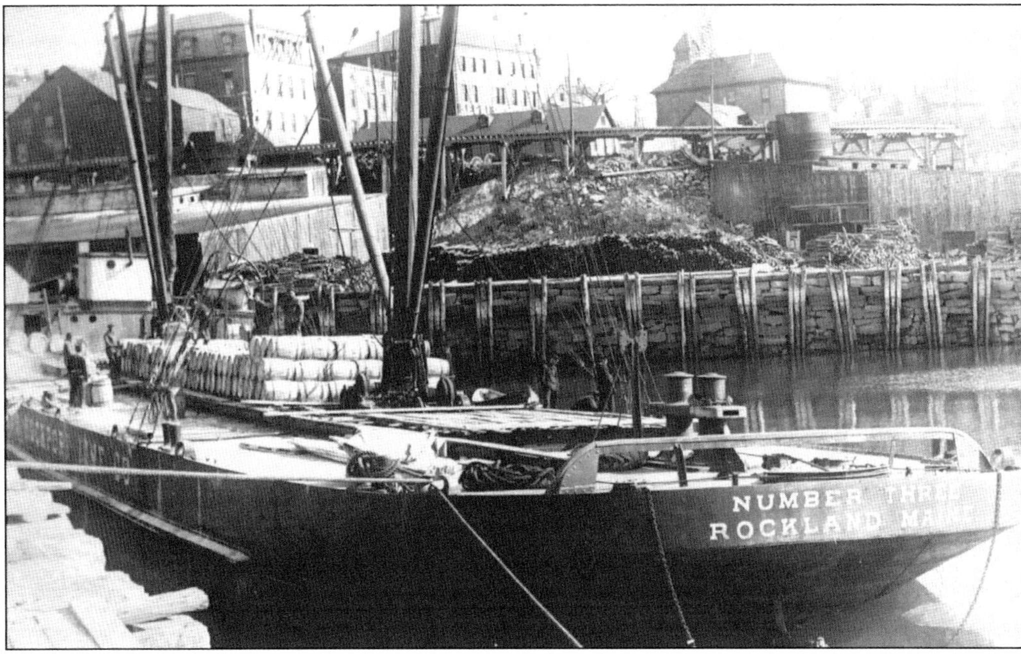

Barge No. 3 of the first barge fleet is being loaded with lime at the head of Rockport harbor. In the background are the kilns where the Rockport Yacht Club is now, and above that is the railroad trestle. This image was taken around 1913. (CRHS.)

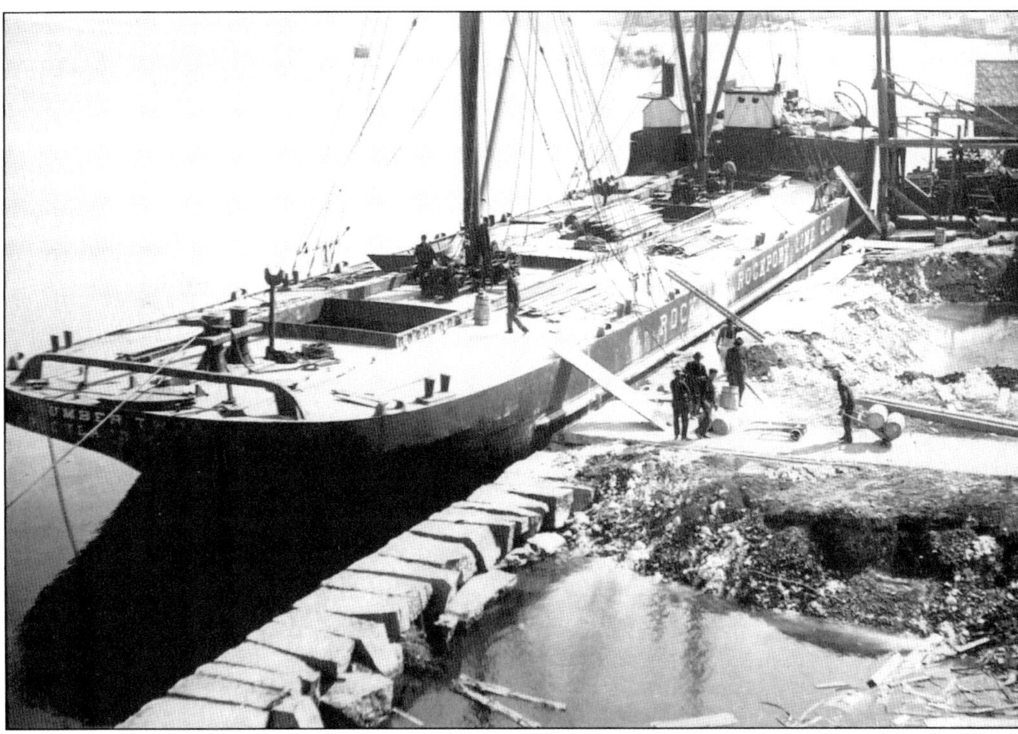

This is the last lime barge that was loaded in Rockport. According to a notation on the picture, it carried 16,000 barrels of lime when fully loaded. (CRHS.)

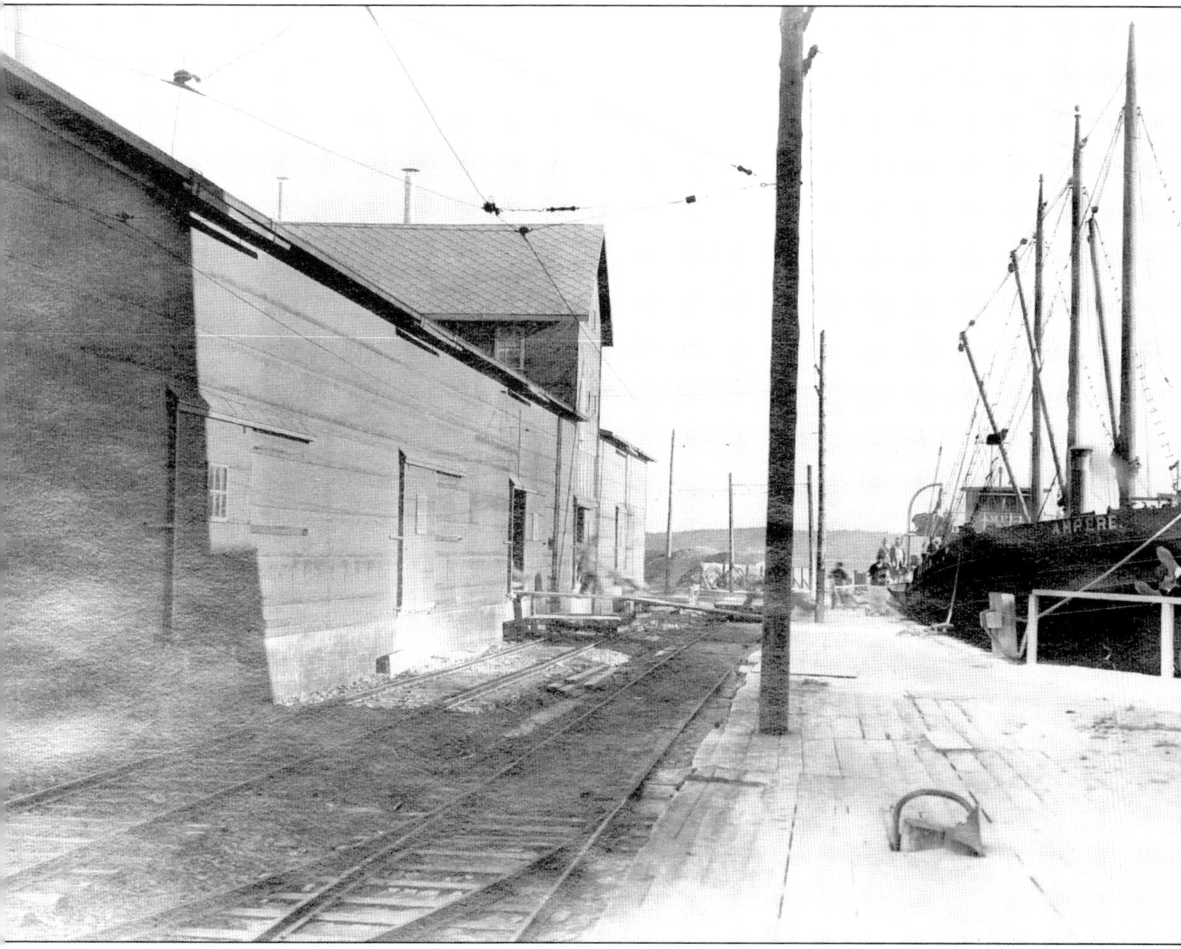

Sitting high in the water, an empty barge is docked at Rockland Harbor. This named barge may not be part of the Rockland-Rockport Lime Company fleet, which had numbered vessels. If all its fleet was in use, the company sometimes chartered other barges.

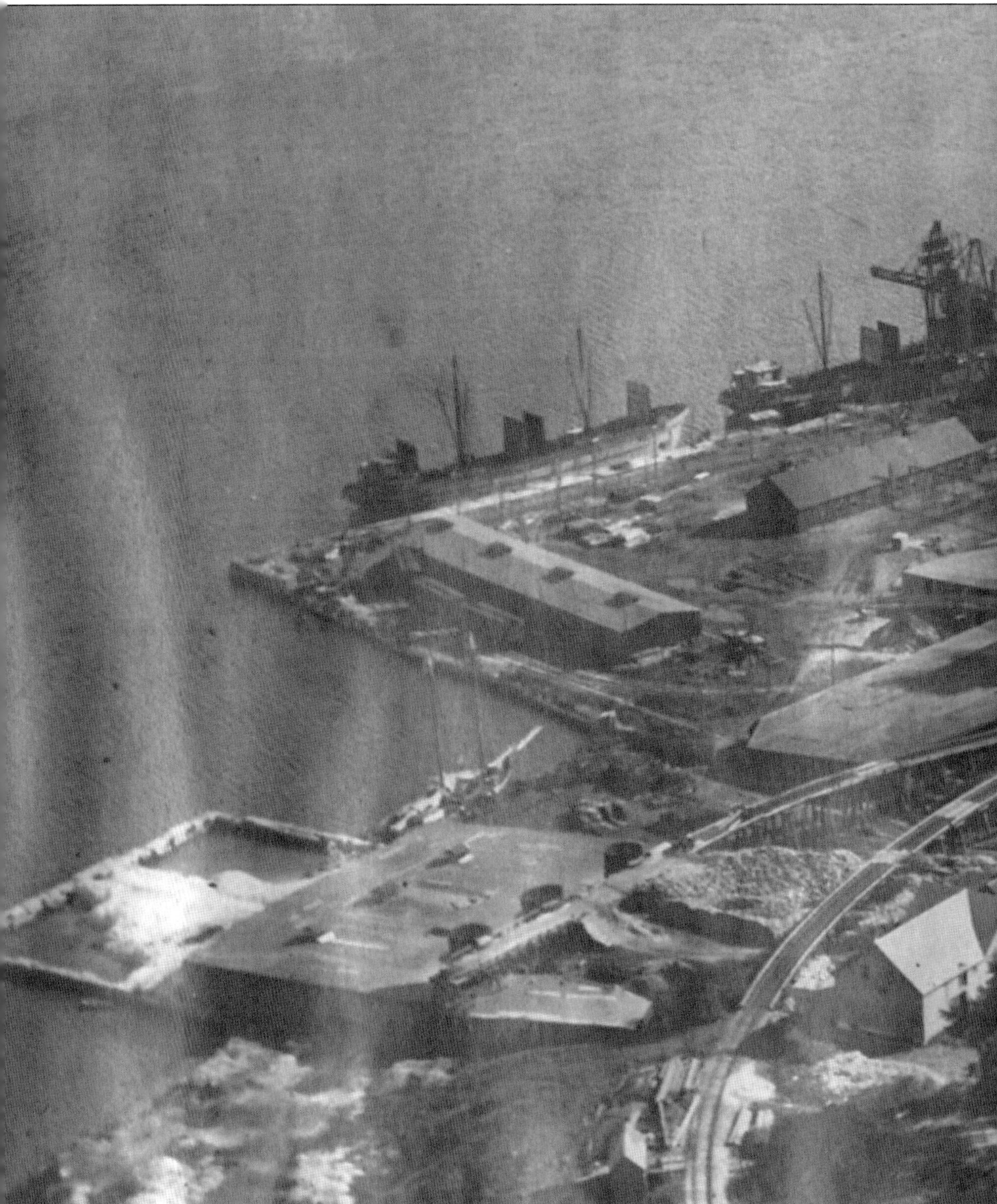

The North End of Rockland Harbor was the main area of operations for the Rockland-Rockport Lime Company. Two steel barges are unloading coal into the coal pockets, and they will return to New York carrying cargoes of lime. The steam and smoke come from the kilns. Rock cars

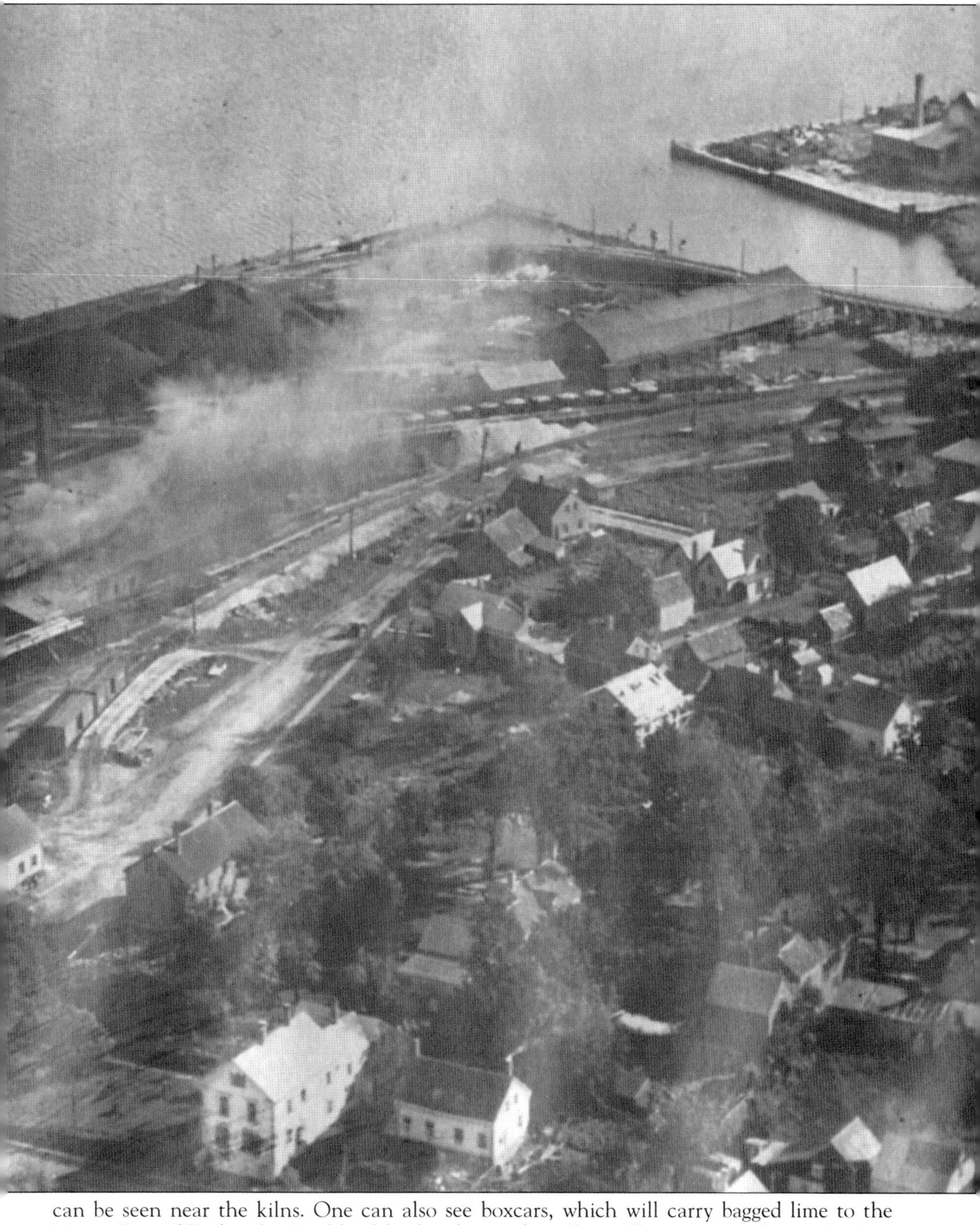

can be seen near the kilns. One can also see boxcars, which will carry bagged lime to the Maine Central Railroad in Rockland for distribution from there. The cooperage shop is the long building to the left of the coal pockets and coal tower. (DH.)

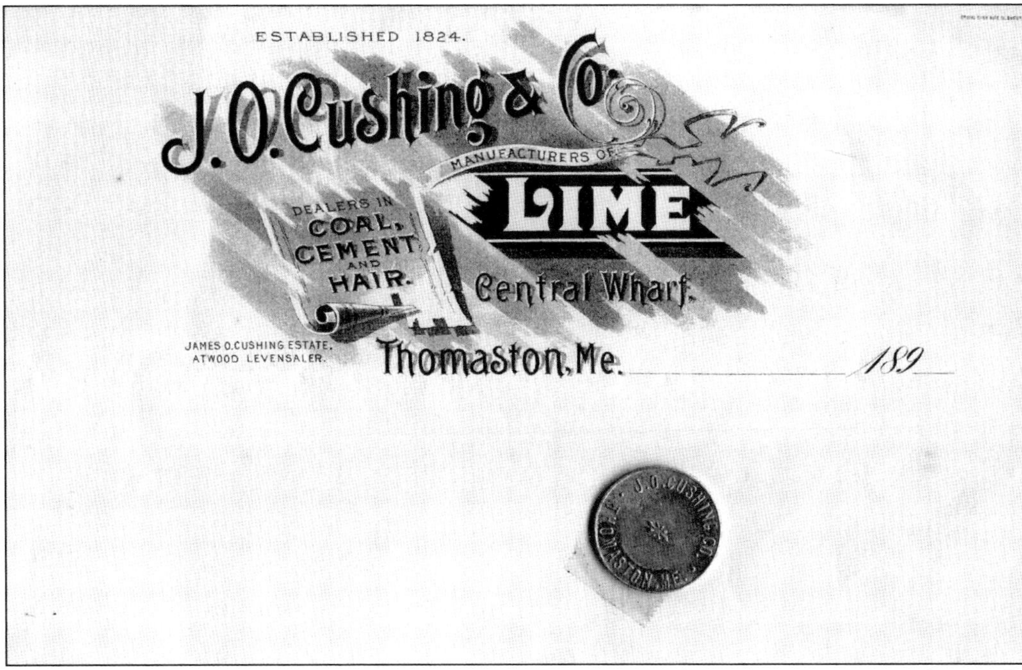

A letterhead from the J. O. Cushing Company in Thomaston from the 1890s is seen here. The company also dealt in coal, cement, and hair. Hair was used in the manufacture of horsehair plaster, common in the 19th century. It was added as a binder, and it also retarded the hardening process, allowing the plasterer more time to work while the plaster was malleable. (THS.)

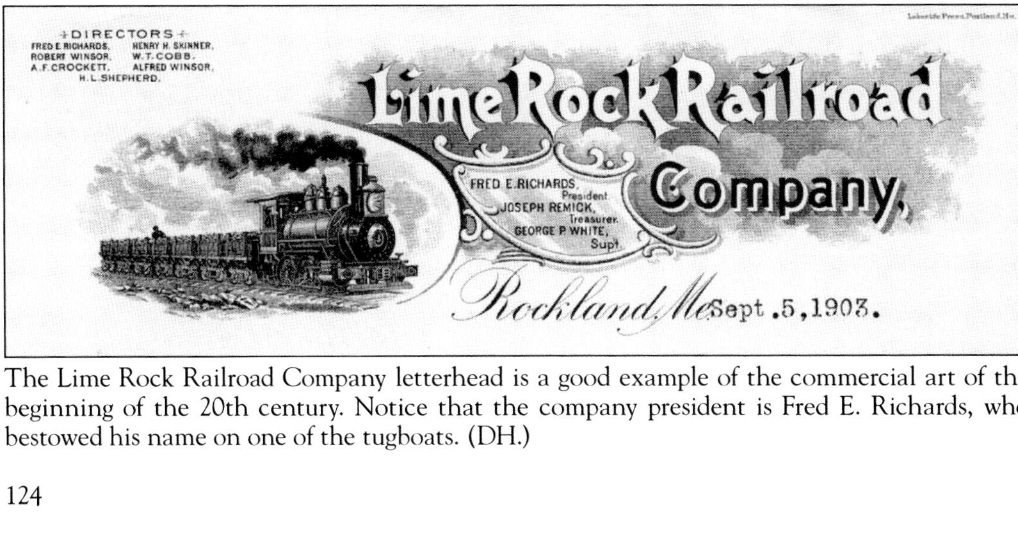

The Lime Rock Railroad Company letterhead is a good example of the commercial art of the beginning of the 20th century. Notice that the company president is Fred E. Richards, who bestowed his name on one of the tugboats. (DH.)

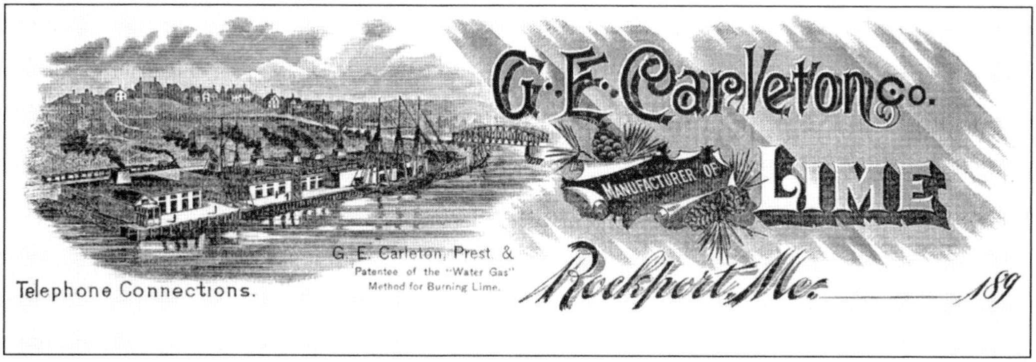

A letterhead from the G. E. Carleton Lime Company in Rockport shows the head of Rockport harbor in the 1890s. Kilns and their sheds line the side of the harbor. The rock train is delivering lime rock to the kiln tops. The Goose River is spanned by the old iron bridge, which was replaced after the 1907 fire. (CM.)

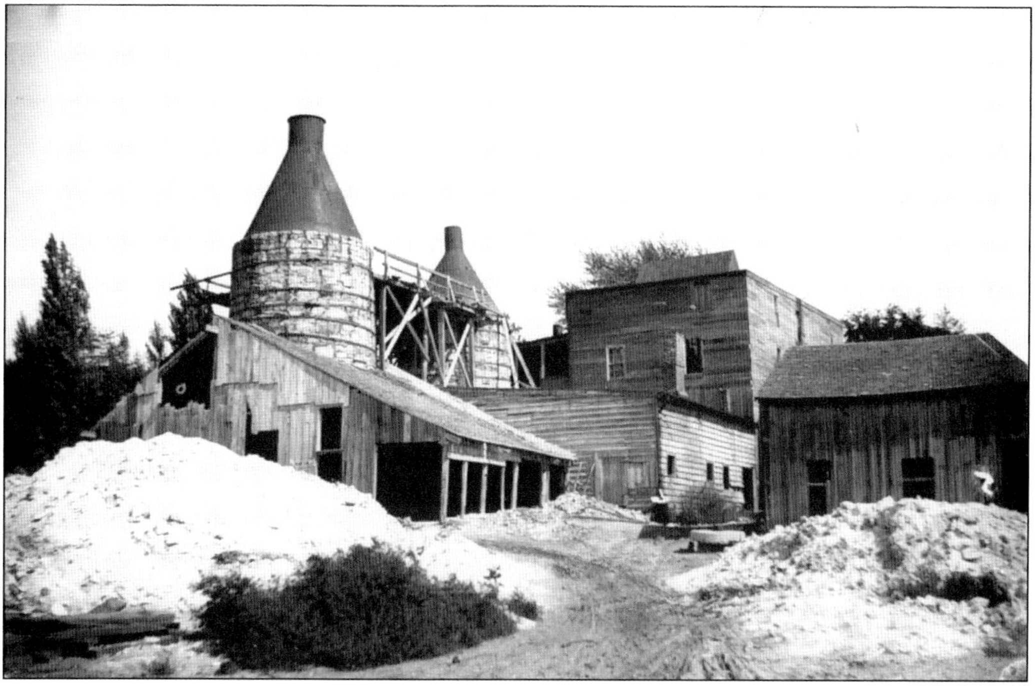

This iron-topped kiln was probably owned by the G. E. Carleton Company, but its location is unidentified. The cone-shaped, iron-topped kilns helped to burn the lime rock more efficiently, and they were safer. The G. E. Carleton Company experimented with special methods of burning soft coal, and this kiln could have been part of the experimentation. (CM.)

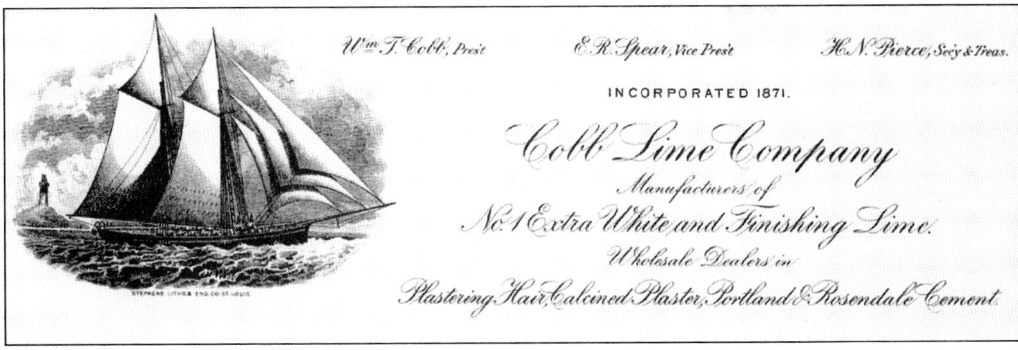

This is the dramatic letterhead of the Cobb Lime Company, done by Stephens Lithographers and Engravers of St. Louis. The Cobb Lime Company was very successful, manufacturing about one-quarter of all the lime produced in Knox County.

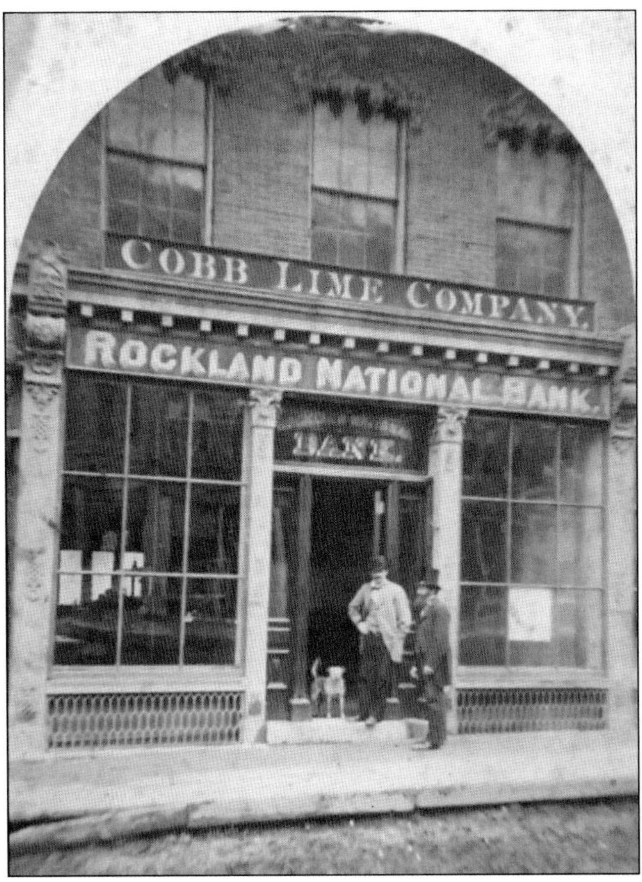

The headquarters of the Cobb Lime Company was above the Rockland National Bank on Main Street. The largest lime manufacturer in Knox County, the company was started by Francis Cobb in 1871. The men standing at the door are Orris Andrews (left) and G. Hawes Wiggin. (DH.)

For Further Reading

Bunting, W. H. *A Day's Work: A Sampler of Historic Maine Photographs 1860–1920*, Parts I and II. Gardiner, ME: Tilbury House Publishers; Portland, ME: Maine Preservation, 1997.
Duncan, Roger. *Coastal Maine: A Maritime History*. New York: W. W. Norton, 1992.
Fagan, William Francis. *From Lime Kilns to Art Galleries: Anthropogeography of the Maine Coast City of Rockland*. Ph.D. diss., Louisiana State University, 2003. (On file at Rockland Public Library.)
Grindle, Roger. *Quarry and Kiln: The Story of Maine's Lime Industry*. Rockland, ME: Courier Gazette, 1971.
Harden, Brian R., ed. *Shore Village Story: An Informal History of Rockland, Maine*. Rockland, ME: Courier Gazette/Rockland Bicentennial Commission, 1976.
Leavitt, John F. *Wake of the Coasters*. 2nd ed. Mystic, CT: Mystic Seaport Museum, 1984.
Packard, Aubigne. *The Town That Went to Sea*. Portland, ME: Falmouth Publishing House, 1950.
Rowe, William Hutchinson. *Maritime History of Maine: Three Centuries of Ship Building and Seafaring*. New York: W. W. Norton, 1948.
Snow, Bertram G. *The Main Beam: An Informal History of Documented Vessels Built at Rockland, Maine, from 1795–2005*. Rockland, ME: Lakeside Printing, 2005.